The Dynamics of Auction

Each year some billions of pounds of art and antiques are sold at auction. These auctions consist of numerous intense episodes of social interaction that rarely take more than thirty seconds and yet they enable the valuation and exchange of goods worth anything from a few pounds to many millions. Analyzing video recordings of auctions in Europe and the United States, Christian Heath examines the fine details of the participants' talk, bodily comportment and their use of various tools and technologies. He addresses such matters as order, trust and competition and demonstrates how a complex institutional arrangement with its substantial global turnover is accomplished through embodied action and multimodal interaction.

Christian Heath is a professor at King's College London and codirector of the Work, Interaction and Technology Research Centre. He is co-editor of the Cambridge University Press Learning in Doing series.

LEARNING IN DOING: SOCIAL, COGNITIVE AND
COMPUTATIONAL PERSPECTIVES

SERIES EDITOR EMERITUS
John Seely Brown, Xerox Palo Alto Research Center

GENERAL EDITORS
*Christian Heath, Work, Interaction and Technology, The Department of
Management, King's College London*
*Roy Pea, Professor of Education and the Learning Sciences and Director,
Stanford Center for Innovations in Learning, Stanford University*
*Lucy A. Suchman, Centre for Science Studies and Department of Sociology,
Lancaster University, UK*

BOOKS IN THE SERIES

(continued after index)

The Dynamics of Auction

Social Interaction and the Sale of Fine Art and Antiques

CHRISTIAN HEATH
King's College London

CAMBRIDGE
UNIVERSITY PRESS

CAMBRIDGE UNIVERSITY PRESS
Cambridge, New York, Melbourne, Madrid, Cape Town,
Singapore, São Paulo, Delhi, Mexico City

Cambridge University Press
32 Avenue of the Americas, New York, NY 10013-2473, USA

www.cambridge.org
Information on this title: www.cambridge.org/9780521767408

First published 2013

Printed in the United States of America

A catalog record for this publication is available from the British Library.

Library of Congress Cataloging in Publication data
Heath, Christian, 1952–
    The dynamics of auction : social interaction and the sale
    of fine art and antiques / Christian Heath.
        pages   cm. – (Learning in doing)
    Includes bibliographical references and index.
    ISBN 978-0-521-76740-8 (hardback)
    1. Art auctions – Psychological aspects.   2. Antique auctions – Psychological
    aspects.   3. Social interaction.   I. Title.
    N8602.H43   2012
    381'.457–dc23   2012015691

ISBN 978-0-521-76740-8 Hardback

Contents

Series Foreword

This series for Cambridge University Press is widely known as an international forum for studies of situated learning and cognition. Innovative contributions are being made by anthropology; by cognitive, developmental, and cultural psychology; by computer science; by education; and by social theory. These contributions are providing the basis for new ways of understanding the social, historical, and contextual nature of learning, thinking, and practice that emerges from human activity. The empirical settings of these research inquiries range from the classroom to the workplace, to the high-technology office, and to learning in the streets and in other communities of practice. The situated nature of learning and remembering through activity is a central fact. It may appear obvious that human minds develop in social situations and extend their sphere of activity and communicative competencies. But cognitive theories of knowledge representation and learning alone have not provided sufficient insight into these relationships. This series was born of the conviction that new exciting interdisciplinary syntheses are under way as scholars and practitioners from diverse fields seek to develop theory and empirical investigations adequate for characterizing the complex relations of social and mental life and for understanding successful learning wherever it occurs. The series invites contributions that advance our understanding of these seminal issues.

Christian Heath
Roy Pea
Lucy A. Suchman

Preface

As part of their series of regular sales of art, antiques and general effects, Bainbridge's, a small auction house in Ruislip, West London, had the opportunity to sell a Chinese *yang-cai*, or double-walled vase. The vase had been consigned as part of the house clearance of a bungalow in Pinner not far from the auction rooms. It was one of more than 400 lots to be sold that day. The sale included furniture, pottery, silver, plate, jewellery, pictures, small collectables and the like – the stuff of auctions of art, antiques and general effects sold throughout hundreds of salerooms in Britain, mainland Europe, North America and Australasia each week. Most lots sell for less than £1,000 and many for less than £100. During the days running up to the sale, the vase was on view to potential buyers in the cluttered storeroom at the auction house, placed on a table close to the kitchen. On the day of the sale itself, the auction room was remarkably busy with people sitting on the furniture that was to be sold, standing at the back of the room and crowded along the staircase that rises to the mezzanine floor above. By now the auctioneer, Peter Bainbridge, realised there was substantial interest in the vase but had little idea what price it would achieve.

The auctioneer began the sale of the vase at £500,000 and bidding soon rose by increments of £1 million. As the price rose past £20 million, it fell to two buyers, or at least their representatives, sitting alongside each other on a settee that was to be sold as part of the same sale. The vase was finally sold to a 'leading mainland Chinese collector' for £43 million, surpassing the previous record for a Chinese work of art, £37 million paid earlier the same year for an eleventh-century calligraphic scroll sold at the Beijing Poly auction house. The hammer was brought down to gasps and applause. In his excitement, the auctioneer struck the gavel a number of times on the rostrum. After the sale, when a television crew turned up to film a short piece for the evening news, it was reported that the auctioneer removed the masterpiece from its carrying case – a cardboard box from a local super-market – a masterpiece that with the premium had cost the buyer some £51.6 million and may well have increased the auction house's coffers by some £10 million.

The sale raises a number of interesting issues, not least perhaps how a vase believed to have been commissioned for one of the palaces of the Quianlong emperor during the eighteenth century happened to find a home in a small bungalow in West London. It demonstrates the remark-able way in which an auction can establish the price of a rare work of art or antique through open competition and legitimately transfer its own-ership – in this case – from the niece of a deceased relative to a leading collector on the Chinese mainland. This seemingly simple mechanism in which the price of goods rises in response to bids from interested par-ties seems almost anachronistic, more characteristic of traditional, agrarian societies than twenty-first-century capitalism. Yet each year auctions serve to establish the price and exchange of art and antiques worth many billions of pounds. Indeed, the prices achieved at auction are frequently used as 'reference values' and serve as a barometer of the market for works of art and antiques – whether paintings by Dutch masters, early eighteenth-century walnut chairs, long case clocks or, as in the case at hand, Chinese *yang-cai* or double-walled vases.

Over the centuries, auctions of art and antiques have become institu-tionalised with numerous provincial, national and international houses in Europe, North America, Australasia and, increasingly, the Far East holding sales of art, antiques, objets d'art and general effects on a regular basis. The press and publicity that arise when a Picasso or Turner, the jewel-lery collection of a Hollywood actress or a Chinese vase sells for many millions of pounds draw attention from the hundreds and thousands of pictures, paintings, clocks, toys, posters, bronzes, sculptures, cameras, clas-sic cars, musical instruments, watches, tea caddies, books, jewels, costumes, garden ornaments, pieces of china, silver and the like sold each and every year through auction. Each one of these transactions, transactions that may involve the sale of goods worth anything from a few pounds to many mil-lions, is accomplished through a brief intense episode of social interaction, an episode that rarely lasts for more than a minute and, in most cases, sig-nificantly less.

It is this interaction, its characteristics and organisation, that forms the focus of this book. Drawing on ethnomethodology and conversation analy-sis, it considers how a complex institutional arrangement is accomplished through embodied or multimodal action and interaction. It examines the ways in which participants – auctioneers, buyers and sale assistants – through talk, bodily comportment and the use of various tools and technologies determine the price and exchange of goods worth many billions of pounds each year – transactions that rarely lead to dispute or difficulty. It addresses matters of *order, trust and competition*, matters central to economic action and market activity, and explores the ways in which they are managed and resolved within the practicalities of the event itself, the routine and recurrent forms of social interaction through which auctions are accomplished.

The book is primarily based on the analysis of a substantial corpus of video recordings of auctions in Britain, mainland Europe and North America gathered over a number of years. Recording was accompanied by extensive field work of both auctions and the activities that arise behind the scenes – in preparing and cataloguing auctions, in displaying the goods for sale and in dealing with vendors and buyers before and after the event. Much time was spent talking to auctioneers, experts, saleroom managers and administrative staff concerning such matters as securing consignments, planning and structuring sales, listing commissions, dealing with accounts, negotiating fees, introducing technical systems and a whole host of related issues that arise in the operation of an auction and auction house. Field work also included numerous discussions and meetings with buyers, members of the trade as well as collectors and private buyers, many of whom provided highly insightful observations concerning the operation of auctions and their own participation and buying practices. On a personal note, having been in the antiques trade for a few years and having attended auctions on a regular basis since I was young, the video recordings proved a remarkable 'aid to sluggish imagination', to borrow Harold Garfinkel's phrase, revealing features of the auction's accomplishment that had passed unawares to myself and others who frequently participate in these events. While analysis primarily involved extensive transcription and scrutiny of the video recordings, the recordings also provided a useful resource in provoking comments and reflections from auctioneers, saleroom assistants and buyers.

As analysis developed, it became increasingly clear that it was necessary to improve the quality of the recorded data and in particular to secure more reliable access to buyers and sale assistants as well as auctioneers. With the generous assistance of Robin Meisner, Anthony Morris and Menisha Patel, I was able to build a substantial corpus of video recordings using three or more cameras that enabled more detailed scrutiny of the interaction that arose between the auctioneer, prospective buyers and their representatives as well as the telephone and Internet communications that play an increasingly important role in the auction. With the support of a number of auction houses, I was able to progressively broaden the range and types of auction we recorded. This substantial corpus of recordings includes sales undertaken in regional, national and international auctions houses in the United Kingdom and abroad, and auctions that range from sales of old masters to antiquities, early English furniture to modern and contemporary art, from high-end sales of fine art, through to rural auctions of general household effects. For convenience, throughout the book I use the term *art and antiques* to encompass a broad range of merchandise including paintings, prints, clocks, china, porcelain, jewellery, books, furniture, metalwork, toys, objets d'art, watches, boxes, maps, carpets, musical instruments, photographs, mirrors, statuary, costumes, cameras, trinkets, drawings, antiquities, weapons and much more besides.

Other material and data were also gathered as part of the project. Aside from field work, video recording, discussions and interviews, a number of auction houses generously provided access to a range of internal documents including the confidential sale sheets used by auctioneers during a sale. Also, in collaboration with Hideaki Kuzuoka and Jun Yamashita (University of Tsukuba), Paul Luff and Dirk vom Lehn (King's College London) and two willing and enthusiastic auctioneers, Robert Stones and Nick Allsopp (Peter Wilson Fine Art), we undertook an experimental auction involving students and staff at King's College London. The aim of the auction was to evaluate the use of a prototype system to enhance Internet participation in live auctions. One or two of the findings from the experiment are discussed in Chapter 6. Aside from these materials, it is worth mentioning that for anyone interested in auctions of art and antiques, there is a wealth of readily available material including histories of the auction and auction houses, light-hearted biographies of auctioneers, delightful descriptions found in novels and an interesting and insightful trade press. In Britain, for instance, we have the excellent trade weekly, the *Antiques Trade Gazette*, commonly known as the ATG, from which I liberally quote extracts throughout this book.

For all of us who engage in field work and ethnography, we are well used to relying on 'the kindness of strangers' to cite that wonderful phrase of Tennessee Williams in *A Streetcar Named Desire*, but even for a well-seasoned academic, the kindness and generosity that I have received from auctioneers, specialists, saleroom managers and assistants and buyers have proved remarkable. Despite the cynicism that is sometimes levelled at auctioneers and the auction houses, I have found nothing but openness and encouragement for the research with few, if any, limits placed on access or the topics that people were willing to discuss. Members of the art and antiques trade as well as collectors and other members of the public who attend auctions have also shown extraordinary generosity – enabling us to record sales and discuss the practicalities of buying and selling at auction. It is not possible to thank all those who helped with the research, but without their kindness and support it would have been a great deal more difficult and less enjoyable to undertake this project. I would like to express my thanks in particular to Nick Allsopp, Paul Barthaud, James Bradburne, James Bruce-Gardyne, Richard Cratchley, Andrea Fiuczynski, David Gregory, Ian Guild, Jane Hay, Richard Heath, Carlo Karrenbauer, Chris Large, Cornelia Pallavicini, Marie Poole, Michael Pritchard, William Summer, George Wade, Tom Woolston and the late Brian Higgins. Robert Stones and Hugh Edmeads deserve very special mention in this regard. They provided wide-ranging access for field work and recording and demonstrated extraordinary willingness and patience to discuss at length the numerous questions and issues that arose as a naive 'outsider' attempted to come to grips with the intricacies of auctions and the demands of running an auction house.

For a number of years, the research discussed in this book has formed the basis of presentations, talks and papers given at conferences, colloquia and seminars in Britain and abroad. Audiences have shown much patience and I have greatly benefitted from their comments and in some cases liberally incorporated their ideas into the analysis. I am sure the following does little justice to their observations and insights and for any mistakes or misrepresentations I am very sorry indeed. A number of academic colleagues to whom I am very grateful indeed have provided particular support for and contribution to the study; they include Robert Dingwall, Charles Goodwin, Marjorie Goodwin, Howard Gospel, Adam Kendon, Hubert Knoblauch, Karin Knorr-Cetina, Hideaki Kuzuoka, Per Linell, Lorenza Mondada, Stephen Pratten, Alex Preda, Bernt Schnettler, David Silverman, Aksel Tjora and members of Work, Interaction and Technology Centre at King's College London, Jon Hindmarsh, Dirk vom Lehn, Helena Webb, Menisha Patel, Lewis Hyland and Francesca Salvadori. Paul Luff deserves very special mention in this regard – he has helped at every stage of the project – in data collection, analysis and preparing the many presentations and papers. Last, but by no means least, I would like to thank Phineas Cleverly for his tremendous efforts in the production of the numerous images and drawings, Helena Webb and Ami Naramor for their careful scrutiny of the manuscript and Simina Calin, Joshua Penney and Adina Berk of Cambridge University Press, New York, for their editorial assistance.

The research for this book was assisted by a number of research grants and fellowships. These include: 'Interactions with Artefacts in Public Spaces: Informing the Design of Advanced Technologies' British Academy and the Japanese Society for the Promotion of Science (2007); 'Pervasive Computing and Market Trading' EPSRC WINES Programme (2005–10); 'The Social Production of Value' Alexander von Humboldt Foundation Fellowship (University of Constance 2008/2009); and 'Enhancing Interpretation: New Techniques and Technologies for the Arts and Decorative Arts' AHRC (2004–8).

I would like to dedicate the book to my wife, Gillian Heath for her inspiration and kindness during the preparation of this book, and to my mother, Joan Heath.

Christian Heath
King's College London

1   Auctions

Institutional Form and Interactional Organisation

> Going, going gone. £40m record price for money, money, Monet. High
> drama at Christie's in London sent the largest of Monet Waterlilies ever
> sold to an astonishing £40.1 million, a record price for artist. Art's mira-
> cle in 2008 of climbing ever higher into the sky while the real economy
> crumbles on the ground saw no fewer than 11 bidders join in the Monet
> scramble last night. "Twelve million pounds to start it!" cried Christopher
> Burge, the auctioneer and chairman of Christie's America. At racing speed
> he galloped the bids so fast that arms were waving at him. Some of the des-
> perate super-rich waited for calm before entering late. "26 million new bid-
> der!" cried Mr Burge when we were already far above the Monet record.
>
> *London Evening Standard* 25.6.2008: 3

Each year some billions of pounds of art, antiques and objets d'art are
sold at auction. We have become accustomed to reading of the spectacu-
lar prices that the work of certain artists such as Rembrandt, Picasso and
Warhol achieve at auction, and yet it still comes as some surprise when a
Lucian Freud, a Damien Hirst or a Lucio Fontana sells for many millions
of pounds. These 'tournaments of value', to borrow Appadurai's (1986)
splendid phrase, with their drama and intensity, frequented by the international super-rich or as they are sometimes known, high-net-worth individuals, have achieved an almost mythical status, providing a momentary
glance into a world way beyond our wildest dreams. These high-profile
sales, however, are just a small fraction of the tens of thousands of auctions
of art and antiques that take place every year – from small salerooms in
provincial towns in the west of England selling numerous lots worth little
more than £100 to the sophisticated emporia found in the leading international auction houses in London and New York.

Auctions appear a somewhat anachronistic method of selling goods,
more common perhaps to traditional agrarian societies than post-industrial

capitalism. Merchandise of differing quality is presented to a gathering of prospective buyers, and an auctioneer rapidly announces the price in response to bids received from interested parties. The bids themselves rarely consist of little more than a gesture or a nod of the head, and yet the price of the goods may rapidly increase to five sometimes ten times the starting value. The price increases until only one bidder remains, and at that point the goods may be sold on the strike of a wooden hammer or gavel on the rostrum. This seemingly crude mechanism is successfully used to sell merchandise worth little more than a few pence or goods worth many millions of pounds ranging, at least in the area of antiques and art, from fine English furniture to nineteenth-century lemonade bottles, from neoclassical garden urns to the most charming Fragonard drawing. The sale of each lot typically takes little more than thirty seconds, and yet it provides interested parties with the opportunity to, literally, show their hand, and to buy the goods if they are willing to pay the highest price. And despite the relative absence of legislation in many countries governing auctions and auctioneering, surprisingly few disputes or difficulties arise.

Auctions markedly differ from the more familiar methods used to establish price and enable transactions in contemporary society. Put very simply, the most common arrangement is the fixed price mechanism through which the seller sets the price that the buyer or consumer pays for the particular goods in question. Prospective buyers may reject the price by not purchasing the merchandise. The price is not subject to negotiation, and price adjustments are made over a period of time. In contrast, private treaty involves negotiation in which the final price of the merchandise is the outcome of offers and counter-offers, with adjustments made until both buyer and seller can agree on a price. Auctions differ from both these methods. In auction, at least the form of auction discussed here, the price of the goods or service is the outcome of direct competition among prospective buyers who attempt to outbid each other. The final price is dependent upon the highest bid received and expresses the buyers' demand for the merchandise. Unlike more familiar processes of exchange, therefore, in which the price of goods or services reflects complex processes of valuation, in auctions value is constituted at least in part by virtue of the price that buyers are willing to pay on a particular occasion (see, for example, Cassady 1967; Smith 1989, 1991). Auctions are ideally suited to transactions that involve the sale of merchandise that varies significantly in terms of quantity, quality and supply, be it fish, cattle or in the case at hand, art, antiques and objets d'art.

Auctions provide a solution to a social problem. They enable the price of goods of uncertain value to be systematically established through open and direct competition and provide a vehicle through which legitimate transactions are secured between a seller and a buyer. As a social arrangement that enables a particular form of market activity, auctions have become increasingly institutionalised over many years, and in the case of art and antiques, auction houses are now responsible for a significant proportion of the annual transactions and sales. Moreover, in terms of the value of works of art or antique objets d'art, auction prices, rather than retail prices, have increasingly become the principal source of valuation, the 'reference values', and form the basis to various lay and professional price guides, market analyses and indexes. How auctions and auction houses have come to achieve such a dominant position in the market for art and antiques deserves a study in its own right (see, for example, Learmount 1985; Herrmann 1980; Herbert 1990; Lacy 1998; Towner 1971; Cooper 1977; Watson 1997), but here we are concerned with rather a different matter. Despite a substantial corpus of research within the social sciences, mainly within economics and econometrics, we know little of the interaction that arises at auctions and still less of the ways in which the auctioneer, in concert and collaboration with buyers and others, deploys an organisational arrangement that enables the price and exchange of goods to be legitimately accomplished in seconds. In other words, the complex social and interactional organisation that underpins and enables auctions remains largely neglected. Before discussing one or two studies that have begun to draw our attention towards this 'seen but unnoticed' organisation, Garfinkel's (1967), it may be helpful to provide a brief history of auctions of art and antiques and how this particular form of social arrangement has become increasingly institutionalised over the past few centuries.

A Brief History of Auctions of Art and Antiques

The first known reference to auctions is found in *Histories of Herodotus*, in his discussion of the customs of the Babylonians where he describes the annual village sales of women of marriageable age. The custom is dramatically portrayed in Edwin Long's enormous *The Babylonian Marriage Market* (1875), a painting that achieved a record price in 1882 of sixty-three hundred guineas and was owned until recently by one of the colleges of the University of London. It is the Romans, however, who are largely credited with first formalising auctions; arguably the importance of auctions derived in part from the need to efficiently dispose of general merchandise plundered by Roman armies. Indeed it is said that 'business agents accompanied military expeditions in order to be on the spot when these auctions were held' (Learmount 1985: 8).The word *auction* derives from the Latin *auctio*, meaning an increase, and the Romans established a range of terms to describe the key participants including the *argetarius*, who organised the sale; the *praceo* or promoter, who served as the auctioneer; the *dominus* and *emptor*, namely the seller and the buyer; with the sale held in an *atrium auctionarium*. It is suggested that the method of selling was much like auctions today, with auctioneers announcing successive increments in response to bids from prospective buyers. Following the decline of the Roman Empire we find little reference to auctions of general merchandise and works of art until the fifteenth century in Venice and a little later in the Low Countries, in particular the towns of Antwerp and Amsterdam in the sixteenth century.

In his insightful analysis of the records of the Orphan and Bankruptcy Chambers in Amsterdam in the late sixteenth and early seventeenth centuries, Montias (2002) demonstrates the increasing importance of the auction to the sale of household belongings as well as works of art, with dealers in particular buying stock at auctions or buying on behalf of clients. Masters of a particular chamber or guild, such as the Orphan Chamber, undertook the sales. On different occasions, sales involved one of two different methods to sell goods by auction. On one hand, the English or Roman auction method was used – the model most familiar to us today, characterised by an ascending price that increases in response to bids from prospective buyers, with the goods sold to the party willing to pay the highest price. On the other hand, the Dutch auction method was also used; sometimes known as the 'upside-down auction'. The auction begins at a high price with the auctioneer announcing successively lower prices until a buyer calls out '*mijnen*', or 'mine'. It is the method still used for flower auctions in Amsterdam, by some street traders in England (see Clark and Pinch 1995) and more curiously perhaps, by a number of television shopping channels. In the Dutch auction method, the first, and in some cases the only, bid secures the lot in question. It is suggested that the Dutch method was prone to dispute, with participants arguing as to who called out '*mijnen*' first, and despite remnants of the Dutch method appearing in contemporary auctions, sales of art and antiques overwhelmingly follow the English or ascending price method.

It is interesting to add that the auctions of general merchandise held in the Low Countries beginning in the sixteenth century reflected many of the conventions and difficulties associated with auctions to this day. For instance, the vendor (or vendor's estate) paid a commission for the selling of merchandise and chambers provided buyers with a period of credit to facilitate the purchase of goods. Problems of collusion arose, and the existence of 'rings' dampened the credibility of auctions. Evidence suggests that vendors or their agents placed bids in order to 'puff up auction prices above the competitive value of the objects sold' (Montias 2002: 25) – a practice that, for example, has caused eBay and other Internet auction sites some difficulties in recent years. Indeed, it is said that Rembrandt attended a sale in 1636 or 1637 to bid up the price of paintings by his friend Jan Uijl and received a small payment for his trouble.

Alongside the increasing importance of auctions of general merchandise including pictures and works of art in the Low Countries, we find the French government passing an act in 1556 to establish the Huissiers Priseurs (Baliff Auctioneers), who had the exclusive right to undertake auctions of property left by death or taken in execution, a civil position that remained in place, much to the frustration of the international auction houses, until recently. An early seventeenth-century charter in England attempted to restrict selling by auction to an officer called an *outroper*, but these restrictions were soon abandoned. By the end of the seventeenth century, encouraged in part by a Dutch king on the throne in England, we find an increasing number of references to auctions. Perhaps most familiar in this regard are the extracts from Pepys' diaries and his descriptions of the 'sales by candle' held in coffeehouses. These auctions primarily used the English or Roman auction method, but to restrict the length of the auction, an inch of candle was lit at the beginning of the sale and the person who made the highest bid before the flame went out secured the goods in question. The annual sale of French wines is still held in this way, but more surprising perhaps is the way in which eBay and other Internet sites have introduced a similar procedure (though without candles). At the beginning, the auction of each lot specifies the precise time at which the sale will end. As with eBay and other Internet auction sites, however, it was soon found that the majority of bids were submitted during the final few moments of the sale. It was also said that experienced participants could cunningly anticipate the flame going out and place a bid at the final moment – a seventeenth-century version of what is now commonly known as 'sniping'.

Towards the end of the seventeenth century and the first half of the eighteenth century we witness the emergence of the auctioneer and auction house dealing not only in general merchandise but also in more specialist goods including pictures, art, jewels, china and books. We also find the development of auction catalogues describing the lots and the conditions, including, for example, forbidding vendors from bidding on their own goods in order to raise the price. The English or Roman auction method, without lighting candles to prescribe a time period, became the principal method for sales by auction of general merchandise, including art and antiques. Learmount (1985) suggests the most important figure at this stage was Christopher Cock, who established his 'Great Room' in Covent Garden in the 1720s and foreshadowed the emergence of the auction house as we know it today – a specialised institution with permanent rooms with sales undertaken by a professional or at least a celebrity auctioneer. Learmount states that Christopher Cock was 'more than simply the first major auctioneer, he is in fact the link between the world as it was and the auction more or less as we understand it today' (Learmount 1985: 27). Parallel developments emerged in France, transforming the auction from a casual to a full-time business with the establishment of auction rooms in which to present goods and undertake sales.

By the mid-eighteenth century in England, two leading auction houses came to dominate sales of art and antiques throughout the world and do so to this day. Sotheby's was founded by bookseller Sam Baker and held its first auction in 1745, and James Christie established his auction rooms in 1766 (Figure 1.1). Both Phillips and Bonham's, who still hold an important position in sales of art and antiques, were founded towards the end of the eighteenth century. From the outset, Christie's held sales that dealt with a broad range of goods; one of its first auctions featured household furniture, pier glasses, Madeira, china, carpets and the like, albeit of some quality. In contrast, Sotheby's specialised in book sales and indeed only following the First World War did it begin to hold regular auctions of art and antiques, a strategy that flourished from the 1950s onwards. Aside from establishing permanent rooms and holding specialist auctions, a number of key elements begin to emerge that are now commonplace amongst the leading auction houses of art and antiques. These include the provision of specialist expertise that enables auction houses to discriminate, discover and evaluate goods – expertise increasingly reflected in the sophisticated catalogues that accompany auctions of art and antiques. It involves a widespread, increasingly global, network of clients, both vendors and buyers, that enables auction houses to secure merchandise and market sales to those with the interest, resources and wherewithal to purchase works of art and antiques – be they wealthy individuals, dealers or private or public sector institutions (including leading museums and galleries). It also includes 'professional' auctioneers who are able to conduct auctions with authority and not infrequently to secure high prices for the goods in question. In the eighteenth century, for example, James Christie – nicknamed 'the King of Epithets' (Cooper 1977) – was renowned for his rhetoric

CHRISTIE'S AUCTION ROOM.

Figure 1.1. *The Auction* by George Cruickschank (late eighteenth or early nineteenth century).

and powers of persuasion, and today auctioneers such as Tobias Meyer of Sotheby's and Christopher Burge of Christie's have become celebrities in their own right.

Notwithstanding the growing institutionalisation of auction houses in the nineteenth century and their growing influence on the market of art and antiques, problems remained concerning the integrity of the auction process and the trustworthiness of auctioneers. The general scepticism towards auctions and auctioneers is exemplified in the ways in which they are portrayed in novels and pictures, particularly nineteenth-century caricatures. In *Middlemarch*, for example, George Elliot describes the ways in which a provincial auctioneer attempts to cajole the innocent to bid for goods of little value:

> Meanwhile Joseph had brought a trayful of small articles. 'Now, ladies' said Mr Trumbull, taking up one of the articles, 'this tray contains a very recherchy lot – a collection of trifles for the drawing room table – and trifles make the sum of human things – nothing more important than trifles. This I have in my hand is an ingenious contrivance – a sort of practical

rebus I may call it: here you see it looks like an elegant heart-shaped box, portable – for the pocket; there again it becomes like a splendid double flower – an ornament for the table; and now ... 'a book of riddles! No less than five hundred printed in beautiful red ... Four shillings sir? Four shillings for this remarkable collection of riddles with the et caeteras.... Four and sixpence – five shillings. The Bidding ran on with warming rivalry. (Elliot 1871–2, 1992: 653)

There have been successive attempts to regulate auctions and auctioneers with the introduction of licensing for auctioneers in England, first in the 1770s and once again in 1845 (the Auction Act), though some argue this was more concerned with generating revenue for the exchequer than trying to regulate auctions. Doubts concerning the legitimacy of auctions and the integrity of auctioneers are perhaps exemplified by the anti-auction movement that arose in America in the early nineteenth century with pamphlets issued entitled 'Reasons Why the Present System of Auction ought to be Abolished', with a similar movement emerging in England some years before that included explicit references to Christie's and Sotheby's. Learmount quotes from a pamphlet published in London concerned with the 'Ruinous Tendency of Auctioneering' that includes a reference to 'that irresponsible body of men called Auctioneers, who know no laws or restrictions in their mode of business' (Learmount 1985: 94). It continues:

> Ruinous as this system is to trade, it is perhaps not so mischievous in that point of view, as for the grudging and grovelling spirit it engenders in that portion of society which ought to be above illiberality and meanness. What progress can we make in the work of civilisation, when we see a clergyman, a barrister, or a physician, truckling among a parcel of 'low fellows' at Squibb's, Robins's or Leigh and Sotheby's, for permission to get a fortunate nod at the Auctioneer, that is to enable him to save a few shillings in the purchase of trinkets and books? (1812 pamphlet quoted in Learmount 1984: 95)

Despite widespread reservations concerning auctions and those who bought at auctions, exacerbated perhaps by the ability of certain auctioneers to charm, persuade, cajole and even mislead buyers, there are few restrictions, at least in Britain, 'placed upon carrying on the business of an auctioneer, and no special formal qualifications required' (Harvey and Meisel 2006: 35). The 1848 Licensing Act was repealed and – notwithstanding legislation designed to curtail 'rings' or coalitions among buyers between the

Wars (1927 Auction Bidding Agreement Act) and to outlaw fictitious or mock auctions (Mock Auction Act 1961) and the emergence of a host of regulations at the national and European levels to protect consumers – auctions and auctioneering remain surprisingly unregulated. In the United Kingdom, a number of professional associations have emerged, including the Auctioneers' Institute of the United Kingdom, RICS (Royal Institute of Chartered Surveyors) and SOFA (Society of Fine Art Auctioneers and Valuers), yet there is no necessity, or widespread commitment amongst the auction houses, for auctioneers to belong to these associations. Moreover, members of the leading international auction houses are not formally members of the associations and certainly are not required to be so in the terms of their employment. Even in the United States, for example, where particular states such as New York regulate and license auctioneers, Sotheby's and Christie's have an 'arrangement' empowering them to 'license' their own members of staff to take sales. In Britain, anyone, with no formal qualification or license, can establish an auction house and become an auctioneer as long as they place their name and address over the door of the premises. And while one or two of the leading auction houses have introduced training courses for their auctioneers, most auctioneers with whom I have spoken received little or no training. Indeed, they claim to have 'learnt the hard way'; 'one day I was clerking and the next told to climb on the rostrum and take over the sale'. It is not surprising that we have heard auctioneers jokingly say 'we're just a bunch of public-school Del boys' – the name of a character in a popular British television programme who lives by his wits, wheeling and dealing.

Even in the second decade of the twenty-first century, some 350 years after they became increasingly institutionalised in Britain and elsewhere in Europe, auctions of art and antiques provoke scepticism and even protest. Only recently, for example, we find a Sotheby's sale of modern and contemporary art disrupted by a group opposing the 'orgy of the rich', a group which then staged a mock auction on the street outside in which £50 notes were thrown into the air.

Beginning in the 1950s, a small number of leading auction houses increasingly dominated the market for art and antiques. Through the extraordinary energy and influence of its director, Peter Wilson, Sotheby's recognised the potential of the international market for modern paintings, and, following the de-restriction of the U.S. wartime currency regulations, held its first sale devoted entirely to Impressionist paintings in 1955. By the 1960s, Sotheby's opened an office in New York and purchased the leading U.S. auction house, Parke-Bernet. According to Cooper, these developments:

> changed the whole balance of the art market, which had previously favoured international dealers such as the Duveens, the Kugels, the Partridges and the Wildensteins, and which now allowed the auctioneer to assume a natural right to many of the major deals. (1977: 90)

Notwithstanding the financial difficulties that emerged in the 1970s by virtue of the oil crisis, the late 1950s onwards brought – at least until the last decade or so – an extraordinary expansion of the leading international auction houses and a flourishing of provincial salerooms dealing in art and antiques in Europe and North America. Sotheby's and Christie's developed a range of specialist departments and for some years expanded both the number of sales and the range of merchandise they sold at auction under the broad rubric of art and antiques and objets d'art. We saw, for example, the subdivision of picture sales into a number of specialist subcategories, including old masters, watercolours, Impressionist and contemporary art and old master prints, as well as the creation of new 'disciplines' and accompanying sales specialising in costumes, toys, scientific instruments, cameras, photographs, posters and the like. These developments were funded through substantial increases in turnover, year on year, and the growing number of million-dollar sales. Both houses developed an increasingly global market for certain goods and opened offices and salerooms in many major European cities and cities in the Far East, Australia and, more recently, in Russia, India and China. The net turnover of Sotheby's in 1938 was just over £3 million and reached £98 million in 1976. In 2007, it peaked at $1.9 billion (U.S. billion).

Despite these developments – the growing institutionalisation and internationalism and their increasing domination of the market for art and antiques – there remains some mistrust of auctions and auctioneers. The price-fixing scandal of the early 1990s involving Sotheby's and Christie's, the introduction of guarantees for vendors to enable the auction houses to secure major works of art and collections, loan arrangements, 'financial interests' in some of the goods sold, the increase in commission rates and the introduction of the 'buyer's premium', the substantial profits of the leading auction houses – all served to cast doubt on the operation of auctions and the validity of the prices, and, in some cases, the transactions that arose. How these matters of trust and legitimacy are resolved within the practicalities of the auction and the interaction that arises poses an important question for those of us interested in the ways in which this seemingly simple method of selling goods transacts sales worth billions of pounds each year.

Beginning in the 1990s, we witnessed significant changes in the market for art and antiques, changes that have had an important impact on auctions and the ways in which the auction houses select and market merchandise. For some it began to look as if this was a 'boom with no bust'.

> Art prices leap as new buyers enter the frame. New buyers entering the art market are causing prices to 'leap' beyond all expectations according to auction house Sotheby's that has raised the highest sum ever realised in its sale of impressionist and modern art. The sale on Monday raised $88.7m, with 20 works selling for more than $1m. Bidding came from as far afield as Russia, the Middle and the Far East … during parts of the auction, the traditional increments of 10 per cent were evidently too modest for the more determined buyers. (*Financial Times* 21.6.2006: 3)

> This was a historic moment for the London art market, yet such was the almost machine-like efficiency with which Sotheby's were 'choreographing' bidding from their global network of private clients, some of whom had never bid at auction before, that the atmosphere in the room at these record breaking sales was at times strangely subdued. "There was a much broader interest than in the late 1980's" says Henry Wyndham Chairman of Sotheby's Europe who was on the rostrum at the Bond Street Part 1 sale. "Here are now many more nations bidding at these sales and a lot of new people in the market. There was a man in the front row who'd never been to a sale before who was bidding up to £4m." (*Antiques Trade Gazette* 1.6.2006: 1)

Record prices have been achieved for little-known works by contemporary artists, with Hirst ranking fourth, just after Warhol, in the 'art market heavyweights' in 2008, while stalwarts such as Picasso, Monet and Degas continue to attract substantial interest and achieve prices well in excess of the boom in the early 1990s. Until 2007, the revenue generated by the leading international auction houses went from strength to strength, revenue increasingly derived from the sale of highly selective, top-of-the-market merchandise, in particular modern and contemporary art. In contrast, middle-range and lower-range pieces, be they eighteenth-century furniture, nineteenth-century pictures, silver and metal work or other goods that have traditionally dominated sales of art and antiques, at best held their price, but in many cases have fallen in value over the last decade or so. In 2007, *Art Market Trends* stated:

> In 2007, the art market posted its 7th consecutive year of price inflation. In global terms, art prices rose by 18% over the previous year. The higher prices were accompanied by a higher total Fine Art market at 9.2 billion dollars, up 43.8% compared with 2006 and driven by a substantially

higher number of sales above the million dollar line: 1254 compared with 810 in 2006 which was already an exceptional year. (*Art Market Trends* 2007: 4)

A number of factors have contributed to the results that have emerged over the past decade and the extraordinary prices achieved for modern and contemporary art. As Henry Wyndham, chairman of Sotheby's, remarked in 2006 following highly successful sales that June, there are 'phenomenal amounts of money around at the moment' (*Antiques Trade Gazette* 1.6.2006: 1). The last decade has brought a significant change in popularity of certain works of art and antiques, more profound perhaps than the rise of Impressionism in the 1950s or contemporary art in the 1980s, a change primarily revealed through auctions, in particular the leading international art sales in London, New York and, to a lesser extent, Paris. This radical change in the 'economics of taste', to borrow Reitlinger's (1982) phrase, has had profound implications for the auction houses, not only for the leading international houses such as Christie's and Sotheby's, but for the thousands of salerooms throughout Europe and North America that hold regular auctions of art and antiques and form the bedrock of the trade and small dealerships throughout many countries. In Britain, for example, while the turnover and the profits of the international houses rocketed during the early years of the new millennium, largely through sales of modern and contemporary art, the fall in the prices of more traditional art and antiques such as brown furniture, silver, watercolours, porcelain and the like has proved highly challenging for the national and smaller regional auction houses, in their ability to both sell merchandise and persuade vendors that they should part with their treasured possessions. In some cases, smaller auction houses have closed or amalgamated; others have been subsumed by larger national companies, sometimes to face further amalgamation or closure after a few years.

Developments in the leading auction houses over the last decade or so reflect these growing divisions in the market. In 2001, for example, Sotheby's relocated and restructured its departments and sales dealing with the lower end of the market, announcing five years later that it was closing its new salerooms and placing a minimum value of £5,000 on goods that it was willing to sell. In contrast, Christie's has attempted to restructure and rejuvenate its auctions and the departments dealing with the lower end of the market, refashioning the salerooms at South Kensington and elsewhere. In a highly ambitious move to bypass the trade, which traditionally bought up to eighty per cent of the lots sold at auction, Christie's introduced non-specialist, regular sales with mixed merchandise, designed to appeal to the private buyer; sales open to view during the weekend and in some cases accompanied by well-illustrated 'mega-catalogues' that enable householders to easily peruse furniture, pictures, objets d'art and the like. As a marketing ploy, it has proved highly successful, with a substantial increase in the value of goods sold directly to private buyers rather than the trade. The profits that these sales contribute to Christie's overall results are small, however, compared to the revenue generated by one or two auctions of leading modern and contemporary art.

The changes in taste that have emerged over the past decade or so have been driven in part by the growing influence of buyers from the newly emerging 'tiger' economies. Whereas the boom in the 1950s was largely driven by North American buyers and the boom of the 1980s was spearheaded by the Japanese, developments in the 1990s were initially fuelled by buyers from the countries of the former Soviet Union. During the 1990s, an almost mythical Russian buyer entered the global market, and whenever extraordinary prices were paid, the press reported that an 'unknown Russian was responsible'. Auctioneers would joke 'well, it is Russian' when absurd prices were achieved for minor works of art, and a lively trade developed in adding fake Russian signatures to Western European landscapes to sell them for high prices in auction. India and China have had a growing impact on the market, not only by buying the more established modern and contemporary art, but in creating a significant demand for their own national treasures and for works by contemporary artists in the East and Far East. By 2007, Christie's posted a premium inclusive sales figure of $6.3 billion, a thirty-six per cent increase on 2006 with substantial growth in a number of sectors – post-war and contemporary (up seventy-five per cent), Asian art (up thirty-eight per cent) and Russian works of art (up thirty-eight per cent). These figures revealed the significant changes in the burgeoning global market for art and antiques, changes that have brought new buyers or their representatives to auctions and that have been accompanied by the auction houses creating sales in new specialist fields and establishing a presence in countries that hitherto had little involvement in the international market for art and antiques.

The financial strength of the leading houses over the past decade, coupled with profound changes in taste and purchasing power, has further entrenched the auction as the principal vehicle through which works of art and antiques are valued and exchanged. The leading international auction houses have increasingly attempted to out-manoeuvre the 'trade' by encouraging buyers to purchase directly from auctions, with dealers increasingly acting as agents rather than trading their own stock. Aside from giving generous guarantees, taking a financial interest in certain major works of art and expanding private treaty sales, the role of the leading auction houses has become even more pervasive as both Christie's and Sotheby's have established independent dealerships, namely the Haunch of Venison and Noortman's, both of which now stand at Maasctricht – the leading European antiques fair.

Unfortunately, the excesses of the new millennium did not mark the end to the 'boom and bust'.

> One by one, the global picture markets which experienced remarkable growth in recent years have begun to unravel in the sale-room. Whichever way the figures are spun, the results for contemporary art in New York, Russian paintings in London, Chinese post-War works in Hong Kong, or modern Middle Eastern pictures in Dubai have made gloomy reading. (*Antiques Trade Gazette* 20–7.12.2008: 26)
>
> 2008 will be remembered in art market history as a turning point, beginning in a mood of speculative euphoria and ending in violent contraction.... At the end of 2008, the total value of the global Fine Art auction sales amounted to $8.3 billion. This figure was down $1 billion on 2007. (*Art Market Trends* 2008: 3–4)

There was some delay, a few months, before the 2008 banking crisis hit auctions of fine art and antiques. Indeed the Damien Hirst sale that achieved such remarkable prices in September 2008 gave temporary succour to those who believed that the art world might be immune to the perilous state of Western economies. This was not to be; within months, selling rates fell, some disastrously, and many of the goods that did manage to 'get away' sold at prices close to their reserve. Both Sotheby's and Christie's suffered severe difficulties, not least as a result of their growing commitment to offer price guarantees to vendors, many of which proved impossible to achieve as the market began to slump. Indeed, both houses quickly abandoned the guarantee system, rendering it all the more difficult to secure merchandise at the top end of the market. By 2009, Sotheby's saw an eighty-seven per cent fall in annual profits, the financial effects cushioned by the large-scale redundancies they had imposed the previous year. The crash provoked further changes in the market, with some areas of the highly inflated modern and contemporary art market suffering particular difficulties whereas old masters and more traditional categories of art and antiques held their own at least for a short time. Ironically perhaps, it is sometimes said that the smaller provincial auction houses both in the United Kingdom and abroad, for whom the boom and change of taste of the last decade proved perhaps most problematic, suffered less during the financial crisis. Indeed it is argued that, in some cases, revenue increased since the downturn, largely due in no small part to the influence of the new markets in the East and Far East.

Irrespective of the boom and bust of the last few decades, auctions have come to dominate sales of art and antiques and the values that inform transactions both in the primary and secondary markets. They also increasingly inform and reflect changes of taste and the rise and fall of particular types of art, antiques and objets d'art. Despite the growing institutionalisation, internationalism and influence of auctions and auction houses, many of the problems and reservations that have accompanied sales of art and antiques from their early beginnings remain. It is still believed, for example, that on occasion vendors scheme with friends or colleagues to escalate the price of goods, or that buyers conspire to stultify genuine competition, and that auctioneers use various tricks of the trade to fabricate competition and drive up the price of a particular work of art or antique. One could argue that these and other practices might serve to threaten the very efficacy and legitimacy of sales, undermining the very principles on which auctions are based – that price and exchange reflects genuine competition amongst able and interested buyers. Yet despite the doubts and uncertainties sometimes associated with auctions, they have become one of the principal vehicles through which art and antiques, as well as many of other types of merchandise, are valued and sold. Notwithstanding the institutionalisation of auctions and the auction houses, even the introduction of legislation and professional associations in some countries, there would appear to be something powerful and pervasive about a social and interactional organisation that enables the legitimate valuation and exchange of goods worth many billions of pounds each year.

Auctions and Social Interaction

Since the 1970s, we have witnessed the emergence of a substantial corpus of research in mathematics and econometrics concerning auctions and price construction. Game theory in particular has made a significant contribution to our understanding of auction models and their applications, as well as their implications for participation and revenue generation. It has also made an important contribution to the development of models of auction behaviour, our understanding of the strategic actions of buyers and to the development of new auction mechanisms that in some cases, for instance in the sale of 3G spectrum licenses, proved highly successful, at least for the vendors. The burgeoning development of auction theory and models of auction behaviour has also been brought to bear on a broad range of economic phenomena and applications (for overviews see Klemperer 2004; Krishna 2002; Menzes and Monteiro 2005; Milgom 2004). Many would agree with Klemperer that:

> Auction theory is one of economics' success stories. It is of both practical and theoretical importance: practical importance because many of the world's most important markets are auction markets, and good auction theory has made the difference between successful auctions and disastrous ones; theoretical importance, because lessons from auction theory have led to important insights elsewhere in economics. (Klemperer 2004: 1)

Within this burgeoning corpus of research there is a growing interest in auctions of art and antiques. In a wide-ranging review, Ashenfelter and Graddy (2002, 2003) underscore the importance of how particular auction models influence price and explore the effects of auction institutions on price formation. Their analysis focuses on studies of estimate, selling rates and reserve prices and the 'declining price anomaly' that sees goods of the same type, when sold at particular auction, successively fall in value. They also touch on whether works of art are 'burnt' when they fail to sell at auctions and the ways in which secret reserve prices may serve to counter collusion amongst buyers:

> The value of the most important works of art is established by public auction, either directly, by an actual sale, or indirectly, by reference to other sales. How the auction system works is thus a critical determinant of how the public's preferences are translated into the evaluation of artistic work. The auction system is central in the determination of the incentives for artistic work, and the efficiency of the system is a key determinant of the cost of creating and distributing works of art. (Ashenfelter and Graddy 2003: 763)

The thrust of their review addresses how auction prices can be used to examine price movement in the art market, underscoring the significance of auctions to the constitution of the value of art. Not surprising perhaps, throughout the growing corpus of research on the economics of auctions, we find a central concern with the efficiency of particular auction models and their application, their outcomes, particularly in terms of revenue, and the strategic behaviour of prospective buyers. How the auction model is deployed on actual occasions, the highly variable and contingent forms of participation that arise and, perhaps most important, the social and interactional organisation that informs its routine and legitimate accomplishment remains epiphenomenal. Like any other form of transaction, auctions rely upon, for want of better terms, socially organised practice and reasoning in and through which participants legitimately accomplish, in concert and collaboration with others, the valuation and exchange of goods. As Lawson (2002) suggests, the analysis of markets and economic behaviour should entail in the first instance 'an elaboration of the human practices responsible'. In the case of auctions, like other forms of market activity, the 'human practices responsible' are inextricably embodied within, and accomplished through, social interaction.

Geismar (2004) suggests that in contrast to economics and econometrics there is a 'dearth of sociological writing about auctions'. There is, however, a small but growing number of studies that in different ways powerfully demonstrate how auctions rely upon a cultural and social organisation, an organisation that underpins the structure and legitimacy of auctions and the ways in which people, both buyers and sellers, participate in the event. For instance, while not a work of sociology or anthropology per se, Cassady's (1967) wide-ranging study of auctions and auctioneering, though now a little dated, discusses the broad range of social, legal and organisational issues that enables auctions to determine the price and exchange of goods and provides some insights into conduct that arises at sales. In a very different vein, Boeck (1990) provides a highly insightful analysis of livestock auctions and examines the ways in which the auction serves to coalesce and preserve a culture and community and in which it structures how buyers and sellers participate in the event. The significance of the community of buyers and sellers to the process and operation of auctions is developed further in Jarvenpa's (2004) study of sales of art and antiques, in which she directs attention to the importance of 'collective witnessing' and the ways in which auction communities contribute to and legitimise the transactions that arise. These and other studies, primarily ethnographic, stand in marked contrast to the forms of analysis that we find within economics and econometrics. They demonstrate how the operation and trustworthiness of auctions are inextricably embedded within a complex of social relationships and communities, including communities of practice and participation.

These studies reflect the long-standing interest in how economic action relies upon social networks and dynamic social relations that inform and enable the agency, order and forms of participation that underpin market activities. Perhaps most critical in this regard is Granovetter's (1985) highly influential work on the social organisation of economy and his application of the laudable concept of 'embeddedness' drawn from Polanyi (1944). Embeddedness directs analytic attention towards the ways in which 'economic actions are embedded in concrete, ongoing systems of social relations' (Granovetter 1985: 487) rather than undertaken by individuals pursuing their own self-interest, primarily to maximize profit (also see Swedberg and Granovetter 1992). The concept of embeddedness serves to powerfully promote the interconnectedness and interrelationality that underpins market activity and treats coordinated, collaborative action as embodied in, and deriving from, common understandings and shared cognitions that can become, as Abolafia (1996) suggests, institutionalised. Callon (1998) suggests that the 'notion of social network or more broadly embeddedness' provides a vehicle with which to address the question of coordination in market activity, social interaction, the 'primitive reality' that underpins market activity and lies 'beneath the contracts and the rules'.

The commitment to understanding economic action with regard to its embeddedness, in particular to the ways in which market activities rely upon dynamic social networks, has informed a number of studies of auctions including, for example, Bestor's ethnography of Tsukiji, the Tokyo fish market. Bestor demonstrates how an understanding of the organisational forms and institutional arrangements of a market that includes seven auction houses and numerous daily sales provides a framework for economic activity sustained by and accomplished through the dynamics of social relationships, patterns of interaction and a cultural order that is continually produced and reproduced (Bestor 2004: 16). He suggests 'the economic life of Tsukiji, in Granovettor's terms, is embedded in an institutional structure, that in turn is shaped by historical and cultural understandings that the market's participants, both individual and institutional, continually revisit and revise' (2004: 15). These commitments provide a vehicle for a wide-ranging study of the market's social, spatial and material organisation that includes a brief description of the auctions themselves and the characteristic forms of hand signals that participants use to bid. While concerned with market makers rather than auctions, it is also worthwhile mentioning Abolafia's highly insightful study of traders in which he suggests that 'financial markets are socially constructed institutions, i.e. that stable and orderly market arrangements are produced and reproduced as a result of purposeful action and interaction of interdependent powerful interests competing for control.' The approach treats the trading floor as an institution that relies upon 'a set of relatively stable arrangements for the repetition of exchange relations between buyers and sellers' (Abolafia 1996/2001: 8). Both studies are primarily concerned with exploring the formal and informal networks and inter-relationships that enable the constitution, performance and preservation of particular forms of market activity. Like Granovetter in his original discussion of embeddedness, they acknowledge that social interaction underpins the order, character and institutionalisation of the markets, including the social relations and networks that contribute to their accomplishment.

The emphasis on the importance of social relationships, even a sense of community, to the constitution of value is developed by Velthuis (2005) in his analysis of the contemporary art market, an analysis that is not primarily concerned with auctions but explores the ways in which dealers, through networks of established artists and clients, are able, and find it necessary, to establish secure distinct boundaries between the gallery and the auctions and the respective price of works of art. As Coslor (2009) shows, the differentiation between the two markets has become increasingly flexible, even problematic, in recent years, with examples of leading artists bypassing their dealers to sell in auction, for example the Hirst sale at Sotheby's (see Velthuis 2011) and auction houses such as Christie's establishing their own galleries. Notwithstanding these developments, as Velthuis demonstrates, dealers rely upon their ability to sustain a network of relationships that allow them to configure how an artist and the work is perceived and valued – 'webs of meaning … that connect prices with quality, reputation and status' (2007: 159). In contrast, the auction is 'parasitic', prices volatile and highly contingent, an event that, as far as dealers are concerned, transforms art into commodity.

The volatility of price at auction draws attention to the operation of the event, the transaction and the contingencies that arise during the course of its accomplishment. This is not to suggest that social relationships are not important to the operation of auctions like any other market activities, but rather to point to the ways in which those relations coalesce in and are sustained through the social interaction that enables the legitimate and ordered accomplishment of actual transactions and the valuation and sale of works of art and antiques. In this regard, two very different studies raise a number of key issues concerning the organisation of auctions and the ways in which social interaction underpins their accomplishment and serves to resolve matters of trust, order and legitimacy.

Perhaps the most important contribution in this regard is Smith's analysis of the social construction of value, in particular the ways in which 'establishing and maintaining ... a sense of community' (1989: 13) is critical to the legitimate determination of price at auction. Smith continues by suggesting that the legitimation of auctions, and the ability of sales to enable the trustworthy valuation and exchange of goods, is grounded in a social context and the 'process is totally dependent on the social interactions intrinsic to the auction and cannot be explained in terms of individual self-interest or rationality' (1989: 90). In a wide-ranging analysis of various types of auctions, Smith powerfully demonstrates how, in contrast to the neoclassical model of economic behaviour, sales rely upon a social organisation, rules, practices, a community of understandings, conventions and the like that inform how people, buyers, sellers and auctioneers participate in auctions. Whilst this wide-ranging ethnography is not primarily concerned with the interaction that arises at auctions, in a Goffmanesque and insightful analysis of the 'show', Smith provides a range of observations into the ways in which auctioneers conduct sales and attempt to maintain control over the participation of buyers and prospective buyers. Smith draws attention to the critical matters of order, trust and participation and the ways in which the characteristic forms of interaction that arise in auctions enable the fair valuation and exchange of goods.

In a very different vein, Kuiper and colleagues have undertaken a series of studies of the talk or speech that arises at auctions (Kuiper 1992, 1995; Kuiper and Hago 1984; Kuiper and Tillis 1986). They develop a model of Proto-English Auction Speech based on the comparative analysis of different types of auctions in North America, the United Kingdom and New Zealand, in which they describe characteristic features of auctioneers' speech including its discourse structure, oral formulas and prosody (intonation, rhythm and vocal quality). Despite the underlying theoretical concern with identifying the ways in which the formulaic speech patterns are a consequence of cognitive demands, 'processing pressures on speakers', the analysis reveals the complexity of an auctioneer's talk even though it largely consists of the announcement and repetition of numbers. Similarly, as part of a study of the speech styles of particular occupations, Dargan and Zeitlin (1983) demonstrate the importance of the ways in which characteristic features of an auctioneer's talk are concerned with maintaining the pace and rhythm of bidding and organising how buyers participate. I cannot resist the temptation to quote a teacher at the Nashville Auction School who tells his students, 'you went to school for twelve years to learn how to speak proper English; now we're going to teach you how to butcher it' (Dargan and Zeitlin 1983: 13). Both studies powerfully demonstrate the complexity of the stock phrases used by auctioneers and the ways in which small variations in the articulation of speech are consequential to the organisation of the event and the ability to facilitate, encourage and structure bidding.

This growing corpus of ethnographic studies raises a number of issues critical to the social organisation of auctions and the interaction that underpins valuation and exchange. First and foremost they draw our attention to the problem of order and the social arrangements through which participants engage and contribute to auctions. They point to the ways in which these arrangements enable the deployment of particular auction models, including the English or Roman auction method, and reveal aspects of a social organisation that underpins their operation. While these studies are largely concerned with exploring and demonstrating how the order of auctions, including auctions of art and antiques, rests in part upon, and is sustained through, dynamic networks of social relations and communities, they recognise that auctions, like other forms of economic activity, are systematically accomplished in and through routine forms of social interaction. The character of this interaction, its organisation and complexity, is touched on in these studies, but, one suspects as a consequence of both their conceptual and methodological commitments, rarely forms a principal focus of enquiry. Directing analytic attention towards the 'interaction order' of auctions, to use Goffman's (1983) terms, would seem of some importance if we are seeking to enrich our understanding of the social organisation that underpins the operation of this particular form of economic activity.

Second, these studies demonstrate how matters of trust and legitimacy are critical to the ability of auctions to establish the value of goods and enable their exchange. They show how trust is not simply achieved by virtue of the deployment of a particular model or as a consequence of the status or standing of a particular auction house, but rather chart the ways in which the legitimacy of sales rests, in part, on communities and the communities of practice that shape and enable participation. How people participate and are seen to participate in auctions therefore is critical to the legitimacy of the transactions that arise and in turn the ways in which the results of sales are treated as evidence of the value of goods and indices of the market. Trust in auctions and their outcomes is accomplished in and through the action and interaction that arises at auctions. The character and organisation of this interaction and the ways in which buyers and auctioneer participate in the event provides the resources with which to examine how these highly contingent episodes of economic activity achieve an integrity, a legitimacy that is critical to the successful operation of the market for art and antiques.

Third, these studies draw attention to the complexities of competition and the contingencies that feature in the construction of price and value. In contrast to the conventional neoclassical model of markets and its conception of the rational actor motivated by the maximisation of utility, they demonstrate how a range of cultural, institutional and personal characteristics bears upon people's participation in the market and the meanings and practices that inform the production of price and exchange. This concern with the rationalities that buyers themselves bring to bear in engaging in market activities, such as auctions, points to the importance of the contexts of economic action and the ways in which circumstances and contingencies bear upon how people participate in transactions. They point to the ways in which auctions provide a vehicle to address and reflect upon the social organisation of competition, not just in terms of the range of commitments, conventions and considerations that might inform the price that goods might achieve, but with regard how the interaction that arises at an auction may bear upon how people participate and the competition that arises. In other words, the interaction that arises in auction provides an opportunity to explore the occasioned production of price and exchange and the ways in which competition and the impression of competition relies upon socially organised practice that enables interests and commitments to be deployed with regard to the contingencies at hand, not least of which is the emergent participation of others during these brief, intense episodes of concerted activity.

The themes of *order*, *trust*, *competition* and *participation* pervade the following analysis of auctions and their social and interactional organisation. They are brought to bear on materials, data, generated over some years through field studies, interviews of auctioneers, sale-room personnel, buyers and vendors, and most importantly video recordings of live auctions of art and antiques. Recording was undertaken in the United Kingdom and abroad and included small provincial salerooms in rural counties as well as leading international auction houses in London, New York and Zurich. It is video recordings that provide the critical resources with which to explore the details of the conduct and participation of buyers, sale-room assistants and auctioneers, and with which to begin to explore the complex forms of embodied action and interaction that arise at sales by auction and that underpin a long-standing social institution of some contemporary economic importance.

A Note on the Approach and Presentation of Materials

Over the last two decades or so, we have witnessed the emergence of a growing body of research concerned with talk and interaction in institutional environments. Some of the most significant contributions in this regard have been informed by ethnomethodology and conversation analysis. These studies have addressed the social, interactional accomplishment of a broad range of activities that arise within institutions, activities that include legal interrogation, news interviews, political speeches, diagnosis, the delivery of bad news, counselling and therapy and classroom instruction and teaching (see, for example, Atkinson and Drew 1979; Boden and Zimmerman 1991; Clayman and Heritage 2002; Drew and Heritage 1992; Heritage and Maynard 2006; Maynard 2003; Perakyla 1995; Silverman 1997). They have demonstrated the ways in which institutional activities are constituted in and through talk and provide a template for the distinctive forms of participation that arise within these specialised environments. As Heritage points out, the sequential and turn-by-turn organisation of talk has proved a critical resource for these studies as they examine the ways in which highly specialised forms of activity embody a re-specification of the interactional practices that inform conversational organisation, a re-specification that enables 'institutional realities and their unique characteristics to be talked into being'(1997, 1984).

It has long been recognised that institutional activities, like other forms of social interaction, are accomplished through embodied action and not infrequently rely upon the material and digital – objects and artefacts, tools and technologies. Alongside studies of talk in institutional environments, there is a growing interest in what is sometimes characterised as 'multimodal' interaction, in particular, perhaps, the ways in which organisational activities are accomplished through the interdependence of talk, bodily comportment and the use of material and digital resources. This research has been gathered under the rubric of 'workplace studies'; research that draws on ethnomethodology and conversation analysis to examine the embodied and embedded character of practical action in institutional environments. It includes studies of work and interaction within a broad range of organisational environments, including, for example, offices and call centres (Moore et al. 2010; Murphy 2004, 2005; Whalen 1995; Whalen and Vinkhuyzen 2000; Whalen et al. 2002), operating theatres (Hindmarsh and Pilnick 2002, 2007; Koschmann et al. 2006, 2007; Mondada 2007; Sanchez-Svensson et al. 2007, 2009), control centres (Goodwin and

Goodwin 1996; Heath and Luff 1996; Luff and Heath 2000; Suchman 1996) and medical consultations (Beach and LeBaron 2002; Greatbatch et al. 1993; Heath 1986). Workplace studies have generated a distinctive corpus of findings and insights that address the concerted, multimodal production of organisational activities (also see Engestrom and Middleton 1996; Llewellyn and Hindmarsh 2010; Heath and Button 2002; Streeck et al. 2011; Szmanski and Whalen 2011). As yet however, save for one or two important exceptions, including Clark and Pinch (1995), Llewellyn and Burrow (2008) and, in a very different vein, Anderson et al. (1989) and Harper (1998), few of these studies have been brought to bear on the analysis of economic behaviour and market activities.

Drawing on ethnomethodology and conversation analysis and its foundations in the work of Garfinkel (1967), Sacks (1992), Sacks et al. (1973), Schegloff (2007) and Goffman (1981, 1983), workplace studies provide methodological resources with which to examine the interactional accomplishment of organisational activities, embodied and embedded action (see, for example, Goodwin 1994, 1995; Knoblauch et al. 2006; Mondada 2001, 2008, 2011; Streeck et al. 2011; Suchman 2007; Heath and Luff 2000; Heath et al. 2010). They drive analytic attention towards the situated, emergent production of organisational activities and the ways in which institutional forms are reflexively constituted in and through embodied action and interaction. The central concern with the occasioned production of action foregrounds the fine details of the participants' conduct – their talk, bodily comportment and use of various tools and artefacts – and prioritises the ways in which participants accomplish action and activity in situ in concert and collaboration with others. Interaction is both a topic and a resource; it forms the principal vehicle through which institutional activities such as an auction are accomplished and provides the analytic resources through which we can examine how participants orient to each others' actions in the emerging course of an activity's production. The social organisation, the resources, methods and reasoning, on which participants rely in the occasioned production of the activity, in this case the auction, forms the focus of these investigations and enables the contingent yet routine accomplishment of daily transactions in and through intense, passing moments of social interaction.

These analytic concerns, coupled with the complex forms of embodied action and interaction that arise in auctions, render conventional forms of qualitative data problematic. Field observation is highly insightful and yet provides limited access to the talk and bodily conduct through which participants accomplish these momentary transactions. So while our own field studies of auctions and auction houses provided invaluable information concerning the practice and practices of auctions and auctioneering, it was only through video recording the events themselves that it became possible to begin to scrutinise the interactional accomplishment of the participants' actions and activities. It has long been recognised that film and, more recently, video provide unprecedented resources for the analysis of human conduct as it arises in its natural habitats, not only by enabling the repeated scrutiny of (versions of) social action and interaction, but in the ways in which recorded materials provide the opportunity to show and share data and its analysis with fellow researchers and on occasions with participants themselves (see, for example, Mead 1974/1995; Goodwin 1995, 1993; Goodwin 2006; Knoblauch et al. 2006; Laurier and Philo 2006; Mondada 2006, 2008; Streeck and Mehus 2005; Heath et al. 2010). Given the potential contribution of video to social science research, in particular ethnography, it remains surprisingly neglected, perhaps more as a consequence of the conceptual commitments that inform much qualitative research rather than a reticence to exploit the opportunities afforded by the technology. However, the inclusion of video data in publication remains problematic and it can prove difficult to publish even still photographs in many social science journals. Over the past decade or so, there has been an increasing interest in enabling textual materials to be accompanied by pictures, even sequences of images, accessed, for example, through an accompanying DVD or via a website. These solutions are not unproblematic; it can prove challenging to enable a 'reader' to easily discover relevant phenomena within sequence of video images that show for example the movement of a gesture, and, in some cases, the ethical strictures that guide data collection, for example to preserve the anonymity of the participants, can undermine the reproduction of images from the original data corpus. To make matters more demanding still, unlike speech, for which there is a conventional method to transcribe spoken actions, there is no conventional orthography for the transcription of visible or bodily conduct.

The solution adopted here, as in other articles and books concerned with embodied action and interaction, though by no means ideal, consists of a mixture of textual description, pictures and drawings, coupled with selected transcripts of talk and accompanying diagrammatic representations of visible conduct – versions of the complex transcripts of talk and visible conduct used in the analysis of the original recordings. Where possible, the transcripts of talk have been simplified or reconfigured to draw out a particular phenomenon or issue. Names and references to people and organisations have also been changed to help preserve the anonymity of the participants, the particular sales and the auction houses. Images reproduced from the original recordings have been used to present fragments, but in cases in which I discuss buyers and their bidding behaviour we have used drawings to preserve their anonymity. It is very much hoped that these fragments from the original recordings provide at least some sense of the action and its organisation and do not prove too tedious for the reader.

At the end of the book, I have included a brief description of the transcription conventions. I have also included a brief glossary of terms for those less familiar with auctions and the nuances of language that arise.

2　Orders of Bidding

Discovering fresh delights. London dealer beats rivals and Getty to take a
newfound Italian Old Master at record £6.6.m – and says he got it cheap
at the price.

Antiques Trade Gazette 22.7.2006: 18

Lot 45 was a 'newfound Italian Old Master' by Ludovico Carracci entitled *Salamacis and Hermaphroditus*, a picture that had been 'languishing
unnoticed' in the storerooms of Knowle House, Kent for many years. It
generated significant interest at an evening sale of old master pictures at
Christie's in London. With a relatively conservative estimate of £800,000
to £1,200,000, the auctioneer started bidding at £550,000, and, following
intense competition, the painting finally sold for £6,600,000, a record price
for the artist.

Fragment 2.1. Transcript 1

   A:　Lot Forty Fi̲:ve:: the Ludovico Carracc̲i (5.5) Five hundred and fifty
       thousand pounds (.) to open it

       (0.8) Six hundred thousand pounds, I see already.

       .

       .

   A:　At <u>six million</u> (0.8) six (0.5) h:undred (0.5) <thousand pounds (2.3) Last
       chance (0.6) Anywhere (0.5) at six million (0.2) six (.) hundred (0.2)
       thousand pounds (0.2)

   A:　{knock} <u>Sol:d</u>

Aside from the Carracci, the auction featured a number of pictures by
leading artists, including works by Robert, van Huysum, Dou and what is
known in the trade as a 'sleeper', a portrait catalogued as 'the studio of van

Fragment 2.1. Image 1 & 2.

Dyck' that achieved a price some ten times its upper estimate. Such was the interest in the sale that Christie's opened adjoining rooms to enable more than 200 people to attend and arranged for more than thirty members of staff to take bids from prospective buyers via the phone. The following pictures show a section of the principal saleroom and one of the two banks of telephones manned by sale assistants.

The auctioneer knew of significant interest in the Carracci painting and a number of the other paintings included in the sale. He knew there was a leading North American museum and some members of the old masters' trade interested in the picture, but who would actually bid for the picture on the night and the price that people might be willing to pay remained unclear. As with any lot that comes up for sale in an auction, the auctioneer has to encourage people to bid and bid with dispatch and to coordinate contributions from those in the room as well as those bidding on the telephone represented by sale assistants and, increasingly, prospective buyers who bid through the Internet. The auctioneer has to establish competition and deploy an organisational arrangement through which the contributions of multiple participants, many of whom might wish to bid if the price is right, are organised through an orderly sequence of turns, where those turns, to corrupt Sacks, Schegloff and Jefferson (1973), are 'valued', indeed literally in this case of auctions:

> Turn-taking is used for the ordering of moves in games, for allocating political office, for regulating traffic at intersections, for the servicing of customers at business establishments, for talking in interviews, meetings, debates, ceremonies, conversations, etc (these last being members of the set of what we shall refer to as "speech exchange systems"). It is obviously a prominent type of social organization, one whose instances are implicated

in a wide range of other activities. For socially organized activities, the presence of "turns" suggests an economy, with turns something being valued, and with means of allocating affecting their relative distribution, as they do in economies. An investigator interested in the sociology of some sort of activity that is turn organized will want to determine, at the least, the shape of the turn-taking organization's device, and how it affects the distribution of turns for activities it operates on. (Sacks, Schegloff and Jefferson 1973/1974: 7–8)

The auctioneer's problem reflects an important analytic issue that pervades studies of markets and economic behaviour. Put most simply, the problem consists of the question of order. It directs analytic attention towards the social organisation, the processes and mechanisms of coordination that enables participation in economic transactions and serves to ameliorate the conflict that might arise by virtue of unfettered competition for scarce resources (see, for example, Beckert 2003; Fligstein 2002; Thevenot 2007). Rather than address this problem in terms of the formal institutional arrangements that might be thought to govern auctions, the following chapter explores the orders of interaction that arise at sales and the organisation that enables people to participate in the event in a transparent and systematic fashion. Critical to these forms of participation are the procedures and practices that enable the production and coordination of turns, namely 'bids', the expression of demand that underpins the valuation and exchange of goods.

Projecting Prices

In all, five potential buyers successfully bid during the sale of the picture. These included a member of a syndicate of the London old master trade headed by Johnny van Haefen, a buyer on behalf of a major North America museum said to be the Getty and the successful buyer, the St James's dealer Jean-Luc Baroni representing a private client. There were also a number of other potential buyers both in the room and on the telephone who attempted to bid but did not have the opportunity within the price range they were willing to pay. Nonetheless, determined bidding from a number of potential buyers, coupled with the low estimate and the 'fresh to market' condition of the picture, led to a series of lengthy bidding battles, and the audience spontaneously burst into applause when the picture sold for more than £6 million.

It is worthwhile considering one or two phases of the sale in a little more detail. For convenience, each bidder is numbered in the order in

which they first enter the bidding, for example B.1or B.2. Sale assistants
who bid on behalf of clients on the telephone are identified by SA and
numbered in terms of the order in which they first enter the bidding, for
example, SA.1 or SA.2. The transcription system for talk was developed by
Gail Jefferson. It is widely used within ethnomethodology, conversation
analysis and cognate studies of talk and social interaction. Details of the
orthography can be found in Appendix I. Where possible, transcripts have
been simplified for ease of reading.

Fragment 2.1. Transcript 2

    A: Lot Forty <u>Fi</u>:ve:: the Ludovico Carra<u>cci</u> (5.5) Five hundred and fifty
        thousand pounds (.) to open it

        (0.8) [B.1]

→A: Six hundred thousand pounds, I see already. (0.4) At six>h<u>un</u>dred
        <u>thous</u>and p<u>ou</u>nds::

        (0.3) [B.2]

→A: Six hundred an fifty thousand

        (.) [B.1]

→A: Seven <u>hun</u>dred thousand (0.4) At seven hundred thousand pounds

        (1.0) [B.2] [*SA.1 attempts to bid*]

    A: At seven hundred and fifty thousand

        (0.4) [B.1]

    A: At <u>eight</u>, <u>hund</u>red, th<u>ous</u>and, p<u>oun</u>ds:

        (0.6) [SA.1]

    A: Eight hundred and fifty thousand

        (0.3) [B.1]

    A: Nine hundred thousand

        (2.6) [SA.1]

    A: Nine hundred and fifty thousand

        (0.3) [B.1]

    A: One million pounds.

        .

        .

    A: <<u>Six million pounds</u>

        (0.4) [B.5]

    A: Six million two hundred thousand

        (4.4) [B.4]

A: Six million four hundred thousand

    (0.2) [B.5]

A: Six million six hundred thousand

    (5.6) [B.4 withdraws]

A: At six million, six hundred thousand pounds.…

A: Last chance (0.6) Anywhere (0.5) at six million (0.2) six (.) hundred
    (0.2) thousand pounds (0.2) {Knock}

Irrespective of the values that potential buyers may have in mind, following
the introduction of the painting, bidding is organised in terms of a series
of increments that rapidly escalate the price of the lot. These increments
remain stable through certain values: £50,000 until £1 million, £100,000
until £2 million, and from then on £200,000 until the lot is sold. The increments used at auction are roughly ten per cent of the current price of the
goods. The leading international auction houses detail the bidding increments that they use for many sales in the rear of the sale catalogues alongside the 'Absentee Bids Form'. These will include, for example, '£10,000 to
£20,000 by £1,000s' or '£50,000 to £100,000 by £5,000s'. There is, however,
normally a maximum price over which the incremental structure is at the
auctioneer's discretion, for example, at Christie's in New York $200,000, in
London £200,000. In the case of our Carracci we can see that the incremental structure remains stable from £2 million at increments of £200,000.
The following is an extract from the catalogue of the sale of Important Old
Master Pictures at which the Carracci was auctioned.

Bidding Increments

Bidding generally opens below the low estimate and advances in increments of 10% subject to the auctioneer's discretion. Absentee bids that do
not conform to the increments set below may be lowered to the next bidding interval.

UK£50 to UK£1,000	by UK£50s
UK£1,000 to UK£2,000	by UK£100s
UK£2,000 to UK£3,000	by UK£200s
UK£3,000 to UK£5,000	by UK£200, UK£500, UK£800
UK£5,000 to UK£10,000	by UK£500s
UK£10,000 to UK£20,000	by UK£1,000s
UK£20,000 to UK£30,000	by UK£2,000s
UK£30,000 to UK£50,000	by UK£2,000, UK£5,000, UK£8,000
UK£50,000 to UK£100,000	by UK£5,000s

UK£100,000 to UK£200,000   by UK£10,000s

above UK£200,000   at auctioneer's discretion.

The auctioneer may vary the increments during the course of the auction at his or her own discretion. (Christie's London 6.7.2006 Important Old Master Pictures: 193)

Notice that in Fragment 2.1, the auctioneer does not state a price and then attempt to have someone bid that increment. Rather, the auctioneer announces the bid after it has been made, for example, 'six hundred thousand pounds, I see already'. The auctioneer then seeks a further bid, and when it is issued, announces the bid, for example, 'six million four hundred thousand'. The pauses or silences that follow the announcement of each increment are occupied by the auctioneer seeking the next bid and waiting for the potential buyer to accept or decline the opportunity.

In smaller provincial auction houses, increments may be less formalised and are not necessarily described in the catalogue that may accompany the sale. Consider the following fragment drawn from a sale of household goods and antiques at an auction house in rural England. The lot in question is a small Doulton figurine charmingly known as 'Bunnykins'.

Fragment 2.2. Transcript 1

    A: The Royal Doulton (.) Mother, Father and Victoria Bunnykins ninety ninety, ninety eighty (.) eight >lot four sixty(s) lot number:? (0.4) Er: what we going to say we're nearer to:: (.) twenty pounds, start me off, ten:?

       (0.2)

  B.1: Five [B.1]

→A: Five I'm bid five lot number four sixty five (I've got) five (couple of five:s)

       [B.2]

→A: Si:x:

       (.) [B.1]

    A: Eigh:t↑

       (0.4) [B.2]

    A: Te:n:

       (0.2) [B.1]

    A: Twelve

       .

A: Out at eightee(n) bid at eightee(n) bid (I'm) eightee(n) now [B.3}
Twenty (.) fresh bid twenty (lot) Twenty pound (.) don't lose it f.fer a
couple of pound? (.) At twenty bid at twenty I'm selling at

[B.4]

A: Twenty two::

(0.4) [B.3]

.

A: At twenty eight, twenty eight I'm selling (away) (for the last count)
twenty eight pounds::: (0.2) {Knock}

In this case, four bidders compete for the figurine with bidding starting at
five pounds. The increments used by the auctioneer are initially one pound
and then two pounds until the figurine is sold for twenty-eight pounds.
Once again, save for the first bid, the auctioneer announces each bid after it
has been made and then seeks a further contribution. The potential buyer
does not bid, therefore, at the increment announced by the auctioneer, but
rather *against the current price with the expectation that the price bid corresponds
to the relevant next increment.*

Once an incremental structure is established, it projects the series of
prices that will serve to increase the price of the goods, at least for a certain
range of values. In consequence, following the announcement of the second bid, all those present know, or at least can envisage, what it should take
to advance the price of the goods. In other words, even though auctioneers may not necessarily announce the price at which buyers are invited
to bid, in announcing the current price, buyers can bid with confidence
that the price at which they bid is the projected next value. Establishing an
incremental scale enables the auctioneer to escalate the price of goods in a
systematic and transparent fashion that does not favour or respond to the
whim of particular buyers and prices they may have in mind. It allows the
price of the goods to be rapidly and efficiently escalated in values transparent to all those present, including those with a particular interest in the
goods.

The Run

Within the twenty seconds or so it takes to sell Bunnykins, four potential
buyers bid, and, while only five people successfully bid for the Carracci, a
number of others attempt to bid as the sale proceeds. It may appear surprising to find that, despite significant interest in the two respective lots,

bidding appears to alternate between two prospective buyers. In both cases, on receiving the first bid, whether £600,000 in the one case or £5 in the other, the auctioneer looks for and successfully identifies a second bidder, B.2. Rather than seeking bids from other interested parties, such as the sale assistant, SA.1, who attempts to bid at £750,000, the auctioneer returns to and invites a further contribution from B.1. When one of those two participants declines the (projected) next increment, the auctioneer then seeks contributions from a new potential buyer or their representative. For example, during the sale of the Carracci, B.2 withdraws at £800,000 and the auctioneer finds a new buyer represented by a sale assistant, SA.1, who had attempted to place a bid earlier. B.1 remains in the bidding until £1,800,000, whereupon a new bidder is found and so on. B.4 and B.5 battle it out from £4,000,000 with the lot selling to B.5 at £6,600,000. Similarly with the sale of Bunnykins, the auctioneer takes bids from B.1 and B.2 until the bids have reached eighteen pounds, at which point B.1 withdraws. B.3 then joins the bidding, B.2 withdraws, and B.4 ultimately buys the figurine for twenty-two pounds.

The escalation of price at auctions of fine art and antiques is based on what is known as the 'run'. The auctioneer establishes, or seeks to establish, *two bidders and no more than two bidders at any one time*. The procedure is applied irrespective of the value of the object or the scale of the increments, whether £2 or £200,000. It is applied irrespective of the number of bidders who may wish to bid or attempt to bid. With a stable incremental structure that project a series of standard values, the run forms the foundation of the organisation through which sales by auction are accomplished in an orderly, rapid and transparent manner.

Establishing two bidders and no more than two bidders at any one time enables the auctioneer to establish competition between two principal protagonists. It also provides resources for discouraging, even disregarding, the potential or actual contributions of other buyers that, if acknowledged, might well disrupt the evenness, rhythm and tempo of bidding. In the case of the Carracci, for example, we have mentioned that SA.1 attempts to bid at £750,000, but is disregarded until B.1 withdraws at £800,000. At that time, the auctioneer accepts a bid from the sales assistant and establishes a new run. Similarly, B.3 attempts to bid eight pounds when there is slight hesitation by B.2 to bid the next the increment. With the withdrawal of B.1 at eighteen pounds, B.3 once again raises his hand and the auctioneer accepts the bid. In these and almost all cases, the introduction of a new bidder is postponed until a current participant declines to bid the projected next increment. The auctioneer then accepts a bid from a new participant and establishes a run between the new bidder and the remaining buyer.

Establishing and maintaining two bidders and no more than two bidders at any one time also enables the auctioneer to incorporate contributions from remote participants. A significant source of bids in many auctions of fine art and antiques, especially those dealing with more valuable goods, is the telephone. Potential buyers book telephone lines with the auction house so that they can bid on particular lots. They bid through sale assistants who communicate the current price to the remote participants and when relevant bid on their behalf. The exchanges between the sale assistants and the remote buyers lead to a slower pace of bidding. This is reflected in the following example, where the pauses between bids are longer than in the previous fragments. In this case, in receiving a bid, the auctioneer announces both the current and projected next increment. The piece in question is an early eighteenth-century bracket clock with a catalogue estimate of £3,000 to £3,500. We join the action at £7,800.

Fragment 2.3

    A: Seven eight. Eight thousand
         (0.7) [SA.2]
    A: Eight thousand. Eight two?
         (1.6) [SA.1]
    A: Eight two. Eight five
         (0.7) [SA.2]
    A: Eight five. Eight eight
         (0.9) [SA.1 declines to bid]
    A: Eight five your bid Henry. At eight thousand five hundred, at eight thousand five hundred, I'm looking for eight eight
         (0.8) [SA.3]
    A: Eight eight? Is that a bid?
         (0.3) [SA.3 confirms bid]
    A: Andrew eight eight fresh bidder. Nine thousand

Two sale assistants, standing to one side of the rostrum, bid on behalf of the prospective buyers. The auctioneer alternates bidding between the two sale assistants until it reaches £8,500, when one of the two bidders withdraws. A further member of staff then bids on behalf of a new bidder, once again on the telephone: 'Andrew eight eight? Is that a bid?' After one bid, he also

Fragment 2.3. Image 1 & 2.

withdraws, and SA.2 secures the lot at £9,000 for his client. The sale consists entirely of bids announced by sale assistants. The auctioneer successfully establishes and sustains two runs between remote buyers mediated through sale assistants; the successive bids are voiced publicly and at each increment, the auctioneer turns from one member of staff to the other.

Bids from prospective buyers via the telephone are not the only source of contributions received from remote participants. Increasingly bids are received through the Internet and as we will discuss in a later chapter, these are also integrated into the orders of bidding in the sale.

There is a further source of bids that plays a critical role in auctions of art and antiques. These are bids placed with the auction house in advance of the sale by potential buyers who are unable or unwilling to attend the event. Known as 'absentee bids' or 'commission bids', prospective buyers provide the auction house with the details of the highest price they are willing to pay for particular lots. These bids are then entered on the confidential sale sheets or in the 'auctioneer's book'. The sale sheets also include information concerning each lot, often an abbreviated version of the description in the catalogue, coupled with the name or reference of the vendor and the catalogue estimate of the goods in question, for example, in the case of the Carracci, £800,000 to £1,200,000. The sale sheets or auctioneer's book also detail the 'reserve', that is the lowest price that the vendor is willing to accept for the goods in question. When the lot is sold, the auctioneer enters the sale price and the buyer's number or name on the sale sheet. The sheets are then passed to the accounts department of the auction house and form the financial basis to the transaction (Figure 2.1).

The payment made by the purchaser includes the commission charged by the auction house, known as the 'buyer's premium' and taxes such as VAT. The vendor receives the price at which the goods are sold, the

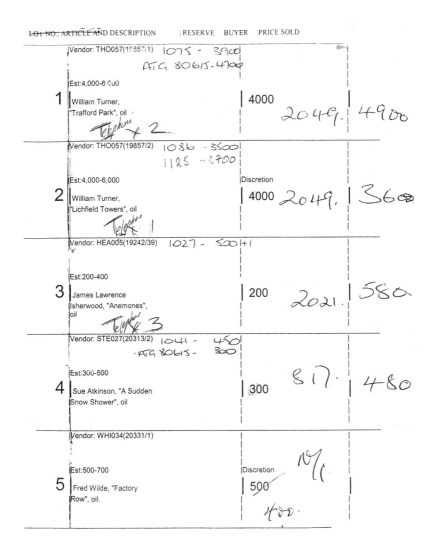

Figure 2.1. An auction sale sheet. Note the series of lot numbers and the details of commission bids on certain lots. The figures on the right-hand side are the selling price of the lots entered by the auctioneer.

'hammer price', excluding the commission charged by the auction house and other costs incurred in selling the goods, such as the cost of photographs, transport and taxes. The buyer's premium can be up to twenty-five per cent and the vendor can pay a commission of up to twenty-five per cent of the 'hammer price' for the sale of the goods. The commission rates and buyers premium vary significantly between auction houses and are graded with regard to the price scale at which the goods sell. Suffice it to say that the houses gain a significant proportion of revenue from the goods sold at auction, up to fifty per cent in some cases, and this forms a frequent source of comment and complaint by both vendors and buyers, especially from members of the trade.

The auction houses go to some trouble in handling commission bids. For example, to avoid the difficulties that might be caused by receiving two commission bids at the same value, the administration, sometimes known as the 'commission bids office', will systematically time the arrival of each and every commission bid. These bids may be received over a period of weeks leading up to the sale. In cases in which two commission bids are received at the same price, the timing of their receipt is critical. The first commission at a particular price takes preference over subsequent commissions received at the same price. When preparing the sale sheets, the administration will typically document no more than the three highest commissions for a particular lot. At his or her discretion, the auctioneer bids on behalf of the potential buyer until the lot is secured or the commission is beaten by a bid in the room, via the telephone or issued through the Internet.

Commission bids make an important contribution to the auctioneer's ability to facilitate bidding during the auction. Consider the following example, the sale of a painting by Joan Mitchell at a post-war and contemporary art sale in New York. For convenience, the bids placed by the auctioneer on behalf of the commission are represented by [A.].

Fragment 2.4. Transcript 1

    A: One Seven Nine is Joan Mitchell (0.4) here it is showing here↑ (0.3) Ar:: Fields for Two (.) an::d interest is strong...

→A: [A.] Here with me now at four eighty
       [B.1]

→A: Five hundred, [A.] Five fifty against you
       (0.4) [B.1]

    A: Six hundred, [A.] Six fifty (1.8) Six hundred an fifty dollars it's here with the absentee bidder (1.2) <Six hundred and fifty thousand: and dollars... Here with me now at six fifty
       (.) [SA.1]

    A: Seven hundred [A] Seven fifty (0.2) Ahead of you Ami
       (.) [SA.1]

A: Eight hundred (0.3) I'm out (.) It's here on the phone with Ami now (0.4) At eight hundred thousand dollars (0.5) Is there any advance

[B.2]

A: Nine hundred thousand

The auctioneer places successive bids on behalf of the absentee buyer. She decomposes the maximum price that the buyer is willing to pay and bids at successive increments. She announces a bid from commission, 'here with me now at four eighty', and secures a bid from B.1 in the room at $500,000. She then establishes a run between the absentee buyer, the commission and the bidder in the room. The potential buyer in the room withdraws at $650,000 and the auctioneer then establishes a new run between the absentee buyer, the commission and a sale assistant representing a buyer on the telephone. At $800,000, the auctioneer announces 'I'm out'; she has reached the maximum price of the commission. At that place, she looks for a new bidder and successfully finds a willing participant in the room, B.2. She establishes a further run between Ami and the new bidder, who finally secures the picture for $1,200,000.

Decomposing a commission into a series of increments enables the auctioneer to play fair by the absentee buyer. It enables the goods to be secured for less than the maximum commission price if at any point no further bids are received. It also allows the auctioneer to establish competitive bidding with a potential buyer in the room, via the telephone or the Internet, and can prove particularly useful when few interested parties are willing to bid for a particular lot. Commission bids, therefore, are integrated into the structure of bidding in a similar way to contributions from those in the room or via the phone or the Internet – they are decomposed into standard increments and juxtaposed with the contributions of a particular participant forming a run until the maximum price is achieved or the participant declines to bid the next increment.

A clear and consistent series of increments coupled with securing two bidders and no more than two bidders at any one time, even when those bids are placed by the auctioneer on behalf of an absentee buyer, renders transparent the process through which the price of goods is established at auction. At any place during the course of the proceedings all those present or participating in the event know the current price and what it will take to advance the value of the goods. They can discern the distinct contributions of buyers or their representatives and have a sense of the source of each and every bid. Imagine in contrast a situation in which the auctioneer randomly took bids from any participant within the developing course of the proceedings and accepted bids at any price at the whim of particular buyers. The lack of clarity might not only undermine the legitimacy of the process but threaten the ability of participants to produce and coordinate their contributions with each other.

A clear and consistent series of increments coupled with the run enables an extraordinary economy of behaviour that allows the sale of goods at auction to take, in many cases, less than thirty seconds. Indeed, it is not unusual to find auctioneers selling 120 lots an hour, and that includes the time it takes to check goods and to document the selling prices and details of the buyer. A stable set of increments that projects a series of prices enables the auctioneer to announce a current price and allows buyers to know, in advance, what will constitute an appropriate next bid and to bid against the current increment in confidence that the price will correspond to the projected next increment. Moreover, in alternating bidding between two principal protagonists, a bidder knows at any point during the proceedings who has the current price and who has the next turn to bid. This organisation selectively orders successive contributions and enables auctioneers within the course of a run to invite the next bid by simply announcing the current increment and, as we will see, by turning towards and looking at the underbidder.

Transitions in the Run

A run comes to an end when one of the two bidders declines the opportunity to bid the next increment. In the case of commissions, the auctioneer ceases to bid when he or she has reached the maximum price that the potential buyer is willing to pay. It is relatively rare for a bidder to attempt to re-enter the bidding at a later stage in the proceedings, so, in general, the increment at which a buyer withdraws reflects the price that the buyer is willing to pay. When a buyer declines to bid the next increment, the auctioneer will seek bids from new prospective buyers and attempt to establish a run between the remaining participant or the commission and the new bidder. In the case of the sale of the Ludovico Carracci, the auction consists of five runs, with the painting selling at £6,600,000 when no new bidder is found. It is worthwhile considering an earlier transition at £1,700,000.

Fragment 2.1. Transcript 3

    A: One million three hundred thousand

        (0.2) [B.1]

A: One million four hundred thousand

(.) [B.3]

A: One million five hundred thousand

(0.2) [B.1]

A: One million six hundred thousand

[B.3]

→A: °hhh One million seven hundred thousand

(0.8) [B.1 declines to bid]

A: At one, million, seven, hundred, thousand

(0.2)

A: near <u>me</u>

(0.7)

→A: At one mil(lion) [SA.2] <One million eight hundred, (.) against you

(0.5) [B.3]

A: One million <u>nine hund</u>red thousand

(1.1) [SA.2]

A: Two million

The run involves two bidders seated towards the right-hand side of the saleroom, B.3 in the front row, B.1 a few seats behind. As the auctioneer announces 'one million seven hundred thousand', the auctioneer turns from B.3 to the underbidder, B.1. B.1 shakes his head, turning away from the auctioneer. The auctioneer pauses, repeats the current increment and attributes it to a prospective buyer, 'near me'. The repetition of the current price, coupled with the word 'at' and the attribution, serves to display that one of the two participants in the run has declined to bid the next increment. It also serves to establish an opportunity for any interested parties to show their hand and foreshadows the search for a new bidder. With 'near me' the auctioneer turns from B.3, who holds the current increment, and begins to look to the left and then the right of the saleroom to find anyone attempting or preparing to bid. As he repeats 'At one mil(lion)', a sale assistant, SA.2, raises her hand and bids. The utterance is cut short as he announces the next increment. He immediately establishes a new run between the sale assistant and the remaining bidder, B.3.

Early in the sale of the picture by Joan Mitchell, the auctioneer announces the current price and that she has reached the maximum of her commission: 'Eight hundred (0.3) I'm out'. With 'Is there any advance' she begins to look around the saleroom to see if anyone is attempting to bid. B.2 raises his hand and the auctioneer establishes a further run between Ami, SA.1 and the buyer in the room, B.2.

Fragment 2.4. Transcript 2

    A: Seven fifty (0.2) Ahead of you Ami

        (.) [SA.1]

→A: Eight hundred (0.3) I'm out

        (.)

    A: It's here on the phone with Ami now (0.4) At eight hundred thousand dollars (0.5) Is there any advance

      [B.2]

    A: Nine hundred thousand

In declining the opportunity to bid the next increment, the run is brought to completion. The auctioneer then invites prospective buyers to declare their interest, and on receiving a bid seeks to establish a new run between the remaining participant and the new bidder. The repetition of the current increment, preceded by a brief pause and the word 'at', shows that the underbidder has declined the opportunity to bid (including the auctioneer on behalf of a commission), and, coupled with the onset of the search, it is now opportune for other prospective buyers to show their hands if they have an interest in the goods in question.

It is not unusual for more than one prospective buyer to attempt to bid following a break in the run. Consider for example the scenes witnessed at an auction of contemporary Asian art before the stock market crash.

> The enormous potential of the market for contemporary Chinese art was dramatically underlined by the almost frenzied scenes at Sotheby's eagerly awaited Contemporary Art Asia sale in New York. Numerous multiple-estimate bids were frantically screamed across the packed saleroom at auctioneer Tobias Meyer helping to generate a record breaking total of $13.2m far above the pre-sale valuation of $6–8m. (*Antiques Trade Gazette* 15.4.2008: 1)

It is not uncommon for the auctioneer to have to choose between competing bidders. Consider, for example, the sale in London of a pair of early eighteenth-century landscapes by Robert Griffier. The auctioneer receives a bid of £50,000, then undertakes a search for a new bidder. No bids are immediately forthcoming, and he calls out, 'Any more at fifty thousand pou<u>nds</u>?' Two sale assistants begin to raise their hands to bid. On close

fifty thousand pounds::? (0.2) Fifty five thousand

Fragment 2.5. Images 1, 2, 3 & 4.

inspection, SA.1 begins to raise his hand first, and it is SA.1 from whom the auctioneer accepts the bid. *SA.2* is italicised to indicate that though she attempts to bid, the auctioneer does not accept the bid.

Fragment 2.5

A: Lot <u>Ten</u>::::: (0.6) the er:: (0.6) pair of Griffier(s) showing there (0.3) an::: (1.0) <u>forty five thousand</u> to open this... [B.1] Bidding? (.) Fifty thousand (0.2) At fifty thousand pounds::.

→A: Any more at fifty thousand poun<u>ds</u>::?

→   (0.2) [SA.1 bids] [*SA.2 bids*]

→A: Fifty five thousand in several places. (0.3) At fifty five thousand with
      Bill

      [B.1]

A: Sixty thousand

      fifty thousand poun<u>ds::</u>? (0.2) Fifty five thousand

Irrespective of the number of individuals who attempt to bid at a break in the
run, or even what may be known about the particular buyers, the auctioneer
takes the first bid he or she receives. The principle of *first come first served*
underpins transitions within the run and identifies one prospective buyer,
in some cases one amongst many, as the next bidder. In taking and ascribing
the bid to Bill, the auctioneer disregards others who attempt to bid at that
moment and immediately returns to the previous bidder, B.1, and invites
him to bid at the next increment. It is worth noting that the sale assistant to
the immediate right of Bill is sensitive to the ways in which her bid emerges
after the onset of his hand movement; she begins to raise her hand to bid,
but abandons the movement after seeing Bill's hand thrust in the air. First
come first served provides the auctioneer with an efficient and economic
way of choosing one bidder amongst many. It enables the unproblematic
allocation of the next turn to one amongst many potential participants and
provides a vehicle through which a new potential buyer comes to participate
in a run. The participant who fails to have his bid acknowledged typically
withholds further attempts to bid during the subsequent run, confident that
further opportunities will arise to place a bid at the next break in the bidding. In this way, a smooth and rapid transition between one run and the
next is accomplished with little delay or difficulty.

Preserving the Run

Notwithstanding having more than one participant willing to bid, the auctioneer routinely selects just one new bidder and juxtaposes their contributions with the remaining potential buyer. If one of those participants
withdraws, the auctioneer may then turn and see whether a prospective
buyer who failed to have his bid accepted is still willing to bid and enter
the running. The sale of Bunnykins is interesting in this regard, since both
the third and fourth bidder indicate their willingness to bid at eighteen
pounds. The auctioneer accepts the bid from B.3 and then returns to the
underbidder, B.2, to see whether he will go to the next increment. He
declines, and it is only at that point that the auctioneer seeks and accepts a
bid from B.4 and establishes a new run. First come first served enables the

auctioneer to preserve two and no more than two active participants at any one time, and thereby establish competition, if only briefly, between two principal protagonists.

To preserve the integrity of the run, auctioneers will disregard attempts from other potential buyers, including members of their own staff representing buyers on the telephone, to submit a bid during a run until that run has come to completion. So, for example, during the sale of the picture *Great Innocence* by John Chamberlin at an auction in New York, we find the auctioneer preserves a run between two potential buyers, a 'lady in the room', B.1, and a second represented by Andy, SA.2, despite a delay in the lady responding to the invitation to bid and an attempt by the clerk, standing alongside the auctioneer, to point out a new bidder.

Fragment 2.6

    A: At two hundred, an eighty thousand dollars now, two (.) <two eighty, [B.1] three hundred lady's bid (0.5) At three hundred

        (0.2) [SA.2]

    A: An twenty with Andy now °hh

        (0.2)

→A: Three fifty? [*Clerk points to bidder*]

        (0.5) [B.1]

    A: Back to the lady

        (0.5) [SA.2]

    A: Three eighty with Andy again

        (0.2)

→A: At three hundred [*Clerk points to bidder*] an eighty thousand. At three eighty (.) [B.2] Four hundred (0.6) In the far back there (0.2) Four hundred

One of the bidders withdraws at $280,000 and the auctioneer finds a willing participant in the saleroom – the 'lady's' bid. She then seeks to establish a run between the lady and Andy. Andy bids the next increment, and with 'at three hundred', the auctioneer turns back to the lady. The auctioneer is looking at the lady by the word 'twenty'. There is no immediate response, and, following a pause, the auctioneer specifies the increment that the lady should bid and invites her response 'three fifty?' Again there is no immediate response and at this moment, the clerk points out a bid on the right-hand side of the room to the auctioneer. The new bidder is sensitive to the potential transition that would appear to be emerging by virtue of the delay

Fragment 2.6. Images 1, 2 & 3.

in the lady issuing a bid, and in turn, the clerk takes the trouble to point out the bid to the auctioneer. The auctioneer ignores the clerk and turns back to the lady. The clerk once again points to the bidder. This time the auctioneer raises her left hand to hold the clerk and the new bidder at bay – at least for the time being. They do not have to wait long. The lady withdraws at $380,000, and the new bidder bids $400,000.

While going to some trouble to preserve the run, auctioneers may well use the visible presence of others attempting to bid to encourage a particular participant within the run to decide whether to bid the next increment. So for, example, in the following fragment, the auctioneer has established a run between a commission and a sale assistant, Bibi. He invites Bibi, or rather Bibi's buyer, to bid at the next increment, $48,000, and waits as she speaks to her buyer over the phone. After a couple of attempts to elicit a response, the auctioneer takes the unusual step of placing two further bids on behalf of commissions, and, continuing to look at Bibi, awaits a response. Unsurprisingly, a new bidder attempts to bid, namely Ami, and the auctioneer uses the attempt to encourage Bibi to respond 'Coming to you Ami (0.2) Fiftythousand (0.2) Bibi (.) have to hurry you Ami wants it'.

Fragment 2.7

    A: At forty thousand

         (1.0) [SA.1]

    A: >Forty:,two: thous:and, Bibi

         [A.]

→A: Forty five: [A.] thousand with me (.) Forty five thousand (1.2) My bid (.) at forty five: [A.] Forty eight (.) [A.] I've got fifty: (.) [SA.2] <Coming to you Ami (0.2) Fiftythousand

         (0.2)

→A: Bibi (.) have to hurry you Ami wants it (.) Fifty thousand (.) I'll go to (0.2) fifty five I want sixty

Reconfiguring Increments

At some point during the developing course of the proceedings, no new bidder will be found, and, if the goods have reached their reserve, the auctioneer will sell the lot to the outstanding bidder on the strike of the hammer. One can see, for example, why auctioneers go to some trouble to create and in some cases sustain an opportunity for anyone to bid during what turns out to be the closing moments of the sale, since the absence of a second participant with whom to (re)establish a run determines the final price that goods achieve, even whether they can be sold at all. Preserving a run can be of some financial importance, not just for the vendor, but also for the auction house. It can help secure the sale of goods that might otherwise fail to achieve their reserve, and in some cases can make a significant difference to the monies received by the vendor and the auction house. When increments are of five or ten pounds, a few extra bids may make little difference, but in cases in which the increments are £50,000 or even half that figure, sustaining a run for a further one or two bids can have an important impact on the revenue generated by an auction.

Consider the following fragment drawn from the sale of the Photobooth Strips of Holy Solomon by Warhol. Bidding begins at $6,000; we join the action at $24,000 during a run between a buyer in the room and a buyer on the telephone represented by Tina, SA.3. The increments stand at $2,000. The auctioneer turns to Tina and invites her to bid the next increment.

Fragment 2.8. Transcript 1

    A: Twenty Four:. Thank you sir (0.2) Tina?

        (1.2)

    A: Gentleman no(w):::: in the room:: has it for twenty four thousand dollars:: (0.5) Going to <u>sell</u> to him Tina (0.6) Twenty four

        (0.3)

→A: Just for you twenty five

        (0.5) [SA.3]

→A: I'll take twenty six from you sir

    A: Twenty five (0.2) with Tina (0.2) sure sir? Thank you very much (0.2) <u>Twenty five</u>: with↑ Tina↓ (0.2) Twenty five thousand dollars:::::s:::

        (0.3)

        {Knock}

There is a delay in Tina responding to the invitation to bid the next increment. The auctioneer remains oriented towards Tina as she speaks to the
buyer on the phone. He attempts to elicit a further bid, upgrading the
urgency with which she (or her buyer) should make up their mind with
'Going to <u>sell</u> to him Tina'. No bid is forthcoming, but neither does Tina
decline the opportunity to bid. Rather than move towards the close of the
sale and sell to the 'gentleman in the room', the auctioneer transforms the
invitation; he invites Tina and her buyer to bid $25,000, half the current
increment. The move proves successful. The auctioneer then turns from
Tina to the underbidder once inviting a bid at the reduced increment. It is
declined and the goods are sold to Tina's buyer at $25,000, some $10,000
more than the upper estimate of the photographs.

In reducing the increment to encourage a further bid, auctioneers routinely establish a new incremental structure – each subsequent bid typically half the value of the previous scale. By establishing a new incremental
structure rather than, for example, simply taking a reduced bid from one
of the buyers, the auctioneer plays fair by both protagonists and preserves
a consistent price structure that maintains the transparency of the process.
It is interesting to note in the following fragment, having invited a bid at a
split increment, twenty-five pounds rather than fifty pounds, the auctioneer rejects the sale assistant's attempt to shift the increment still further by
reducing the price to twenty pounds.

Fragment 2.9

    A: Late Regency giltwood wall mirror

          .

    A: [A.] Six hundred on the books >six hundred pounds out on the
          phone(s) again six hundred

          (0.3) [SA.2]

    A: Six fifty

          (0.6)

    A: [A.] Seven hundred. On the book at seven hundred pounds.

    A: I'll take twenty five if it helps you. At seven

 →SA.2:   <u>Seven twenty</u>

  →A: Seven twenty five::

          (0.5)

    A: [A.] Seven fifty on the book. Out on the phone.

An incremental structure may not only be reconfigured in the light of an auctioneer's attempts to encourage further bids, but also in response to a potential buyer attempting to remain in the bidding. Bidders in response to an invitation may offer a reduced price, ordinarily half the current increment. So, for example, during the sale of the Carracci, one of the bidders, B.3, offers to split the increment at £3,400,000, offering £100,000 rather than accepting a £200,000 increase. The auctioneer rejects the offer and the bidder does indeed bid the full increment, but withdraws following a further bid by the competition. The auctioneer is more likely to accept a split increment when it looks as if no further buyers wish to enter the fray and it will make the difference in whether the goods are sold or are 'bought in'. It is interesting to note, for example, that, in the case of the Carracci, while the auctioneer declines to split the increment at £3,400,000, at £5,600,000, after a lengthy delay, he accepts an increment of £100,000 rather than £200,000 – thereby maintaining the run.

Fragment 2.1. Transcript 4

    A: <u><Five</u> mi<u>ll</u>ion po<u>und</u>s:
          (0.3) [B.5]
    A: Five million two hundred thousand
          (7.2) [B.4]
    A: Five million four hundred thousand
          (0.2) [B.5]
    A: Five million six hundred thousand
          (12.4)
    B.4   °Seven hundred?
          (2.0)
 →A: Five million seven hundred thousand
          (.) [B.5]
    A: Five million eight hundred thousand

Whether proffered by the auctioneer or requested by the bidder, reducing the increment can encourage a buyer to remain in the bidding and thereby sustain the run for at least another 'turn' and in many cases, as we will see, for at least two turns. In reducing the increment, auctioneers routinely halve or split the value of the increment and from then ordinarily establish and sustain a run involving the two remaining participants using the new scale of increments. In this way, bidders and all those present are able to anticipate the scale of price increase that will constitute each and every subsequent bid. It also enables the auctioneer to announce a current price and invite a next bid, without necessarily stating the price that the buyer will have to accept. In other words, splitting the increment and establishing a new scale of prices that simply halves the values used up until that point provides a coherent structure for the auctioneer to implement and participants to follow. It enables a run to be sustained while preserving the transparency and economy with which bidding is organised.

Differentiating Contributions

While the success and integrity of auctions relies upon the principle that no favour or disfavour is shown towards any particular buyer, the allocation of opportunities to bid is sensitive to the source or type of bid. Take commission bids, for example. In principle, bids from commission could be announced at any point within the proceedings and one might imagine that if the auctioneer failed to find a willing participant in the room, he might simply take a bid from the book or sale sheets. This rarely happens. Consider the following fragment involving the sale of a 'nice little bracket clock'. The auctioneer takes the first bid from commission and then searches the room for a potential buyer, forewarning any potential buyer of the increment that that will be used by asking, 'one ten do I hear?' He receives a bid from the room. Rather than seeking a second buyer within the room or from one of the sale assistants manning the phones he immediately announces a third bid on behalf of the commission.

Fragment 2.10

    A: One Forty Two:: a nice little bracket clock here for selling. [A.] Hundred pounds I'm bid. At one hundred one ten is it now one ten do I hear. One hundred [B.1] <One ten. One ten [A.] One twenty with me: One thirty are you bidding? (.) [B.1] One thir(ty) [A.] One forty One fifty? [B.1] One fifty (0.2) One fifty [A.] One sixty

        [B.1]

→A: One seventy now. Your bid at one seventy (0.7) *Seventy (0.5) One eighty anywhere else (.) One seventy

        (.) [B.2]

    A: One eighty fresh bidder [B.1] One ninety. One ninety [B.2] Two hundred. [B.1] Two ten

From the outset, the auctioneer establishes a run between the absentee buyer, A., on whose behalf he bids, and a participant in the room. He reaches the maximum price of the commission at £160 and then, and only then, does he look for a bidder to replace the absentee buyer and establish a further run. Finding a prospective buyer in the room, the auctioneer establishes a new run between B.1 and B.2, a second buyer in the room. Even in cases in which an auctioneer has two or more prospective buyers in the saleroom attempting to bid early in the sale, he will take the first bid off commission and then select one of the potential participants with whom to establish a run. In the following fragment, the auctioneer announces the first bid on commission A. and then invites bids. The attempts to bid disregarded by the auctioneer are in italics.

Fragment 2.11

    A: Lot One Sixty Fi<u>ve</u> (.) an::: (0.2) [A.] nine hundred is already <u>bid</u> (.) with <u>me</u> (.) at nine: hundred pounds:. At nine hundred pounds and against the ro<u>om:</u>

         (0.7)

→A: At nine hundred. [SA.1. *SA.2*] Nine fifty

         [A.]

    A: One thous:<u>and</u> with me

→   (0.2) [*SA.3*]

    A: At one thousand

→   (0.5) [SA.1, *SA.3*]

    A: Eleven hundred with Midgy

         [A.]

    A: Twelve hundred with me and against the you <u>both:</u>.

Two sale assistants attempt to bid at £900, SA.1 raising her buyer number slightly in advance of SA.2. The auctioneer takes the first bid but disregards the second, establishing a run between the absentee buyer and the sale assistant. A third sale assistant, SA.3, attempts to bid at 'One thousand'; the auctioneer disregards the bid and repeats the increment 'At one thousand'. SA.3 attempts to bid again, and once more is disregarded in favour of SA.1, preserving the run between commission and the original participant, SA.1. 'Against the you <u>both:</u>' reveals that the commission has reached its maximum price, £1,200, and that statement seeks an actual bid from one of the two sale assistants, SA.2 and SA.3, who attempted to bid earlier.

Aside from prioritizing commission bids, auctioneers will also attempt to take bids from the room before accepting contributions by telephone or over the Internet. Consider the following fragment involving the sale of a pair of pictures in the manner of Vernet.

Fragment 2.12

A: Showing there <u>pair</u> of <u>Vernet</u>s (.) or: (.) the manner of Vernets on:: commission bids <u>here</u> of: (2.5) nine hundred an fifty pounds to open it.

[A.]

A: At nine hundred an fifty pounds

→   [*SA.1*]

(0.3)

A: At nine hundred an fifty pounds.

→   [B.1] One thousand [A.] Eleven hundred

[B.1] Twelve hundred [A.] Thirteen hundred with me. At thirteen hundred (.) Still my bid (.) Bidding?

(0.5) [B.1 declines]

→A: At thirteen hundred pounds: (0.5) Anyone?

→   [SA.1]

A: Fourteen hundred [A] Fifteen hundred (0.5) Make it sixteen? [SA.1] Sixteen hundred with Sam: (.) I'm out

A: Sixteen hundred pounds

(.) [SA.2]

A: Seventeen hundred (0.3) At seventeen↑ hundred↓ Near me at seventeen (0.3) hundred pounds

(0.4)

{Knock}

A sale assistant attempts to bid towards the beginning of 'At nine hundred an fifty pounds', well in advance of a bid in the room, which arises a few moments following the announcement of the bid. The sale assistant thrusts the bidding number well above her head and the auctioneer looks directly at her. As he continues to announce 'at nine hundred an fifty pounds', the sale assistant energetically waggles her buyer number. The auctioneer does not accept the bid, but rather turns to the room to see whether anyone is willing or preparing to bid. A catalogue is raised and the auctioneer announces the bid from the room.

Fragment 2.13. Image 1, 2 & 3.

The auctioneer establishes a run between a participant in the room and a commission until £1,300, at which point the bidder withdraws. Even then it is interesting to note that the auctioneer searches the saleroom before turning towards the sale assistants manning the phones to see if anyone wishes to bid. As he turns to the phones, he utters 'anyone?' an invitation that is then, and only then, directed towards the sale assistants. Almost immediately, a sale assistant bids and becomes part of a run bidding against the auctioneer representing the absentee buyer on commission.

Auctioneers suggest that prioritising bids from the room in preference to bids from buyers on the telephone or the Internet at the beginning of the sale of each lot provides recognition of those who have bothered to attend the sale. It can also avoid the impression that the auction primarily involves remote participants – with buyers in the saleroom failing to get a look in. Aside from showing regard for those who trouble to attend sales, there is also a practical issue that encourages auctioneers, and in some cases auction houses, to give initial priority to prospective buyers in the sale-room. Given the delays that frequently arise in the issue of telephone bids, taking bids off commission and from the room in the first instance enables the auctioneer to establish a rapid pace of bidding and a clear incremental structure from the outset.

With a clear incremental structure and the selection of two and no more than two bidders at any one time, we can see the ways in which orders of bidding contribute to the transparency and legitimacy of the process through which price and exchange is determined at auctions. While avoiding discrimination against buyers in terms of their enthusiasm, appearance, nationality, representation, institutional membership and the like, differentiating the source of a bid at certain transitions in the run contributes to the orderliness of the process, enabling everyone to participate at some place within the proceedings. It also allows auctioneers to progressively encompass all those present and not present and to systematically provide opportunities for anyone to bid, whether they are an absentee buyer, in the room, represented by a sale assistant or bidding through the Internet. The principle of first come first served is contingently applied with regard to the source of the bid and provides a vehicle for the systematic selection of the 'next' prospective buyer at transitions that arise between runs. The run, whilst enabling the rapid and efficient escalation of price, effectively excludes particular participants at various phases of the process, whilst at some places enabling all to exercise their interest in a lot. *First come first served* provides an ordering principle for the inclusion of a participant in a run within a framework that favours bids from different sources at different stages within the proceedings.

Ordering Contributions

Like other forms of institutional activity, auctions rely upon a characteristic turn-taking organisation, procedures that structure how people participate. These procedures structure the opportunities to participate and the types of action that people legitimately produce within the developing course of the activity. In other words, problems and issues posed by transacting goods of an uncertain value are resolved by virtue of a social organisation, an interactional arrangement, which selectively focuses participation whilst creating specific opportunities for anyone who is present (or represented) to bid for the goods in question. The organisation enables the auctioneer to establish competition between specific individuals whilst simultaneously rendering that competition, their participation and the eventual sale of the goods transparent to all those who happen to participate in the event. At its most basic, we find that the systematic escalation of price is accomplished through the successive creation of runs, in which bidding involves two, and no more than two bidders, at a time. Attempts by others to bid during a run are largely disregarded and in some cases postponed until the run has come to completion. A specific incremental structure renders the escalation of price predictable and transparent insensitive to the whim or wishes of particular participants. It also provides a structure that projects a series of values and, coupled with the run, enables prospective buyers to know in advance the value at which they have to bid to advance the price. In other words, the organisation that underpins sales by auctions not only enables people to know when they have an opportunity to bid, when indeed it is their turn, but also specifies the action required if they wish to successfully advance the price. The introduction of new bidders is localised to places at which one bidder withdraws, the auctioneer then providing an opportunity for others to enter the bidding. The auctioneer selects one of those bidders, and whilst prioritising an order of bidders, in terms of commission, room, telephone and, as we will see, the Internet, all being equal, the auctioneer selects the first to bid. In these, and various other ways, an 'interaction order', to use Goffman's (1981) term, is deployed, socially organised procedures that systematically reveal demand and through open competition determine the value and exchange of goods.

It is worth adding one further point at this stage. The social and interactional organisation that enables auctions to determine the value and exchange of goods is deployed with regard to the contingencies at hand. Whether it is a Carracci or a Bunnykins, a Warhol or a small Regency mirror, worth a few pounds or many millions, in concert and collaboration with prospective buyers, sales staff and the like, the auctioneer deploys an organisation that is sensitive to and that encompasses the very different interests, commitments and circumstances that bear upon the sale of each lot. Through this organisation, auctioneers establish competition among prospective buyers and shape the ways in which people participate during the sale. In other words, this social and interactional organisation does not determine the conduct of the buyers; it is not a framework in which action takes place, but rather a body of practice and procedure in and through which sales by auction are systematically and legitimately accomplished in ordinary, everyday circumstances.

3   Trust and the Integrity of Bids

The ability of auctions to establish the value of art and antiques and enable their exchange rests upon the integrity of sales and their outcomes. Supply and demand constitutes the price of goods, and auctions provide a forum in which prospective buyers can compete for the merchandise put up for sale. In turn, auctions provide legitimate outcomes used to identify broader trends in the value of art and antiques and underpin the growing trend to produce the summary data and market analysis found in publications like the *Art Price Index, Art Market Confidence Index*, the *Art Market Blog* and the *ACCC Annual Furniture Index*. Auctions have an important impact on the retail market for art and antiques and the prices that dealers can ask and sustain for particular works, ordinarily far in excess of the values achieved at sales. The importance of auctions to the contemporary art and antiques market cannot be overestimated, and the significance of the auction rests upon trust in the process and the belief that the value and exchange of goods derives from open, genuine and legitimate competition among interested parties, namely buyers or prospective buyers with the wherewithal to purchase the goods in question. Corruption or sharp practice, even doubts as to the integrity of particular contributions, can undermine confidence in the prices achieved and, in the longer term, the willingness of people to buy and sell at auction.

Declaring the Source of Bids

Auctions and the legitimacy of the prices that goods achieve at auction and their exchange relies upon the integrity of each and every contribution, that bids are genuine contributions issued by or issued on behalf of prospective buyers. The integrity of contributions is accomplished in and through the interaction that arises during an auction. This is not to suggest that participants do not believe in, or take for granted, the integrity of particular contributions, but rather that the very ways in which bids are elicited, announced and ordered enable prospective buyers and all those involved in the sale to believe in the process and its outcomes. Trust is reflexively accomplished, for the practical purposes at hand, through the interaction that arises at auctions, with the integrity of particular sales or their outcomes, despite general scepticism and doubt, rarely called into question.

It is not uncommon to find auctioneers making explicit reference to the source of bids during a sale. So, for example, in the case of sale assistants bidding on behalf of prospective buyers, they may refer to the bidder by name.

> Eight five your bid Stephen
> Eleven hundred with Midgy
> No (.) it's Ben's bid. Victoria you're out
> Five and a half with (0.5) Camilla
> One hundred and seventy with Sarah
> Twenty fou:r:: (.) >back with Clemence

Or auctioneers may describe the source of the bid by virtue of the sex or location of the bidder.

> Two twenty with the lady. (.) Two twenty
> One million nine hundred thousand (it's) the gentleman's bid
> At eighty five on my right
> One million nine hundred thousand (it's) the gentleman's bid
> At three hundred an eighty in the middle
> Twe:lve: behin:d↑

Or they may characterise the bid in terms of the medium through which it is issued, on occasions coupled with naming the bidder.

> Two fifty on the phone:
> On the telephone now at three hundred thousand pounds
> Against you online (0.3) Last chance Madam
> Six I've got online
> It's with Ami on the telephone
> Sixty five thousand on the Internet
> Six hundred dollars it's here on the book with the absentee bidder

These explicit references to a prospective buyer or his or her representative enable the particular participant to know where he or she stands with regard to the bidding and the current price. They also provide the resources, in principle, for anyone present to know the source of the bid. In practice, it is often rare for members of the audience to turn to look at the particular buyer; rather the ways in which the reference is produced enables all those present to take it on trust that the bid is a genuine bid issued by, or on behalf of, a particular participant.

It is interesting to note that these more explicit references to particular buyers rarely name the participant even in cases in which the bidder is well known to the auctioneer. It is not unusual for prospective buyers to wish to remain anonymous; indeed particular individuals may go to some trouble to avoid being identified as the bidder on, or the buyer of, a particular lot. Perhaps more important, the integrity of an auction relies upon the principle that no favour is shown to particular individuals – with goods sold to the individual willing to pay the price for the lot in question. Even in making these more explicit references to the buyer, therefore, we find auctioneers balancing two almost competing demands – on one hand they reveal the source of the bid, and in many cases provide the resources with which to discover the bidder, and on the other they preserve the anonymity of the prospective buyer.

Explicit references to bids and bidders often arise at transitions in a run, where one bidder withdraws and a buyer joins the action. Indeed, at breaks in the run, auctioneers may go to some trouble to reveal significant changes in the participation of particular individuals to the bidders as well as to all those participating in the event. These more explicit references to particular participants are not infrequently accompanied by gestures that show the source of the bid – the location of the bidder or his or her representative within the saleroom. Consider the following instance. The auctioneer finds a new bidder at £2,400, B.3, and a second at £2,600, SA.1.

Fragment 3.1

    A: Any advance on two thousand four?
        (0.2) [B.3]

→A: Two thousand six in the room. Thank you sir: Two thousand six at the back. Any advance on two thousand six?
        (.) [SA.1]

    A: Two thousand eight on the telephone against you.
        [B.3]

    A: Three thousand. Waving at three thousand now. In the room, at three thousand.

↑ ↑ ↑

six in the room. ....Any advance on ...Two thousand eight against you

Fragment 3.1. Images 1, 2 & 3.

The auctioneer receives a bid – announcing the increment 'Two thousand six in the room'. He simultaneously looks at and gestures towards the new bidder. The gesture and hand are held outstretched towards the bidder during 'thank you sir'. The auctioneer then looks for a second bidder and, rotating his hand as he turns, searches the saleroom. The auctioneer receives a bid from a sale assistant and ceases the rotation of the hand gestures towards the source of the bid. As the auctioneer announces the bid, he turns back to the previous bidder and, while still gesturing towards the sale assistant, describes the source of the competing bid: 'Two thousand eight on the telephone and against you'.

The voicing of the increments, coupled with the auctioneer's gestures and realignment of orientation, enables two particular individuals, in this case a prospective buyer at the back of the saleroom and a sale assistant, to know that they have successfully bid at a particular price. It also enables all those in the saleroom to know the whereabouts of the new bidders and the price that they have bid. The voicing of the increments coupled with the accompanying bodily orientation and gesture reveals the source of the bids and the whereabouts of the buyers entering a run.

The gestures that accompany these more explicit references to bids and bidders display the source of the bid, but rarely involve specifically pointing at a particular buyer. They do not encourage those gathered in the room to turn and look at the particular buyer and rarely provide the resources that would enable participants to easily or unambiguously locate the individual to which they refer. The bodily comportment and gestures of the auctioneer, coupled with the reference to the location, sex or actions of the bidder, instantiate and reveal the bid while preserving the anonymity of the buyer.

Indeed, it is interesting to note that in its guidelines for auctioneers, one leading auction house suggests 'use open handed gestures and do not point at bidders' (Chichester et al. undated: 6).

Auctioneers may also go to some trouble to reveal the withdrawal of bidders from a run. Withdrawal marks the end of the run and prefigures a search for a new bidder. Returning to the sale of the Doulton Bunnykins discussed in the previous chapter, we recall that a run was established at six pounds; we now join the action at fourteen.

Fragment 3.2. Transcript 1

    A: Sixteen

        (0.2) [B.2]

    A: Eighteen

        (0.2) [B.1 declines]

→A: Out at eightee(n) bid At eightee(n) bid (I'm) eightee(n) now [B.3]

    A: Twenty (.) fresh bid twenty (lot)

        [B.2 declines]

    A: Twenty pound (.) don't lose it f.fer a couple of pound? (.) At twenty bid at twenty I'm selling at

        [B.4]

    A: Twenty two::

        (0.4) [B.3]

    A: Twenty four

The second bidder declines the next increment, namely twenty pounds. The auctioneer not only announces the bidder's withdrawal, but simultaneously gestures towards the bidder, waving his hand from side to side as if dramatically discarding the prospective buyer. The gesture first points towards and identifies the location of the participant and begins during the course of its articulation to embody the bidder's withdrawal from the run. As he glances round the saleroom, the auctioneer receives a bid from a fresh bidder. He voices the increment and gestures towards the new bidder.

The transformation of the participation status of particular individuals as they exit or enter the run is rendered visible to the buyers themselves and all those who happen to be in the saleroom. The exit of one bidder, the identification of a new bidder, the attempt to extract a further bid from an underbidder, the discovery of an additional new bidder, is revealed, in and through the ways in which the auctioneer articulates the increments. The

<table>
<tr><td>↑</td><td>↑</td><td>↑</td></tr>
<tr><td>At eightee(n) bid</td><td><u>Twenty</u> (.) fresh bid</td><td>Twenty two</td></tr>
</table>

Fragment 3.2. Images 1, 2 & 3.

auctioneer uses gesture and his visible and bodily orientation to identify particular participants and characterise their actions. Their identification is revealed by virtue of their location within the room, a location that reveals the source of the action by distinguishing particular participants from the many gathered in the saleroom.

When more than two bidders or their representatives attempt to bid at a break in the run, the auctioneer will attempt to delineate where each stands with regard to the current bid and the price. In the following fragment, Robert, SA.1, has failed to confirm the next increment of $380,000. The auctioneer invites anyone to bid '*hh>At *three', and begins to turn towards the left of the saleroom. Two sales assistants attempt to bid and the auctioneer announces the increment. With the announcement 'three hundred an eighty thousand', she gestures towards SA.2. With 'ahead of you', she gestures towards SA.3, and with 'here now' gestures once again towards SA.2.

Fragment 3.3.

> A: °hh>At °three (.) hundred an fifty thousand dollars now my commission still
>
> (.) [SA.2][*SA.3*]
>
> →A: <Three hundred an eighty thousand ahead of you, it's here now, three eighty commission's <u>out</u>. At three hundred an eighty thousand your bidder, against your bidder, against you <u>Ro:bert</u>
>
> A: At three hundred an eighty thousand, <u>Four</u> <u>hund</u>red thousand now

The successive gestures segment the announcement so that each component is addressed to a particular participant, enabling the sale assistants and all those present to see and hear who has the current bid and at what price. The bid then defeats the commission and the auctioneer dramatically

↑   ↑   ↑

an eighty thousand ahead of you, it's here now, three eighty commission's <u>out</u>.

Fragment 3.3. Images 1, 2 & 3.

↑   ↑

three hundred an eighty thousand against your bidder..against you <u>Ro:bert</u>

Fragment 3.3. Images 4 & 5.

displays the exit of the absentee bidder. Going on to seek a bid from either SA.3 or SA.1 to establish a new run, the auctioneer specifically demarcates who has the bid, gesturing towards each sale assistant in turn and revealing their position with regard to the bid and the current price.

The gestures, visible orientation, bodily comportment and talk of the auctioneer that accompany the announcement of increments serve to demarcate and display significant shifts in the participation status of specific individuals, informing and revealing the exit and entry of prospective buyers, the standing of the run and its principal protagonists. Even the names used to refer to sale assistants, though familiar to colleagues in the auction house, will be largely unknown to prospective buyers, and the visible orientation and gestures of the auctioneer provide the critical resource in enabling active participants to know where they stand with regard to the bidding and in revealing to all those present the current state of play. Transition in the run, the exit and entry of particular buyers, the distribution of opportunities to bid and the revelation of significant changes of participation in the auction are accomplished in and through the embodied conduct of the auctioneer.

The Sequential Organisation of Bidding

The organisation of the run and the ability of the auctioneer to secure bids and efficiently escalate the price of goods is dependent upon the ways in which auctioneers announce, elicit and attribute bids through their talk and bodily comportment. The actions of the auctioneer and prospective buyers as they bid during the course of a run rely upon an organisation that informs the production, coordination and intelligibility of the participants' actions and serve to render those successive contributions visible, in principle witness-able to everyone present. In turn, this organisation enables the extraordinary economy of behaviour that we find in auctions, with the most minimal of actions – head nods, waves, hand movements and the like – serving to perform economic actions, actions that in some cases will secure the purchase of goods costing many millions of pounds.

It is worthwhile returning briefly to the sale of the Carracci we discussed in the previous chapter. We join the action during a run involving B.4 and B.5, who eventually secures the painting. With the announcement 'four million four hundred thousand', the auctioneer turns from B.5, standing at the rear of the saleroom, and turns towards B.4, sitting near the rostrum on the central aisle. The announcement of the bid coupled with the realignment of orientation towards the underbidder serves to invite the prospective buyer to bid the projected next increment of 'four million six hundred thousand'.

The auctioneer receives no immediate response and continues to look at B.5. Almost five seconds ensues before the underbidder produces a vertical head nod, accepting the invitation to bid. As soon as he begins his nod, the auctioneer announces the price, 'four million six hundred thousand', and turns from B.4 to B.5.

The visible and bodily reorientation that accompanies the announcement serves to identify and select a particular participant out of the 200 or more gathered in the saleroom. It also serves to display, to all those present who have the opportunity to bid, and with the announcement of the current bid, the value necessary to advance the price. It provides the particular participant with the opportunity to either accept or decline the invitation.

four hundred thousand   Four million six hundred   Four million eight

Fragment 3.4. Transcript 1 Images 1, 2 & 3.

The ways in which the announcement of a bid is produced not only places a particular individual under an obligation to respond and to respond with dispatch, but enables the response to consist of no more than a simple bodily action such as a head movement that can serve to accept or decline the invitation.

It is worthwhile considering in a little more detail how the embodied announcement of the bid serves to secure successive contributions from prospective buyers and reveal to all those present the source and integrity of the contributions.

Consider the following fragment. It involves the sale of an early Egyptian figure. The sale begins with a run between a commission and a prospective buyer seated towards the rear of the saleroom. A second participant attempts to bid at the outset, and at £900, when the auctioneer reaches the maximum commission price, she has the opportunity to bid. A run is established between B.1 and B.2, with B.1 eventually securing the figure for £2,200.

Fragment 3.5

    A: Eight fifty
        [B.2]
    A: Nine hundred
        [B.1 bids]
    A: Nine fifty ma<u>d</u>am thank you
        [B.2 bids]
    A: A thousand <u>the</u>re:
        (0.4) [B.1 bids]

A: Eleven here
        (.) [B.2 bids]
A: Twelve hundred
        [B.1 bids]
A: Thirteen hundred
        [B.2 bids]
A: Fourteen hundred
        [B.1 bids]
A: Fifteen hundred
        (.) [B.2 bids]
A: Sixteen hundred

If we focus on a section of the run, we can begin to see the ways in which the bodily comportment of the auctioneer provides a critical resource in the production and coordination of a rapid succession bids from two protagonists, with each bid issued in less than half a second.

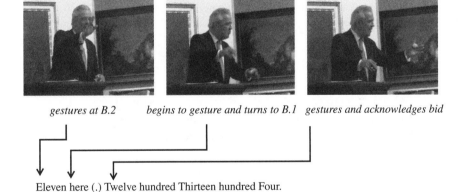

gestures at B.2   *begins to gesture and turns to B.1*   *gestures and acknowledges bid*

Eleven here (.) Twelve hundred Thirteen hundred Four.

B.2 nods

Fragment 3.5. Transcript 2 & Images 1, 2 & 3.

The auctioneer alternates between gestures with his right hand and those with his left. The gestures are accompanied by successive shifts in his visual alignment as he turns from the bidder on his right, B.2, to the bidder on his left, B.1. As he announces 'eleven here', bid by B.1, he turns and gestures towards B.2; the moment he looks at and gestures towards the underbidder, just as he finishes announcing the current increment 'eleven here', the prospective buyer nods, agreeing to the next increment. As B.2 nods in response to the invitation, the auctioneer turns from B.2 to B.1. As he begins to turn, he transforms his gesture, flipping his hand up and then down to acknowledge the bid issued by B.2. The auctioneer then announces the increment 'twelve hundred', and with the announcement withdraws his right hand and begins to gesture with his left towards the underbidder, B.1. By the beginning of the word 'hundred', he is looking at and gesturing towards B.1, who in turn nods her head to accept the invitation to bid. As she nods, the auctioneer turns from his left to the right and begins to gesture towards B.2, announcing the increment 'thirteen hundred'. A moment later, B.2 bids.

The up and down movement of the left hand acknowledging the bid from [B.1].

Fragment 3.5. Images 4, 5 & 6.

The run is accomplished through alternating sequences of action through which two specific participants are provided with successive opportunities to bid. Each sequence consists of the auctioneer issuing an invitation to one of the two participants within the run, namely the underbidder, to bid the projected next increment. The invitation is accomplished through an announcement of the current increment coupled with the auctioneer turning, and in some cases, gesturing, towards the underbidder. The auctioneer's action serves to identify a particular participant amongst many gathered in the saleroom, and projects a sequentially relevant next action, to accept or decline the invitation, an action that properly and routinely occurs immediately following the invitation. An invitation therefore specifies one of two alternative actions that should be undertaken by a particular participant in immediate response to the invitation.

The sequential organisation that underpins the structure of bidding within the run, coupled with the incremental structure of values, enables the response to an invitation to be accomplished with the most minimal of actions – as in this case – a head nod or slight wave of the catalogue and the rapid escalation of price characteristic of auctions. It also enables the auctioneer and all those present to determine both bids and a participant's withdrawal from the run by virtue of declining an opportunity to bid. The sequence has many of the characteristics described by Schegloff and Sacks (1974) as an adjacency pair, a class of utterances in which a first action is sequentially implicative for a next action; it projects one, or one amongst an alternative set of, action(s) conditionally relevant on the first – an action that if it fails to occur is noticeably or accountably absent and can serve to generate remedial action. The sequential organisation of the invitation to bid and its acceptance or declination, the tight ordering of the pair of actions, is a critical feature of the organisation of an auction and the auctioneer's ability to elicit bids and to recognise when a participant has withdrawn.

One further point in this regard: the embodied announcement of the new increment not only serves to invite the underbidder to bid the projected next increment, but also acknowledges the contribution, the bid, made by the protagonist. It operates both retroactively and proactively, simultaneously acknowledging and inviting a bid. In the case at hand, the auctioneer's bodily actions and gesture contribute to the double-edged significance of the announcement. The transformation of the gesture with the one hand serves to acknowledge the bid with its announcement, and the bodily reorientation and gesture with the other invite a bid at the projected next increment. The auctioneer's bodily comportment differentially demarcates the import and significance of the announcement for the two participants.

The incremental structure coupled with the sequential organisation that alternates the opportunities to bid between two principal protagonists at any one time underpins the systematic and transparent escalation of price at auction. It enables particular participants to know with some certainty when it is their turn to bid, what it will take to advance the price of the goods and the source of bids with whom they are competing. It also allows all those present to witness the actions of the principal protagonists by virtue of the conduct of the auctioneer, the embodied announcements serving to display bids and the participation of particular buyers. In other words, it is not necessary to see for oneself the actions of the protagonists but rather to witness those actions through the conduct of the auctioneer. In this way, the social and interactional organisation of bidding and the run enables the principal participants and all those present to take it on trust that the contributions are indeed bids on behalf of actual buyers, buyers that in many cases are present and participating from specific locations within the saleroom – locations shown but not necessarily revealed through the action of the auctioneer.

Establishing the Integrity of Commission Bids

Bids off commission, on behalf of an absentee prospective buyer, raise particular issues with regard to the integrity of bids and trust in the auction and its outcomes. Whereas buyers in the room are at least in principle visible to those present, and sale assistants are an active presence at the auction even though they represent a third party, commissions are confidential and only accessible to the auctioneer. The price that an absentee buyer leaves with the auction house and the buyer number are listed on the sale sheets, but these and the information they contain, including, for example, the reserve, are inaccessible during the auction to all accept the auctioneer. To make matters worse, it is not unknown for auctioneers to create bids as if they have been left on commission in order to encourage bidding or to run a buyer up to have the lot reach its reserve. Indeed, to avoid these possibilities, in countries such as Switzerland an independent state official issues commission bids on behalf of the absentee buyer during the auction. In Britain as in most countries there is no formal procedure to separate commissions from the auctioneer, and the integrity of these contributions, that they do indeed represent actual bids on behalf of a willing and able buyer, has to be accomplished by the auctioneer in the very ways in which they are presented during the sale. In this regard, decomposing a commission into successive increments can serve to play fair by the absentee buyer and lend transparency to the proceedings, but it is the way in which commission bids are announced and displayed that is critical to their legitimacy and participants trust in the contributions.

Consider the following fragment. It is drawn from the sale of a pair of pictures by a follower of Watteau. The auctioneer begins by announcing a starting bid of £900 on behalf of a commission. From then on, the sale consists of three runs, each of which involves a sale assistant bidding against the commission with SA.3 securing the pictures at £2,200.

Fragment 3.6

    A: Lot One Seven Seven (2.2) showing there:: (0.3) two the lot (0.3) an:::d I have commission bids here: (0.2) of nine hundred to open it. [A.] At nine hundred (0.7) At nine hundred [SA.1] Nine fifty [A.] One thousand now:. At one thousand pounds still my bid (0.2) [SA.2] Eleven thousand [A.] Twelve hundred with me. At twelve hundred pounds (0.7) [SA.2] Thirteen hundred [A.]Fourteen hundred with me (0.7) At

fourteen hundred [SA.3] Fifteen hundred [A.] Sixteen hundred with
me (0.5) At sixteen. Make it seventeen [SA.3] Seventeen hundred [A.]
Eighteen hundred (2.3) No:? Commission bid at eighteen. [SA.3]
Nineteen hundred [A.] Two thousand, my bid

(1.2) [SA.3]

A: Two thousand two hundred. I'm out.

A: At two thousand two hundred. Anymore at >two thousand.two hundred pounds:

{Knock}

Unlike contributions from prospective buyers in the saleroom or those
issued by sale assistants, the auctioneer is unable to orient to or gesture
towards the actual bidder or his or her representative. In Fragment 3.5,
we find that the auctioneer announces the source of bid, both when beginning the proceedings 'I have commission bids here:' and at various increments during the bidding, for instance 'Fourteen hundred with me'. He
also announces when the commission has reached its maximum, in a sense
when the absentee bidder has withdrawn: 'Two thousand two hundred. I'm
out.' The voicing of the source of the bid, however, is only one aspect of
the way in which the auctioneer reveals he is bidding on behalf of absentee
buyers. In each and every case in which he announces a commission bid,
he points at the sale sheets on the rostrum, and then immediately turns
and gestures towards the underbidder to invite the next contribution. As
the sale assistant bids, the auctioneer withdraws his gesture and dramatically points at the sale sheets. As he announces the bid, he flips his hand
upwards, as if the bid has sprung independently from sale sheets and now
challenges the underbidder to go to the next increment. The gesture and
the announcement it accompanies gives each of the commission bids a
sense of independence, as if the absentee buyer is embodied within the sale
sheets and actively participating in the auction. In this way, the auctioneer
reveals the source of the bid and gives each contribution an integrity that
it might not otherwise have.

It is worthwhile considering a further example. The auctioneer takes
the starting bid from commission and then looks for and finds a bidder in
the room at £260.

Fragment 3.7

A: One hundred and ten ladies and gentlemen is the lot number and I bid
two fifty again [A.] on this. At two fifty, two fifty I'm bid, at two fifty.
Two sixty do I hear?

(.) [B.1]

A: Two sixty there. Taken the commission out

A: Two sixty your bid

A: Two sixty

A: Two seventy now do I hear? Two six [B.2] two seventy

A: Two eighty: (0.2) two eighty [B.1] two ninety, two ninety

↑	↑	↑
Two sixty there gestures towards bidder	Taken the commission out points at sale-sheets	Two eighty gestures at new bidder

Fragment 3.7. Images 1, 2 & 3.

With 'I bid two fifty again on this', the auctioneer points at and places a finger on the sale sheets, holding his finger in place as he looks up and searches for contributions from the room. He receives a bid, and with 'two sixty there' gestures towards the bidder. Withdrawing the gesture, he once again points at the sale sheets, announcing 'taken the commission out'. A moment later he repeats the current bid, 'two sixty your bid', gesturing towards the bidder. With 'two seventy now do I hear', he partially withdraws the gesture, but holds his hand out in a state of readiness. On receiving a bid, he then gestures towards the new bidder.

The gestures and visible orientation that accompany the announcement of each bid identify the source of the contribution and delineate the different prospective buyers. The contribution of the absentee buyer is given an equivalent standing in the emerging competition as if he or she is actively participating in the event. The sale sheets and the details of commission bids they contain stand as a surrogate for the absentee buyer, enabling the auctioneer to produce actions on his or her behalf as if those actions are distinct contributions within the developing course of the auction. By decomposing a commission into a series of bids, the auctioneer can integrate the contributions of the absentee bidder into the run, establishing competition between the two prospective buyers. The embodied announcement of each successive commission bid is used to invite a contribution from the underbidder, the commission providing the resources to establish the sequential relevance of a bid from a particular participant. In turn, on the production of a bid by a prospective buyer, whether in the room, represented by a sale assistant or through the Internet, the auctioneer is obliged to issue the next commission bid if the absentee buyer's maximum price has yet to be achieved. So whereas the auctioneer is not subject to the invitation sequence characteristic of bidding within a run, the routine interactional organisation of bidding exercises constraint upon the position and timing of bids on behalf of the absentee buyer. The ways in which they are integrated into the routine interactional organisation of bidding, coupled with the ways in which they are articulated, lend commission bids an integrity, a legitimacy, they might not otherwise have.

The Pace and Rhythm of Bidding

It is not uncommon to find a remarkable evenness in the pace at which bids are issued within a run with, in some cases, little delay between successive contributions. For example, in the sale of the Egyptian figure (Fragment 3.5), a series of bids are issued by the two protagonists with less than half a second between each consecutive contribution and the pace of bidding by each of the buyers remains stable throughout the run. Similar patterns are found within the sale of many lots at auction and even within the small number of cases we have discussed so far, whether it's the sale of Doulton Bunnykins, the Carracci or a picture in the manner of Vernet, bids within a run by particular bidders are frequently issued with a regular piece and timing. Even in cases in which contributions are issued more slowly, with, for example, some seconds emerging between the announcement of successive bids, for example, in one or two of the runs during the sale of the Carracci, we can find a regular pace and rhythm of bidding by particular participants.

A number of considerations bear upon the ability and commitment of buyers to bid and to bid with dispatch. First and foremost, the alternating sequential organisation of the run enables the principal protagonists to know and to envisage when it is their turn to bid. Second, the sequential organisation of the run coupled with the characteristic incremental structure of values enables the principal protagonists to know and to envisage what price will constitute any next bid and to accept or decline the opportunity with the minimum of actions. Third, through the ways in which auctioneers announce increments and orient bodily towards the particular participant, they can project, even encourage, the pace at which the response is and should be issued. Elsewhere, there is a growing corpus of research concerned with rhythm and timing in speech production and the ways in which it can serve to engender an evenness of pace within and across sequences of talk (see, for instance, Auer et al. 2001). Auctioneers therefore, in the very ways they announce increments, can serve to render visible 'delays' in response and attempt to impose upon particular participants an appropriate pace at which they should respond to the invitation.

What constitutes a delay in issuing a bid, therefore, is sensitive to the way in which the auctioneer announces increments and invites contributions as well as the pace at which a particular bidder has bid up until then. In some cases, a bid issued some seconds after the announcement of the current increment will not seem delayed, whereas in others, half a second or less will be noticeable. One observation is worth pointing out. It is not unusual to find that if a delay does arise in issuing a bid, where the delay is recognisable with regard to the pace at which the buyer has issued bids up until that moment, even if that delay is no more than two-tenths of a second, then we find the buyer declines the next opportunity to bid. In other words, delay in the issue of bids frequently foreshadows the participant's withdrawal from the run, confirming the current price, but declining the next opportunity to bid that arises.

In this regard, it is worthwhile noting that the pace and rhythm that can be established during a run by prospective buyers within the saleroom is rarely found amongst those bidding on the phone via sale assistants or through the Internet. Internet contributions and the difficulties they engender will be discussed in a later chapter, but it is worth making one or two remarks at this stage concerning bids from the telephone. A couple of considerations appear critical to the slowness of pace and unevenness of bidding that is frequently found when sale assistants are issuing bids on behalf of a remote participant. First and perhaps foremost, in responding to an invitation to bid that arises within a run, the sale assistant has to enquire whether the buyer wishes to bid at the projected next increment; the exchange that inevitably emerges delays the sale assistant's ability to respond to the invitation with dispatch. Second, and perhaps more interesting, unlike a buyer in the room, the remote participant is not subject to the interactional demands that arise by virtue of having the auctioneer announce an increment and turn towards him or her to invite a contribution, an invitation that gains its performative force, its sequential impact, not solely by virtue of the demands established through the embodied announcement, but as a consequence of all those within the saleroom witnessing the action and being sensitive to the buyer's response. Dislocated from the immediate environment of action, telephone bidders appear less subject to the demands of auctioneer's conduct.

The Ecology of the Saleroom

> The individual gestures with the immediate environment, not only with his body, and so we must introduce this environment in some systematic way ... while the substratum of a gesture derives from the maker's body, the form of the gesture can be intimately determined by the microecological orbit in which the speaker finds himself. To describe the gesture, let alone uncover its meaning, we ... have to introduce the human and material setting in which the gesture is made. (Goffman 1964: 164)

The legitimacy of valuation and exchange at auction relies upon the integrity of bids and bidding – that bids are genuine contributions on behalf of willing and able buyers and express genuine demand. In this way, the price that goods achieve is treated for all practical purposes as the outcome of open and unfettered competition in which any interested party can participate. The process of auction does not lend itself, however, to the explicit identification of all those who might compete for particular lots and the bids they issue. It would be time consuming and difficult to name or explicitly identify all those who, during bidding, declare an interest, and besides, it is not uncommon for buyers to wish to remain unknown and to go to some trouble to preserve their anonymity. The ways in which auctioneers invite, announce and attribute bids reconciles these different demands. Each and every bid creates a sense of the source of the contribution – that the bid is issued by or on behalf of a genuine prospective buyer – whilst not declaring who the participant is or even necessarily providing the resources through which even a bidder within the saleroom can be found and seen. The incremental structure, the run and its alternating sequential organisation, the announcement of bids and the accompanying visual and bodily comportment, the design of gestures that point towards, rather than at, bidders, serve to establish the integrity of bids – to enable all those present and participating in the sale to take it on trust bids announced by the auctioneer that determine the value and exchange of goods are, for all practical purposes, genuine contributions from interested parties competing for the goods in question.

The legitimacy of auctions and the transactions they occasion derives from their open and public character, that the auction is accessible to all those who have an interest in the goods in question. The presence of an audience, those who may not be bidding at some point, others who may be waiting for lots that have not as yet come up for sale and spectators that enjoy watching the event contribute to the legitimacy of the process. They provide a gathering of interested and non-interested parties who are witness to the proceedings and see for themselves how the price of particular goods escalates and transactions arise. The ways in which the auctioneer undertakes the auction and invites, announces and attributes bids, are critical in this regard. They provide the resources for particular protagonists to contribute to the systematic escalation of price, and reveal those contributions to all those gathered within the saleroom and even those connected remotely. In the ways in which the auctioneer undertakes the auction, the sale is not only witnessed, but rather rendered witness-able; the auctioneer's talk and gestures provide resources not only for the organisation of action but for others to witness the proceedings.

There has been a long-standing interest in the performance of auctioneers and the theatre of the event (see, for example, Cooper 1977; Kuiper 1995; Smith 1989), and certainly there are auctions, including sales of fine art and antiques, that are powerfully dramatic. Undoubtedly, the ways in which particular auctioneers perform their part can make an important contribution to the excitement of the event and the willingness of buyers to participate in the sale. However, the impression of performance and the apparent animated conduct of an auctioneer may have as much to do with the interactional and ecological demands of the event as it does with creating a drama. If you take, for example, the gestures that accompany the announcement of increments, gestures that sometimes appear animated, even dramatic, we can begin to see how these gestures may not only be concerned with identifying particular participants and inviting contributions, but in revealing, to all those gathered within the domain, the action within the course of its production. Moreover, the actions of buyers themselves, so critical to the escalation of price and the legitimacy of the event, are only available and visible by virtue of the conduct of the auctioneer, must be rendered visible within the domain. To make matters more demanding still, the domain in question, the saleroom, consists of a gathering, in some cases involving hundreds of people, with the auctioneer responsible for facilitating and coordinating the contributions of others – for deploying an interactional organisation that relies upon all those present recognising what is happening and knowing the implications for their own participation and engagement. In other words, organising and revealing the conduct of particular buyers, the auctioneer shapes the ways in which all those present participate in the event and enables those gathered within the saleroom to witness the proceedings. Given these constraints and commitments, it is hardly surprising that the conduct of auctioneers may appear dramatic and at times almost theatrical, as they mediate and render visible the successive contributions and participation of particular individuals whose actions are largely inaccessible to observation.

It is worthwhile briefly reflecting on the ecology of the saleroom and the way in which it both allows and restricts the visibility of action. There is significant variation in the size and the shape of salerooms and the facilities provided to auctioneers, saleroom assistants and buyers. Salerooms range from the grand rooms of Christie's or Sotheby's in central London, the warren found in the Hotel Drouot in Paris, the tasteful spaces of leading regional auction houses in Britain, the vast emporiums found in New York, through to the idiosyncratic cabinets of curiosity that remain in the provinces of Europe and North America. The long-standing tradition, derived more from the sale of livestock than art and antiques, in which one wandered with the auctioneer from lot to lot has almost disappeared, and in recent years we have witnessed significant investment in fashioning the saleroom and formalising its structure and facilities. The following pictures taken in Britain and abroad provide a sense of the diversity of salerooms and the resources provided to auctioneers, saleroom assistants and prospective buyers (Figures 3.1–3.4).

Despite their differences, salerooms possess a number of common characteristics. The auctioneer stands or sits at a raised rostrum to the front of the saleroom, and to one side is typically positioned a clerk who might document prices and the names of buyers or their numbers, inform the auctioneer of commission bids that have been submitted late, announce Internet bids and spot bidders who may have passed unnoticed by the auctioneer. Increasingly the clerk or clerk's assistant has a system to receive Internet bids and enter current increments. To the other side of the auctioneer is an area that sometimes includes a table where a porter will show the audience the lot that is about to be sold; increasingly, however, the current lot is displayed on a screen below or to one side of the rostrum. On one or even two sides of the sale room may stand sale assistants who take instructions from buyers who have booked telephone lines. To the rear of the auctioneer may also stand a monitor displaying the lot number and the current price in various currencies including, for example, pound sterling, U.S. dollars, euros or yen, depending on the type of auction. Seating is ordinarily arranged in successive rows and aisles with chairs facing forward towards the rostrum, with space to the rear and in some case the sides of the room where people can stand. It is common for at least some of the goods being sold in the sale

Figures 3.1, 3.2, 3.3, & 3.4. Salerooms.

to be displayed within the room itself with pictures hung on the walls and furniture placed against the skirting and dado. In more provincial rooms, it remains common to have the lots on display throughout the saleroom, and buyers will often sit on the tables and chairs and lounge comfortably in the sofas soon to be sold. One further point worth mentioning: increasingly a camera is positioned above the auctioneer – enabling prospective buyers on the Internet to see as well as hear what is happening.

The ecology of the saleroom has a number of interesting implications for the structure and visibility of action that arises during an auction. First and foremost, the position and height of the rostrum and layout of the seating is arranged to maximise the visibility of the auctioneer for the audience and the visibility of the audience for the auctioneer. Obstructions such as supporting pillars and the like can cause difficulties for the auctioneer in detecting bids, and it is not uncommon for buyers who wish to remain anonymous whilst bidding to stand in doorways, entrances and the like in order to conceal their contributions. Second, the shape and arrangement of the saleroom, with seats facing forward, reduces the ability of prospective buyers as well as all those present, except for auctioneer and sale assistants, to see who is bidding. Third, and perhaps most important, the orientation of those gathered in the room is predominantly towards the auctioneer and those gathered either side including clerks and sale assistants, not just by virtue of the ways in which seating is aligned, but also as a consequence of the necessity to watch the auctioneer if you bid or wish to bid. In other words, both the organisation of the ecology and the action prioritises the auctioneer and his conduct and limits the ability for those within the saleroom to watch who is bidding at any moment during the course of a sale.

In consequence, the auctioneer serves as the principal resource through which those gathered in the saleroom are aware of, and are able to witness, if only indirectly, the actions of prospective buyers and others. The auctioneers' conduct, the announcement and articulation of increments, their attribution to particular individuals and the revelation of significant changes in participation, provide the resources through which those gathered in the space see and know of the contributions of prospective buyers. The very ways in which bids are announced, elicited, attributed and acknowledged through the embodied conduct of the auctioneers render competition and the escalation of price visible, transparent *for all practical purposes*. The announcement, articulation and organisation of bids and bidding enable prospective buyers and all those present to take for granted the validity and existence of the respective contributions in circumstances in which they rarely have independent access to the actions of the principal protagonists.

4   Establishing Competition

Creating an Impression of Demand

> And surely among all men whose vocation requires them to exhibit their powers of speech, the happiest is a prosperous provincial auctioneer keenly alive to his own jokes and sensible of his encyclopaedic knowledge. Some saturnine, sour blooded persons might object to be constantly insisting on the merits of articles from bootjacks to 'Berghems', but Mr Borthrop Trumball had a kindly liquid in his veins: he was an admirer by nature, and would have liked to have had the universe under his hammer, feeling it would go at a higher figure for his recommendations.
>
> George Elliot 1871–2/1992: 651–2

There is a common image of the auctioneer, encouraged by the popular press, as a flamboyant creature who can charm bids from unsuspecting buyers and convince people to pay far more for goods than they might have envisaged. The tragic auction of Lidgate and Rosamand's lavish furnishings in *Middlemarch* is exemplary in this regard, with George Elliot's Mr Trumbull saving his most flowery rhetoric for the sale of lots of little value. And, in introducing just one of the numerous lots of a sale, James Christie, the 'King of Epithets', was said to announce:

> Let me entreat – Ladies – Gentlemen – permit me to put this inestimable piece of elegance under your protestation – only observe – the inexhaustible munificence of your superlatively candid generosity must harmonize with the refulgent brilliance of this little jewel. (Cooper 1977: 23)

Even today it is not unusual to find the press devoting column inches to interviews with leading auctioneers such as Tobias Meyer or Christopher Burge, auctioneers believed to command outstanding prices for works of art and able to entice buyers to bid well in excess of their plans or expectations. Unfortunately perhaps, it is increasingly rare to find contemporary auctioneers introducing lots with the rich and avuncular praise characteristic of James Christie and his followers and indeed, if praise does arise, it is limited to one or two remarks that point to the quality or rarity of the goods in question. One occasionally hears remarks such as 'this bracket clock has got everybody's imagination fired up', 'the little oak side table now, it's a nice pretty one' and 'a very unusual pair of late eighteenth century candlesticks' and yet, to a large extent, the introduction of each lot is typically limited to announcing its number with a brief description of the goods – 'the Andy Warhol Crosses', 'Royal Doulton, Mother, Father and Victoria Bunnykins' or 'Lot Forty Five the Ludovico Carracci'.

The praiseworthy introduction of goods that one finds in novels, films or the occasional biography reflects an interesting problem that arises in sales by auction, a problem of some importance to auctioneers keen to sell and sell with dispatch. It is not uncommon to find that potential buyers, even in cases where there is significant interest in the particular work of art or antique, are reticent to bid first or bid early in the sale of the particular lot. Even when the starting price is significantly lower than expected, buyers can be unwilling to show their hand despite being provided with successive opportunities to bid if they so wish.

Consider the following example drawn from a sale of contemporary art in New York. The picture in question, a Warhol, finally sells for $25,000, nearly four times the starting price and some three times the higher estimate. Before being knocked down, the sale of the lot involved 'spirited bidding' with the price rapidly rising through five successive runs. At the beginning of the sale, however, the auctioneer had to make successive attempts to encourage people to bid, eventually, in desperation, calling out, 'where are you?'

Fragment 4.1

   A: Lot number:: (0.3) Three Hundred an Fifty Seven:↑ (1.0) is the Andy Warhol^

          .

→A: Sev:enty five hundred (.) seventy five hundred dollars (0.2) any advance at seventy five hundred (0.2) For a Warhol, at seventy five hundred

     (0.3) >Seventy five (.) Where are you?

     (0.4)

→A: There you are (.) Than:k you eight thousand. Eight five

          .

   A: Twenty five: with Tina (0.2) Twenty five thousand dollars:::::s:: (0.3 {Knock} And sold at twenty five thousand dollars

Despite receiving successive opportunities to bid, prospective buyers, even those who later show significant interest in the picture, demonstrate a remarkable reticence to participate in the sale at this stage. This is not uncommon. Indeed, one suspects that the praiseworthy descriptions said to accompany the introduction of goods in the eighteenth and nineteenth centuries might well have been more concerned with encouraging people to bid at the beginning of the sale rather than trying to secure high prices for mediocre works of art and antiques. Aside from praising the quality or distinctiveness of a particular lot, auctioneers do have practices they rely upon to encourage bidding at the beginning of the auction, practices used in a number of cases to create an impression of demand and thereby engender competition.

In recent years, there has been a growing interest within economics and econometrics in modelling strategic behaviour, in particular in Internet auctions, though as far as we are aware, few studies have addressed the ways in which auctioneers encourage or attempt to facilitate bids and bidding. It is recognised that the success of an auction, and its ability to legitimately determine price and enable exchange, depends upon access to and participation in the event; indeed Klemperer suggests 'in practical auction design, persuading bidders to take the time and trouble to enter the contest, is a major concern' (2004: 24). One of the more significant difficulties in this regard is known as the 'entry problem', that is to avoid, however inadvertently, discouraging potential buyers from entering or participating in the auction. In economics, the entry problem is ordinarily conceived with regard to the potential costs of participating in an auction and informs discussions concerning the ways in which suitable auction mechanisms can be designed to facilitate participation. How prospective buyers participate during the auction, in particular how they are encouraged to enter the bidding, has received less attention, and yet it is of some importance to the price that goods achieve and the success of the sale. In this regard, it is interesting to note that some research within economic and econometrics relies upon what is known as the 'Japanese' or 'button' model to account for the conduct of prospective buyers at auction. This model assumes that prospective buyers display their willingness to purchase the goods from the outset of the sale, for example by pressing a button or raising their hand until they secure the lot or the price has risen above their valuation of the goods in question. In practice, this is rarely the case. Prospective buyers do not necessarily declare their interest at the beginning of the sale and indeed it is rare for an opening bidder to secure the goods at auction.

There has been a long-standing interest within studies of work and organisation in the tricks of the trade that certain occupations and professions deploy in order to accomplish their everyday commitments and responsibilities. Deriving in part from the initiatives of E. C. Hughes (1958), a wealth of ethnographic studies explore the ways in which ordinary, and in some cases, seemingly mundane, work tasks rely upon skills that conceal certain aspects of an activity whilst drawing attention to others. Goffman's (1952, 1959) contributions are critical in this regard, not only for his extraordinary insights into the accomplishment of a range of conventional and less conventional occupational activities, but by virtue of the ways in which he explores how 'impression management' is crucial to our ability to sustain how others perceive both our activity and our selves.

> Regardless of the particular objective that the individual has in mind and of his motive for having this objective, it will be in his interests to control the conduct of others, especially their responsive treatment of him. This control is achieved largely by influencing the definition of the situation which the others come to formulate, and he can influence this definition by expressing himself in such a way as to give them the kind of impression that will lead them to act voluntarily in accordance with his own plan. Thus when an individual appears in the presence of others, there will usually be some reason for him to mobilise his activity so that it will convey an impression to others which it is in his interests to convey. (Goffman 1959/1969: 15–16)

At the beginning of auctions we find a rather different sense of impression management, with impression management put to the service of encouraging participation in the sale. Here the matter at hand is not so much the impression that the auctioneer might create concerning his own self or the auction house, though this can be of some importance, but rather the ways in which he or she can provide an impression of the conduct of others, even conduct that in some cases may not exist, and through this impression encourage people to participate in the sale.

A further point should be mentioned. The escalation of price at auction and the legitimate exchange of goods are accomplished, in principle, through the competition of at least two interested parties. It is widely recognised, but surprisingly under explored, that there is an important 'psychological' element to participating at auction, to corrupt Keynes' term, and that the auction may serve to establish or undermine a 'state of confidence' in particular goods and, more generally, in the market for goods of a certain 'type'. It is interesting to note, for example, that substantial interest in a lot, involving active contributions from numerous participants – known in the trade as 'spirited bidding' – can serve to further encourage competition and establish outstanding prices both for the lot in question and subsequent lots in the sale, with a state of confidence established in the auction itself. So, for example, at a sale of urban art held at Bonham's soon before the financial crash, the trade press reported:

> Paddles were being waved in the air like aerosol canisters as bidders forced into corners struggled to be noticed by auctioneer Pippa Stockade. (*Antiques Trade Gazette* 16.2.2008: 24)

Conversely, lacklustre bidding can further undermine confidence and have an untoward effect on the prices that successive lots achieve during a sale. Shortly after the financial crash, we find successive reports of the ways in which the failure of certain lots during an auction was thought to deflate the price and sale of subsequent items during the sale. In turn these results were used as a barometer of the art market as a whole and even as a reflection of the state of the economy.

> One by one, the global picture markets which experienced remarkable growth in recent years have begun to unravel in the saleroom. Whichever way the figures are spun, the results for contemporary art in New York, Russian paintings in London, Chinese Post-War works in Hong Kong, or Modern Middle Eastern pictures in Dubai have made gloomy reading. (*Antiques Trade Gazette* 20 and 27.12.2008: 26)

Indeed, even the most jaundiced dealer can be disconcerted by lack of interest in a particular lot and start to doubt whether it is worth the price he was willing to pay. For the auctioneer, therefore, who needs to achieve reserves and set a reasonable selling rate for the sale, generating interest and a sense of competition can be critical to the success of the auction and even the very survival of the auction house.

Tempting Prices

The auctioneer's opening remarks are accompanied by the display of the goods to the audience either by porters or the auctioneer, who will point to the painting or piece of furniture in question. Increasingly an electronic display is used to display the piece, often with the lot number printed below. In this way, the auctioneer and the audience have the opportunity to check that the upcoming sale refers to the correct lot and that there is no ambiguity in what prospective buyers will be bidding for.

Showing the next lot for sale.

Figures 4.1, 2, 3 & 4. Displaying the lot.

There are different ways in which auctioneers attempt to establish bidding from the outset of the sale. It is worthwhile considering the following examples that reflect the more traditional way in which auctioneers attempt to secure a first bid.

Fragment 4.2

    A: On to the little oak side table now:: (0.4) One Eighty Four as shown there (.) What shall we say for this one. It's a nice pretty one again. (.) Shall we say four hundred again? (0.3) three hundred (0.6) two hundred?

→B.1: One fifty

    A: One fifty I'm bid on the side table. One fifty I'll take sixty

       (0.3) [B.2]

A: One sixty
     [B.1]
A: One seventy.

Fragment 4.3

A: Quantity of Royal Crown Derby, Lot Four Five Six.
A: Bid a hundred pounds? (0.6) Eighty? (1.0)
A: if you want this lot.
→B.1:   <u>Forty</u>
A: Forty bid, forty, got forty pound.
     [B.2]
A: Forty five
     [B.1]
A: Fifty
     (0.4) [B.2]
A: Five:

The auctioneer attempts to initiate bidding by inviting bids at a particular price, in each case the lower figure of the lot estimate found in the auction catalogue. He receives no response. He then successively reduces the price, attempting to secure a bid at each reduced figure, in Fragment 4.2 £300 and £200. No bid is forthcoming. A prospective buyer volunteers £150; the auctioneer accepts the bid. He almost immediately receives a second bid and establishes a run. The starting price is significantly less than the estimated value of the goods and indeed, in both cases, the lots sell for substantially more than the price at which the auctioneer attempts to secure the first bid.

The invitation to bid at the beginning of a sale stands in contrast to the way in which bids are elicited during a run. Unlike bidding during a run, when each announcement invites a particular participant to bid, the announcement(s) at the beginning of the sale provide a general invitation for anyone to declare an interest. The first to show his or her hand secures the bid. If, as in these cases, the auctioneer finds a second bidder, then the auctioneer will attempt to create a run, with each successive opportunity returning to the initial buyer until he or she either withdraws from the run or secures the lot in question. The auctioneer will select an incremental structure that reflects the starting price of the lot.

In attempting to initiate the proceedings by inviting bids at a particular price and then lowering that figure to secure a contribution, auctioneers

| ↑ | ↑ | ↑ |
| Bid a hundred pounds? | Eighty? | Fifty to start me off |

Fragment 4.2. Images 1, 2 & 3.

typically have to significantly reduce the starting value, well below expectations, before securing a first bid. Prospective buyers are eventually tempted to bid, to go first, by virtue of the possibility of securing a bargain. This occasionally happens, but, more often than not, as soon as a first bid is issued one or two other interested parties will attempt to bid. In other words, the willingness of one person to show their hand and the possibility that the first bidder may secure the goods at a low price encourages others and establishes competitive bidding. In order to overcome the resistance of prospective buyers willing to bid first, auctioneers therefore deploy a mix of the Dutch and English models of auction, successively reducing the price until an initial bid is secured and then systematically escalating the price and selling to the highest bidder.

As a method of tempting buyers to bid and to bid early in the proceedings, the practice of reducing the opening price to a figure well below the expected value of the goods has a number of disadvantages. In the first place, starting the bidding at a low price can unduly extend the time it takes to sell particular lots and can commit the auctioneer to an incremental scale that becomes increasingly inappropriate as the price rises. Indeed, stories circulate within the trade of an unsuspecting auctioneer finding himself taking some minutes to sell, say, a picture because he failed to spot a 'sleeper' worth many millions of pounds and kicked off the proceedings in the hundreds with increments of fifty pounds or so. Second, it is not unusual for auctioneers to receive no bids at all despite having reduced the price well below expectations. Such failures not only look bad at the time and threaten confidence in the auction, but they can undermine negotiations with prospective buyers that sometimes take place after the auction in an attempt to sell the goods in question. Third, if there is a reserve on the lot or commission bids, then initiating bidding at a low price or a figure volunteered by potential buyers can threaten the sincerity of the process by falsely implying the goods can be sold 'cheap'. For these amongst other reasons, encouraging bids by reducing the opening price to well below expectations has become increasingly rare in auctions of fine art and antiques and is largely only used when the goods have no reserve and can if necessary be sold far below their potential value.

Turning the Opening Price into Bid

Rather than announce successive reductions in the starting price to tempt prospective buyers, auctioneers may state a price and attempt to encourage someone to bid. In the following fragment, the auctioneer announces an opening price of 'eighty thousand pounds, to open it', and receives a bid from the room that takes the price to the next increment, £85,000.

Fragment 4.4

> A: Lot Thirty-Nine (.) is the Baton portrait (1.4) Showing here (0.3) And
>   I have interest here with my commission bids (0.2) of eighty thousand
>   pounds, to open it.
> →A: At eighty thousand pounds commission bid against the room. (0.2)
>   At eighty thousand pounds (.) now (0.2) At eighty thousand pounds.
>   Eighty five thousand. Ninety thousand with me

The auctioneer immediately turns the opening price into a bid 'at eighty thousand pounds commission bid against the room'. He then seeks and successfully secures a bid at the next increment, announcing the price after the participant has bid. In this case, the source of the first bid and indeed subsequent bids placed by the auctioneer, until the price of the picture reaches £120,000, are bids left on commission. Rather than having to secure bids from two prospective buyers, the auctioneer can initiate the proceedings using a commission and seek a contribution from only one active participant. As seen in the previous examples, having the first and opening bid appears to encourage other prospective buyers to show their hand. Similarly, in the following examples, the auctioneer initiates the proceedings by announcing the first bid from commission.

Fragment 4.5

> A: Four Five Two ladies and gentlemen, the solitaire ring seems to have
>   er: (.) captured everybody's imagination.
> →A: [A.] I've got three thousand two hundred pounds bid on this lot
>   straight away (.) Three thousand two hundred

Fragment 4.6

    A: Lot One Sixty F<u>ive</u> (.) an::: (0.2) nine

→A: [A.] Nine hundred is already <u>bid</u> (.) with <u>me</u> (.) at nine: hundred pounds:. At nine hundred pounds and against the ro<u>om:</u> (0.7) At nine hundred.

       [SA.1]

    A: Nine fifty

       [A.]

    A: One thous:<u>and</u> with me (0.2) At one thousand

       (0.5) [SA.1]

    A: Eleven hundred with Midgy

    A: Twelve hundred with me and against the you <u>both</u>:.

In each case, the beginning of the sale does not involve the auctioneer attempting to secure a first bid, but rather the auctioneer announces a bid and then looks for a second bid in order to escalate the price. *In almost all the cases in which the auctioneer states an opening price and does not successively reduce that price to secure a contribution, the opening price is immediately transformed into a bid prior to inviting further bids.*

This practice ordinarily involves stating the starting price and immediately announcing a bid. For example, in the following fragment the auctioneer announces an opening price of $240,000 and immediately transforms the opening price into a bid. She then announces two successive bids, taking the price rapidly from $240,000 to $280,000, where she once again invites anyone to bid at the projected next increment of $300,000.

Fragment 4.7

    A: An:::d:: Tom Wesselman. An two hundred an forty thousand dollars for this. [A.] At two hundred an forty (.) [A.] Two sixty. [A.] Two eighty:

       (0.3)

→A: >At two hundred, an eighty th<u>ou</u>sand dollars now, two (.) <two eighty, (B.1] Three hu<u>nd</u>red lady's bid (0.5) At three hundred (0.2) [SA.1] an <u>twen</u>ty with Andy now °hh (0,2) [B.1] Three fifty? (0.5) Back to the lady (0.5) [SA.1] Three eighty with Andy again.

Commissions are not the only source of these initial bids. Less familiar to the general public, but no less important, is the convention that the auctioneer 'may bid on behalf of the vendor up until one increment below the reserve'. The convention is documented at the rear of sale catalogues by some leading international auction houses.

> BIDDING The auctioneer accepts bids from those present in the sale-room, from telephone bidders, or by absentee bids left with Christie's in advance of the auction. *The auctioneer may also execute bids on behalf of the seller up to the amount of the reserve.* The auctioneer will not specifically identify the bids placed on behalf of the seller. Under no circumstances will the auctioneer place any bid on behalf of the seller at or above the reserve. Bid steps are shown on the Absentee Bid Form at the back of this catalogue. (Christie's London 16.10.2006: 190, my emphasis)

In the United States, the practice is also formally announced at the beginning of the auction. For example, at a sale in New York the auctioneer announced:

> The auctioneer may bid on any lot below the reserve by placing a bid on behalf of the seller. I, as the auctioneer, may continue to bid on behalf of the seller up to the amount of the reserve either by placing consecutive bids or by placing bids in response to other bidders. (Christie's New York 14.5.2008)

The practice, though widespread, is highly contentious and there is a long-standing debate regarding whether it is legitimate for auctioneers to place bids on behalf of the vendor. These concerns are exacerbated by accusations that a few unscrupulous auctioneers 'bid on behalf of the vendor' beyond the reserve and or where there is no reserve at all in order to maximise the price that goods achieve. These bids are sometimes known as 'phantom bids' or more colloquially as 'bids off the wall' or 'bids from the chandelier'. These debates have been further fuelled by the rapid growth of Internet auctions and what has come to be known as 'shill bidding' – the act of bidding on your own goods or on behalf of other bidders in order to raise the selling price. Shill bidding is a violation of federal law in the United States and of eBay rules, and indeed eBay uses various software systems in order to detect shill bidding. Moreover, in the United States a number of states, including New York, are attempting to outlaw the practice of auctioneers placing bids on behalf of the vendor. It is worth adding that in our experience we have found little evidence of auctioneers bidding on behalf of the vendor beyond the reserve, and it is interesting to note that in a number of auction houses the auctioneer's guidelines or conventions firmly exclude such practice.

Commission bids, and bids on behalf of the vendor, provide an important resource for auctioneers. They enable auctioneers to initiate bidding and escalate the price of the lot when only one participant in the room is willing to bid and indeed, in some cases, when no one is willing to bid at the beginning of the sale. By beginning at a price significantly below the reserve, the auctioneer decomposes the maximum commission or the reserve price (the vendor's 'maximum bid') into a series of increments and, for example, creates a run between a bidder in the room and the vendor. As a matter of routine and principle, auctioneers typically exercise bids on behalf of a commission or the reserve at the beginning of the sale, and by formalising the procedure in this way, auctioneers attempt to avoid threats to the integrity of the sale that might arise by auctioneer placing bids on behalf of others at any convenient place during the proceedings.

Bids against a commission or the reserve enable the auctioneer to create an impression of interest in a particular lot before receiving or attempting to elicit any bids in the room. They enable a bid or bids to be issued without delay and the auctioneer to use only one bidder, and in some cases, no bidders at all, to initiate the proceedings and escalate the price of the goods. The way in which bids from commission or against the reserve are announced, revealed and, in some cases, animated, is critical to giving an impression of interest and demand and in encouraging others to actively participate in the sale. Indeed, it is argued that the absence of commission bids, or the opportunity to bid on behalf of the vendor, for example in circumstances where there is no reserve, can severely undermine the auctioneer's ability to attract contributions from prospective buyers and depress demand, not only for the lot in question, but subsequent lots put up for sale during the auction.

Starting on the Right Foot

One other matter should be touched on at this stage: At what price does an auctioneer start the proceedings? If the auctioneer begins significantly below the reserve or estimated value of the lot, then it can unnecessarily extend the time it takes to sell a lot and cause frustration to the audience as well as prospective buyers. If the auctioneer begins at a high price, then there is a danger that buyers will be discouraged from entering the bidding. As a rule of thumb, bidding usually begins at approximately sixty per cent of the low estimate and always below the reserve, but a number of important considerations come into play that can threaten the ability of an auctioneer to successfully sell the lot.

First and foremost, it is critical that at whatever price the auctioneer begins the sale of a particular lot, he seeks to avoid a potential conflict of interests – that is, where he has two bids at the same price and no grounds to choose between the respective buyers. For example, if the auctioneer has a commission bid with, say, a maximum of £10,000, it is critical that he avoids receiving a bid from a second buyer at the same price, creating conflicting bids without grounds to choose between the buyers if no further bids are received. When initiating bidding, therefore, the auctioneer has to envisage where the incremental structure will position the commission with regard to the contributions of others. This matter becomes more complex still when you consider that he may have to proceed through successive changes in the structure of increments as the price of goods rise.

Second, the auctioneer will seek to secure a bid from a prospective buyer at the reserve price, since it is possible that he may receive no further bids and in consequence the goods could fail to sell. In beginning the proceedings by bidding on behalf of a commission, therefore, the auctioneer might choose a starting price that will position the successive increments of the decomposed commission so that it corresponds to the reserve. In contrast, if the auctioneer begins the proceedings by bidding on the behalf of the vendor, then he will make sure that when he arrives at the reserve price it creates an opportunity for a prospective buyer to bid at that price. In this way he can also make sure that he does not bid on behalf of the vendor at the reserve or above the reserve price. These considerations, known as 'getting off on the right foot', involve a complex calculation that takes into account the incremental structure and the distribution of turns to bid as the price rises through successive values. Indeed, the complexity of these matters can serve to discourage potential auctioneers from pursuing a career on the rostrum.

Other considerations come into play. Perhaps the most important is the price at which the auctioneer would prefer to 'buy the goods in' if they fail to sell. Depending on the auction, the selling rate of goods may fall as low as sixty per cent of the total. When lots fail to sell, it is known as 'buying the goods in'. Auctioneers want to buy certain goods in at a relatively low price, well below the estimate, and in so doing use the evidence of little interest or lacklustre bidding to persuade vendors that if the goods are resubmitted for sale at a subsequent auction then the reserve needs to be significantly reduced. In this way the chances of the goods selling are significantly increased. On the other hand, it is not unusual for negotiations to arise if goods have failed to sell immediately following the auction between the highest bidder and the auction house in which a compromise price somewhat below the reserve is reached. So common is the practice that many auction houses include these 'private treaty sales' that occur immediately following the auction in the published reports of the overall selling rate and the figures for the total revenue generated by the sale.

Still other matters may come into play. The auctioneer may, for example, sense a growing detachment and boredom amongst the audience and seek to enliven the proceedings by announcing an almost absurdly low starting price for a work of art known to be highly prized – it is remarkable how quickly hands are thrust into the air by eager bidders. Or, for example, the auctioneer may initiate bidding close to the reserve knowing that there is substantial interest and the lot is likely to sell well in excess of the upper estimate. Notwithstanding these and other considerations, problems do emerge – auctioneers can fail to generate any interest despite having initiated the proceedings at low price; they may inadvertently find themselves heading towards 'tied bids', or landing on the reserve, and like any profession, they have routine ways to manage these difficulties. Auctioneers say that it is not just important to 'know where to start but where you will end up'.

Creating Bids

There is a long-standing tradition within Britain and elsewhere in holding non-specialist sales of art, antiques and 'general effects', which often include a broad range of goods including, for example, paintings, prints, books, silver, porcelain, clocks, furniture, musical instruments, toys and the like. An auction can feature as many as three or four thousand lots with their sale spread over several days. Many of the lots will sell for less than a few thousand pounds, most for less than a few hundred. These sales draw the trade and collectors as well as the general public. Indeed, over the past decade, many auction houses, including the leading international companies, have tailored many of their sales to appeal to a more general audience, in particular to encourage the public to buy at auction. These initiatives, helped by popular television programmes which encourage people to buy and sell at auctions, have proved highly successful, with an increasing percentage of goods sold at auction purchased by the public rather than the trade. At these cheaper, less specialist sales, sales that form the bread and butter of provincial auction houses and one or two of the international salerooms, it is not unusual to find both private and trade buyers bidding 'on spec' for particular pieces if they happen to be selling cheap.

More specialist and, in some cases, high-end sales can be very different. There may be few prospective buyers who have an interest in many of the lots that come up for sale and still fewer who have the funds to pay many thousands of pounds, in some cases millions, for a picture or first-rate piece of furniture. Indeed, at the higher end of the art market, for example, it is not unusual to find a number of specialist dealers grouping together, not as a ring, but in order to raise the capital to purchase a particular painting, especially if they have any chance of competing against leading international museums or the increasing number of high-net-worth individuals. Moreover, ambitious vendors, excessive competition amongst auction houses for outstanding works of art and an inflated market for particular goods leading to high reserves and aspiring estimates can significantly reduce the number of potential buyers for particular lots – in some cases to the point where there may be few seriously interested and able buyers.

For an auctioneer, therefore, a high-end, leading international sale can appear, and sometimes prove, a daunting task – the need to create and sustain interest in a series of lots where there may be relatively few serious or able buyers despite the saleroom full to bursting with members of the trade, collectors, the general public, representatives of museums and galleries and the press.

It is worthwhile returning to an earlier fragment. After introducing the lot and a work by Tom Wesselman and mentioning the picture has been requested for an upcoming exhibition, the auctioneer attempts to initiate bidding at $240,000, less than a third of the price for which it finally sells.

Fragment 4.7. Transcript 2

    A: Lot Seventy <u>One</u> (0.5) Please note that this lot has been (0.3) erm:: requested for an exhibi<u>tion</u> (0.4) ..

        There it is (0.3) showing on the <u>screen</u>:

        (0.4)

    A: An:::d:: Tom Wesselman. An two hundred an forty thousand dollars for this. [A.] At two hundred an forty (.) [A.] Two sixty. [A.] Two eighty:

        (0.3)

→A: >At two hundred, an eighty tho<u>us</u>and dollars now, two (.) <two eighty, (B.1] Three hu<u>n</u>dred lady's bid (0.5) At three hundred (0.2) [SA.1] an <u>twenty</u> with Andy now °hh (0,2) [B.1] Three fifty? (0.5) Back to the lady (0.5) [SA.1] Three eighty with Andy again.

        (0.2)

    A: At three hundred an eighty thousand (1.2) At three eighty (.) [B.2] Four hundred (0.6) In the far back there (0.2) Four hundred.

At $280,000, the auctioneer establishes a run between a 'lady', a bidder in the room, and Andy, a sale assistant. The run escalates the price to $380,000, and at that place in the run we see the entry of a new bidder from the room and a little later, a second telephone bidder represented by Ami. The auctioneer's announcement 'At two hundred, an eighty thousand dollars now' encourages both the lady and the telephone buyer to bid – the lady's hand being raised towards the end of the announcement 'Andy' a moment later.

The announcement 'At two hundred, an eighty thousand dollars now' serves as an invitation to bid. It repeats the current increment; it is prefaced by a brief silence and the word 'At'. It displays that no further bids are immediately forthcoming and bidding is temporarily stalled at $280,000, and it is coupled with the auctioneer turning from one side of the saleroom to the other looking for willing participants.

It is not the first opportunity for buyers to bid for the lot. After introducing the picture, the auctioneer states a starting price of $240,000. She looks up from the sale sheets, turns to her far right and then progressively from the right hand of the saleroom to the left. No one attempts to bid or prepares to bid. As she transforms the starting price into a bid, 'At two hundred an forty', she glances at the sale assistants to her left. No bids are forthcoming and there is little indication that anyone is preparing to bid.

Rather than repeat the opening bid and continue the search for willing participants, the auctioneer immediately announces two successive bids, rapidly taking the price of the picture from $240,000 to $280,000. At $280,000, she once again produces a general invitation for anyone to bid and successfully secures two willing participants, namely the 'lady' in the room and 'Andy' representing a telephone buyer, and successfully establishes a run that rapidly escalates the price of the picture. It is prefigured by an earlier invitation that receives no interest or indication of interest within the saleroom, including from those who moments later bid and participate in the run. The rapid announcement of three bids, from $240,000, $260,000 and $280,000 foreshadows, perhaps encourages, the participation of prospective buyers, in this case the lady in the room and Andy's telephone buyer.

The three initial bids announced by the auctioneer are not produced as if they constitute a run. Each bid is announced as if it were from an independent and distinct source. With the announcement of the first bid of $240,000, the auctioneer looks towards the sale assistant on her far left. She then turns, looks towards the centre of the saleroom, momentarily arrests her gaze and announces the next increment, $260,000. She does not return to the sale assistant to invite a bid at the next increment, but rather places her right hand on the sale sheets, looks down and announces a bid of $280,000. No further reference is made to the sources of these bids either by showing or declaring that the commission has reached its maximum or that a bidder has withdrawn from a run. The organisation of the start of the sale is as follows.

Figure 4.5. Opening the Bidding
    i. A: Starting price
   ii. A: Price bid – open invitation to bid – search for bidders
            [No bids received]
 iii. A: Announcement of 2nd bid
 iv. A: Announcement of 3rd bid
   v. A: Open Invitation to bid – search for bidders
            [B.1] Bids [SA.1] Bids – Run established

The three bids announced by the auctioneer at the beginning of the sale appear as if they are genuine bids on behalf of interested parties. The first is produced as if in response to the action of a sale assistant, the second as if in response to a buyer in the room, and the third as if it is taken from the sale sheets on behalf of a commission bid. The three bids are produced as either responsive to a bid by or on behalf of a prospective buyer or a commission. They have the characteristics of ordinary bids, and whilst they are not structured in terms of a run, they appear, for all practical purposes, as if they are genuine contributions, embodying actual demand for the painting. They are taken on trust. They successfully foreshadow and perhaps encourage the active participation of prospective buyers with the painting selling for substantially more than its opening price.

Whereas in the United States the right to bid on behalf of the vendor by law has to be formally announced at the beginning of the auction, this is not the case in Britain, though the practice may be documented at the rear of catalogues by some auction houses. In Britain, it is said that a number of the leading auction houses have a 'gentleman's agreement' with the trade that no more than three bids will be taken against the reserve, on behalf of the vendor. Ironically, in the United States, where auctions are more strictly regulated, it is not unusual to find the auctioneer announcing significantly more bids on behalf of the vendor at the beginning of the sale of a particular lot. In the following fragment, for example, the auctioneer announces a starting bid of $60,000 and then takes a further six bids against the reserve, only then seeking and successfully securing bids from prospective buyers – one in the saleroom, 'Madam', the other represented by Bret on the phone.

Fragment 4.8

    A: Lot Two Twenty Two:::::::::. I can start at <u>sixty</u> thousand.

         (0.5)

→A: <u>Sixty</u>.(0.2) <u>Five</u>. (.) Seventy(0.2). <u>Five</u>. (.) Eighty. (.) <u>Five</u>. Ninety

         (.)

    A: °hh At ninety thousand. (.) Ninety:

         [B.1]

    A: Fi:::ve thank you Madam in the middle now for ninety five thousand dollars

         [SA.1]

    A: One hundred thank you Bret

The reserve, therefore, is used by auctioneers to initiate bidding and to provide the impression that there is interest in the goods. It is used in the first place to transform the starting price into an actual bid and to use the bid to look for, and if possible secure, a second bid. If no second bid is volunteered, rather than prolong the search for an active participant, the auctioneer may use the reserve to create a series of bids. The bids are produced and displayed as if they are bids by independent and genuine buyers. In this way, auctioneers attempt to create the impression of demand for the goods in question and avoid a protracted search for bidders that can give the impression, sometimes correctly, that there is little interest in the goods in question. It is interesting to note that whereas it may prove difficult to secure bids at the beginning of the sale of the lot, it is not unusual to find buyers willing to show their hand when the auctioneer invites contributions following the production of a series of what are in some cases pseudo bids. In other words, part of the justification for proceeding in this way is provided by the reticence of buyers to bid at the beginning of the sale of a lot and their willingness in many cases to bid subsequently far in excess of these starting prices.

    The way in which the auctioneer announces the general invitation to bid following a series of bids off commission or the reserve can also be used to encourage contributions from particular participants. If we take, for example, the sale of the picture by Tom Wesselman, the general invitation to bid at $280,000 is spoken slowly with staggered articulation and accompanied by a succession of glances directed towards distinct regions of the saleroom. The auctioneer begins by turning and looking at the sale assistants on her immediate left and utters the word 'two'. She then turns towards the rear of the saleroom and arrests her gaze at the end of the word 'hundred'. With the word 'eighty', she looks at those gathered near the centre aisle, and then with the word 'thousand' looks at those sitting to the right of centre. Finally, she turns to and looks at the sale assistants on the right-hand side of the saleroom as she announces 'dollars now'. So while the announcement provides an open opportunity for anyone to bid, its articulation subtlety differentiates those in the saleroom. Turning towards and looking at particular participants or gatherings of participants perhaps encourages those with an interest in the lot to bid and to bid then and there. It is interesting to note that, as the auctioneer begins to reiter-ate the invitation to bid and turns towards the centre left of the room, the lady raises her hand to bid. In other words, the way in which the auction-eer articulates the increment and successively realigns her bodily orienta-tion may serve to search for bids whilst simultaneously encouraging certain individuals to bid and to bid with dispatch.

At two hundred,   an eighty th<u>ous</u>and   dollars now,

Fragment 4.7. Images 1, 2 & 3.

It is important to mention one further point. It is not unusual for auc-tioneers to know who might be interested in a particular lot – even if it is no more than knowing that it is the sort of work or piece that a dealer or collector ordinarily buys. In certain cases, especially at high-end sales, the auctioneer may know with some certainty who is interested in the lot and, for example, whether particular buyers have booked a particular tele-phone line. Indeed, some auctioneers are reputed to prepare diagrams of the saleroom in advance of important sales that detail the location of particular buyers or their representatives expected to bid for certain lots. This geography of expected demand can undoubtedly bear upon the way in which the auctioneer undertakes a search for active participants – if only to make sure that certain potential bidders do not pass unnoticed – and it may well be the case that a glance towards a particular region or gathering by the auctioneer may have particular significance for certain individuals. Nevertheless, the auctioneer cannot be seen to be addressing a particular individual in the general search for contribution or subjecting that individual to particular pressure to bid, not simply from a deference to the prospective buyer and his or her individual choice to bid when and if he or she so wishes, but by virtue of providing an open opportunity for anyone to bid without showing favour to any particular buyer.

Despite the auctioneer's best efforts, it is not uncommon to create a series of apparent bids at the beginning of a sale only to find that when the auctioneer produces an open invitation for anyone to volunteer a contribution, no bids are forthcoming.

The following fragment involves the sale of an important picture with a catalogue estimate of $2,500,000 to $3,000,000. The picture does sell, but for significantly less than the lower estimate and the reserve. The sale of the lot begins with the auctioneer announcing an initial bid, undertaking a brief search and on finding little interest announcing two successive bids taking the price from $1,000,000 to $1,300,000. At that time, the auctioneer produces an invitation for anyone to bid.

Fragment 4.9. Transcript 1

A: One million <u>one hun</u>dred thousand (.) One million <u>two</u> hundred thousand. One million three hundred thousand

    (0.2)

→A: °hh At one million three hundred thousand dollars: (0.2) At one million three hundred thousand dollars now

→A: One million <u>four</u> hundred thousand °hh

    (.)

→A: One million <u>five</u> hundred thousand

    (0.3)

→A: At one million <u>five</u> hundred thousand [B.1] <one million six hundred thousand <u>new</u> bi<u>dd</u>er

    (.)

A: At one million six hundred thousand

A: One million <u>seven</u> hundred thousand °hh

    (0.2)

A: °At one million seven hundred thousand dollars now (1.2) At one mil-
      lion (0.5) <eight hundred thousand? [B.1] <seven fifty:? (0.2) One mil-
      lion seven hundred and <u>fifty thousa</u>nd

      .

      .

A: Selling now for one million seven hundred and fifty thousand dollars
      (0.3) Any advance on one million seven hundred an fifty? (0.4) Are we
      <u>all</u> through?

      (0.3)

A: Fair warning then. Against the phones: an selling to you sir <u>standing</u> at
      one million seven hundred and fifty thousand (1.2) {Knock}

With the announcement '°hh At one million three hundred thousand dollars' the auctioneer progressively turns from the far right to the centre left
of the saleroom. No one bids, and there is little indication that anyone is
preparing to bid. She pauses momentarily and repeats the increment, turning from the centre left to the lengthy line of sale assistants manning the
phones on the left-hand side, progressing down the line until she reaches
the far corner. Neither the sale assistants nor any prospective buyers in the
room attempt to bid.

Rather than repeat the increment for a third time and continue the
search for willing participants, the auctioneer gestures towards the sale
assistants on the left and announces a bid of $1,400,000 and, almost imme-
diately, a further bid of $1,500,000. As she announces the bid, she turns
momentarily to the sale sheets, giving the impression that the bid is taken
from a commission. The failure to secure any response or any willingness to respond has the auctioneer creating a further two bids – giving the
impression of active participation in the sale and avoiding appearing to
struggle to secure bids in the light of the invitation, a struggle that might
further undermine buyers' willingness to bid.

At $1,500,000, the auctioneer once again produces an open invitation
for anyone to bid and turns from the far right to the far left of the saleroom.
As her orientation reaches the centre left, a hand is raised. She immediately
announces the bid – '<one million six hundred thousand new bidder' – the
first bid she has received. The auctioneer once again invites further bids,
'At one million six hundred thousand', turning first to the left side and then
the right of the saleroom. No bid or indication that a buyer is preparing to
bid is forthcoming.

Rather than prolong the search, the auctioneer gestures towards the
right-hand side of the saleroom and announces a bid of $1,700,000. No
actual bid has been issued by a prospective buyer. She immediately turns

to the bidder to invite a bid at the next increment, $1,800,000. Speaking on a mobile phone, he does not accept the invitation to bid straightaway, and the auctioneer, whilst continuing to look at him, begins to reiterate the current increment. He mouths 'seven fifty'; she accepts the split increment and announces the bid.

At this stage, having failed to find any others willing to bid, she reiterates the current bid, 'At one million seven hundred an fifty thousand dollars now', and with the invitation turns from the far left to the right of the room. As she looks towards the right-hand corner of the room, she produces 'it's standing at one million seven hundred an fifty' and pauses. A moment or so into the pause, the auctioneer nods her head in response to a gesture by someone standing in the far corner. She immediately turns back to the prospective buyer, the only bidder, and announces 'Selling now for one million seven hundred and fifty thousand dollars'. Moments later, the painting is sold for $1,750,000, some $750,000 less than its lower estimate. Indeed one suspects, given the immediate juxtaposition of the announcement to sell, with the acknowledgement – the head nod – that at that moment the auctioneer is given permission to sell the painting at a price significantly less than the reserve.

Notwithstanding the seeming lack of interest in the painting in the room, the auctioneer generates a series of bids that escalates its value to a price at which it can be sold. For many of those gathered in the room, the sale of the painting and the price it achieved will appear as routine and unremarkable, the final sale deriving from competition between one or two prospective buyers within the saleroom and represented by sale assistants. There is little evidence to suggest that the auctioneer had commissions or received bids from active participants, but she was able to escalate the price, seemingly in response to the contributions of others, to a price at which it could be sold. The ways in which the auctioneer produced these bids, as if they were responsive to contributions from prospective buyers, and avoided the impression of a lack of interest in the picture, enabled many of those present, including the actual buyer one suspects, to believe that the sale was the outcome of competition between interested parties – a normal state of affairs, indeed a state of affairs in which the buyer may have secured a bargain, a painting by a leading contemporary artist bought at well below its estimated value.

The Design of Vendor Bids

While it is recognised, even accepted, that auctioneers announce bids on behalf of the vendor, the success of these contributions in producing an impression of demand depends on the bids being seen as actual bids on behalf of interested and willing parties. If the bids were seen as fictitious, then it would undermine the way in which they can be used to create demand and the impression of demand. The design of phantom bids, therefore, is crucial to the contributions achieving interactional and economic significance and more generally in preserving the trustworthiness and legitimacy of the auctioneer and the auction. The integrity of these contributions is a local, practical accomplishment, and to misquote W. I. Thomas's dictum, they are 'real, and real in their consequences'. It is worthwhile considering a further fragment.

Fragment 4.10

>   A: Lot number Two Twenty Four::: (0.8) (I'll ask) p<u>lea</u>se: One hu<u>nd</u>red
>   thousand (.) thank you (.) One ten. One <u>twenty</u>
>   (0.4)
> →A: One hundred and twenty thousand pounds (0.3) One h<u>u</u>ndred and
>   twenty down h<u>ere</u>, at one twenty showing on the screens there: (0.3)
>   for a hundred and twenty thousand (0.3) Not yours at the moment sir
>   (0.3) One hundred and twenty thousand
>
>   (0.3) Anymore on this one. (.) Not yours Chris (.) One hundred and::
>   (.) twenty thousand (.) Are you done sir? (0.2) sure? (.) Last ch<u>ance</u>: (.)
>   for twenty (1.0) {Knock} pass

Not unlike a number of fragments discussed earlier, the start of the sale consists of three consecutive bids, whereupon the auctioneer undertakes a more extended search for bids. The announcement 'One hundred and twenty thousand dollars' serves to invite anyone to bid. At this place, the auctioneer undertakes a more extended search for interested parties. It proves unsuccessful and the painting remains unsold at $120,000, some $60,000 below the lower estimate. It is interesting to consider the way in which the first three bids are announced.

As he announces the opening price, the auctioneer looks up from the sale sheets and turns to the far right of the room. His gaze is momentarily arrested as he says 'thank you'. 'Thank you' implies that he has immediately received a bid, and his accompanying visual orientation suggests that the bid has been received from a willing participant on the right of the saleroom. He then turns to the centre left, momentarily arrests his movement and announces 'one ten'. He then turns to the left-hand side of the room, again momentarily arrests his gaze and announces 'one twenty'. There is no attempt following the second 'bid' to return to the right-hand side of

One hu<u>nd</u>red thousand (.) thank you   One ten. One <u>twen</u>ty >one hundred

Fragment 4.10. Images 1 & 2.

the room to invite the 'buyer' to bid the next increment. No further reference is made to any of these participants following the third 'bid'.

The announcement of each increment is produced as if in response to a contribution of a prospective buyer within the room. For instance, 'thank you' explicitly voices the bid as if were received independently from a prospective buyer. In each case, by announcing the increment as his visible orientation is momentarily arrested, it appears as if the contribution is responsive to an action by a prospective buyer. In other words, the announcement of the increment renders the auctioneer's visible orientation retrospectively relevant, giving the impression that the contribution is indeed a genuine bid on behalf of a prospective buyer located within the area looked at by the auctioneer. The announcement of each bid by the auctioneer is produced as if it is an independent contribution responsive to the action of a genuine prospective buyer.

The sale sheets also provide a resource with which to display the source of bids and their independent contribution even if the auctioneer does not distinguish between whether the bid is on behalf of a commission or the vendor. Recall, for example, the sale of the picture by Tom Wesselman. It has been noted in earlier chapters how auctioneers may point towards the sale sheets as they announce a commission bid or place their finger on the sheet, often with their hand erect, seemingly to reveal the precise position of the bid on the page below. Whatever is documented on the sheets is inaccessible to those gathered in the room, and yet the gesture coupled with the announcement enables prospective buyers and the like to presume that the bid is taken from the book. Indeed, the bid may well be taken from the book, but not necessarily on behalf of a commission but rather against the reserve.

The attribution of these preliminary bids to prospective buyers is also performed more explicitly. If we return, for example, to Fragment 4.9, we find the auctioneer not only looking at but gesturing towards particular participants within the saleroom as she announces their contributions.

Despite the clauses included in many of the catalogues issued by auction houses, there are no cases in which the auctioneer explicitly or implicitly, for example through gesture, ascribes the source of the bid to the vendor. In other words, whilst there is a formal commitment to acknowledging publicly that this practice is used in auctions, its deployment on actual occasions remains unspecified. Indeed, even for those familiar with auctions of fine art and antiques, members of the trade and the like, it is rare that they can say or know with any certainty during the actual sale of a lot whether the bid is taken on behalf of the vendor. This is not to suggest that prospective buyers and the like may be not cynical about the auction process in general, but rather, that during the emerging course of a sale, the contributions are taken on trust – that bids are treated as actual bids on behalf of prospective buyers – whether in the room, issued by sale assistants or through the Internet or left on commission.

In some respects, this is an extraordinary achievement – given the number of bids taken on behalf of the vendor, especially at the beginning of the sale of particular lots. The achievement derives from the ways in which auctioneers announce and articulate the 'bids' and the bodily comportment that enables people to assume that the bids are genuine contributions on behalf of actual prospective buyers. It is not that it is simply taken on trust, though indeed it is taken on trust, but it can be taken on trust by virtue of how auctioneers, in the very ways in which they announce and reveal bids, achieve the integrity of the respective contributions. Auctioneers enable bids on behalf of the vendor to be deployed unproblematically by virtue of the ways in which they appear as routine contributions by prospective buyers – they preserve 'normal appearances' – business as usual – by virtue of the ways they are announced and attributed.

Informing this achievement are one or two tricks of the trade that contribute to these normal appearances and amongst those in the profession, there are apothecial stories of when things go wrong. So, for example, as we have suggested, in announcing a series of bids on behalf of the vendor, it is rare for the auctioneer to appear to return to the same 'bidder' or to create what would amount to a pseudo run. Auctioneers argue that the danger of returning to the same imaginary 'bidder' creates the possibility that those in the room might then have the opportunity to turn and see for themselves whether there is indeed a prospective buyer bidding. The announcement of just one bid from a particular source precludes the discovery of the fiction. In this regard it is amusing to watch some of the more dramatic clips of auctions found on Internet sites such as YouTube, where the auctioneer announces a series of opening bids from different regions of the room. Aside from avoiding pseudo runs, it is said that in producing bids against the reserve, it is important to avoid holding your gaze on a particular area of the room as you announce the bid since it might well provide the resources to enable people to try and find the active participant. Most explicit in this respect is the backward head flip that sometimes accompanies the announcement of a reserve bid – the auctioneer throws his head backwards displaying the announcement is responsive to a bid whilst not providing the resources to determine who might have actually bid. In one case, an elderly auctioneer in rural England, slightly worse for wear during an afternoon sale, fell backwards off the rostrum, much to the hilarity of the audience, as he announced a particularly animated bid 'off the wall'.

It is worthwhile raising one further aspect of the attribution of pseudo bids and the ways in which they might contribute to encouraging contributions from willing participants. In the following fragment, the auctioneer announces three bids and then undertakes an extensive search for willing participants. In undertaking that search, the auctioneer repeats the outstanding increment and successively glances at particular regions of the room.

Fragment 4.11. Transcript 1

  A: Lot number Eighty Four::: (0.8) (I'll ask) please: One hundred thousand (.) One ten. One <u>twenty</u>

    (0.4)

  A: One hundred and twenty thousand pounds (0.3) One h<u>und</u>red and twenty down <u>here</u>, at one twenty showing on the screens there: (0.3) for a hundred and

→A: twenty thousand (0.3) Not yours at the moment sir

    (0.3) One hundred and twenty thousand (0.3)

→A: Anymore on this one. (.) Not yours John (.) One

→A: hundred and:: (.) twenty thousand (.) Are you done sir? (0.2) sure? (.) Last <u>chance</u>: (.) for twenty (1.0) {knock} pass

As the search develops and there is little indication that anyone is willing or preparing to bid, the auctioneer attributes interest in the lot to a particular participant in the room. In the first instance, as his gaze is momentarily arrested, he states 'not yours at the moment sir' and immediately turns away; the statement coupled with the shift in orientation suggesting perhaps that a participant, or someone located in that area of the room, has already bid during the rapid series of bids issued before the more extended search. Similarly, with 'not yours John', the auctioneer implies a sale assistant located to the left of the auctioneer has also bid, or at least perhaps shown interest in the lot. And finally, 'are you done sir?' addressed to yet another area of the room, suggests that another prospective buyer has also already bid on the lot. There is little evidence to suggest that any bids have been received.

One suspects that these retrospective attributions are not primarily concerned with attempting to demonstrate that the bids issued at the beginning of the sale were taken on behalf of willing participants in the room. Rather, they are concerned with reasserting the impression of active participation, that there are indeed genuine prospective buyers interested in competing for and purchasing the lot the question. If these (re)attributions are designed to provoke 'further' bids they fail; no bids are received and the painting in question remains unsold.

Encouraging Bids

Auctions rely upon the ability of auctioneers to establish competition and escalate the price of goods so that they can be sold to the highest bidder. Establishing a run, in some cases successive runs, is critical in this regard; it enables the auctioneer to rapidly and transparently escalate the price of goods, establishing competition between prospective buyers. Establishing a run depends upon the ability of the auctioneer to encourage prospective buyers to participate in the auction, not simply to attend the event but to bid on particular lots. Occasionally, an exuberant buyer may eagerly bid from the outset of the sale and bid until he has secured the lot in question or reached his maximum price. In practice, it is rare to find buyers enacting the button model; indeed they reveal resistance to bidding early during the sale of a lot. During the auction itself, the problem of participation rather than entry is of some practical importance, a problem that can be exacerbated by ambitious vendors, high reserves and the small number of buyers who have the available funds to purchase particular lots. For the auctioneer, therefore, the beginning of the sale of each lot is not simply a matter of identifying interested parties and mediating their demand, but encouraging prospective buyers to bid and to bid with dispatch.

The beginning of a sale relies upon an open invitation for interested parties to bid – first come first served. The invitation ordinarily specifies or implicates the price at which the prospective buyer may bid, though as we have seen that price may be reduced to encourage a participant to show his or her hand. Even in cases in which the auctioneer specifies a price and transforms that price into a bid, making the bidding price non-negotiable, the starting value is ordinarily two-thirds or less of the lower estimate and therefore a starting price that might well serve to encourage a prospective buyer to bid in the hope of securing a bargain. The invitation to bid is accompanied by the auctioneer looking for prospective buyers willing to show their hand. This search for bidders can consist of a brief encompassing scan of the saleroom to enable the auctioneer to detect bids or those who might be preparing to bid. But it may also be a more extended search in which the auctioneer looks to particular areas of the saleroom, or even at specific individuals, to determine whether they are willing to bid. In this way, whilst providing an open invitation enabling anyone to declare an interest, the auctioneer can subtly differentiate the audience, enabling, even encouraging, particular participants to respond to the invitation during the emerging course of its production.

Providing an open invitation for anyone to bid at the beginning of the sale can also create difficulties for the auctioneer. If no response is forthcoming, it enables all those present to see that there may be little interest in the goods in question at that price. Repeated invitations with no one volunteering bids can serve to underscore the lack of interest, with the lack of demand further undermining people's willingness to bid. Reducing the price way below the anticipated value of the goods is one way of attempting to resolve this problem – provoking people to bid, but as we have suggested, as a solution it raises various difficulties for the auctioneer and can fail miserably to secure interest. Commission bids and bids on behalf of the vendor are the principal resources through which auctioneers can initiate the proceedings and avoid a protracted search for willing participants. They enable the auctioneer to initiate the proceedings, even in cases in which there is no initial interest in the goods in question, and to reveal demand or at least provide an impression of demand. In some cases, the auctioneer announces a bid from commission or even against the reserve and then undertakes a search for willing participants, in others he announces a series of bids and only then undertakes a more protracted search for prospective buyers willing to declare an interest. In other words, in the ways in which auctioneers initiate bidding in auctions they orient in practice to an issue that has long been of interest to those interested in economic behaviour, namely the 'psychology' of demand. In revealing demand, at times even fabricating demand, auctioneers encourage participation in the auction and enable goods to achieve a reasonable price so they can be sold to the highest bidder.

Bids against the reserve and the creation of consecutive contributions at the beginning of a sale can only serve to establish a sense of demand and encourage prospective buyers to participate if they are believable – treated as actual bids on behalf of willing participants, even if the participant is an absentee buyer. The integrity and the interactional and psychological significance of these contributions is accomplished through the ways in which they are announced and articulated – as if they are responsive to the contributions of prospective buyers. For all practical purposes they are indistinguishable from other bids announced by the auctioneer, including the ways in which they are attributed to particular sources – be they buyers in the room, sale assistants or commissions. Moreover, neither the ecology of the saleroom nor the ways in which reserve bids are produced enable participants, with ease, even if they were so inclined, to detect the source of the contribution or its absence. Their integrity is established by virtue of their 'normal appearances' as ordinary routine bids – or bid announcements – and in this way they serve not to provoke any further inquiry or question. They are, for all practical purposes, taken on trust. Participants bring to bear what Garfinkel (1963 1967), drawing on Schutz (1932), characterises as 'background expectancies': schemes of interpretation that render actual appearances as 'recognisable and intelligible as the appearances-of-familiar-events' (Garfinkel 1967: 36), a world, as Schutz (1932) suggests, is 'known in common and taken for granted'. Indeed, it would seem to take some significant incongruity to have participants question the proceedings and adopt a standpoint of doubt in practice – an event rarely found in auctions of art and antiques. Trust is both taken for granted and accomplished through the ways in which participants themselves produce and make sense of each other's actions.

An important question remains, a question to which there is only a partial and uncertain answer: Does the auctioneer's ability to bid on behalf of the vendor significantly affect the outcome of the auction? In the first place, there appear to be numerous cases in which goods achieve their reserve by virtue of the auctioneer's ability to place bids on behalf of the vendor; the auctioneer starting on the right foot and thereby having the buyer bid the reserve. Second, whereas it is not uncommon for the initial open invitation to bid to receive no response and little evidence of participants preparing to bid, following the announcement of a series of bids prospective buyers are willing to show their hand, in fact in some cases eager to have the auctioneer take their bid. Third, it is widely recognised by the auction houses, the trade and even private vendors that particular auctioneers can have a profound impact on the prices that goods may achieve at auction. It is said that an important aspect of the ability to achieve high prices derives from their ability to create a sense of competition and thereby encourage, even animate, demand. Bids on behalf of the vendor are crucial in this respect, enabling auctioneers to create the impression of demand where little, or in some cases none, may exist.

5   Bidding and the Pursuit of Bids

A boom with no bust? Globalisation fuels the demand, restitution provides the supply $847 sets the record. Guy Bennet (Christie's) "This is a truly international and global market now", he says. "We have clients in many parts of Asia, not just Japan, and of course we have an increasing number of major clients in the former Soviet states".

Antiques Trade Gazette 25.11.2006: 6

Auctioneer Henry Wyndham was perfectly prepared to sell the underwhelming 1885 Alfred Sisley (1839–1899) canvas, La Seine a Saint Mammes, at £650,000 against an estimate of £800,000 – £1.2m but a telephone bidder screamed "eight hundred" making the painting a reassuringly £150,000 more expensive. It was bought at £4,4M by a middle-aged man of unidentified nationality sitting in the front row of the sale-room. According to Mr Wyndham, the buyer had never attended an auction before.

Antiques Trade Gazette 8.7.2006: 23

One of the more remarkable aspects of the boom for modern and contemporary art in the new millennium was the emergence of new private buyers from countries that hitherto were rarely represented at auctions of art and antiques. In its press release for its sale of Impressionist, modern and contemporary art held in London in February 2006, Christie's reported that buyers from fifty-five countries registered to bid. Parallel developments, facilitated by the introduction of Internet catalogues and online bidding, have begun to emerge across a broad range of sales, not just sales of fine art or high-end antiques, but auctions dealing with goods ranging from porcelain to antiquities, jewellery to knick-knacks. These developments have been further enhanced through the growing commitment of auction houses to broaden their appeal and client base, in for particular private buyers and investors. Increasingly, auctions of art and antiques include buyers who are new or relatively unfamiliar with the proceedings, and yet there is little evidence to suggest that they have difficulty following or participating in the proceedings despite the pace and intensity of the event.

Auctions rely upon a well-behaved and properly socialised buyer. The possibility that the price of goods can escalate to four or five times their starting price within less than thirty seconds, that bids have to exercised in a timely and efficient manner and that the value and exchange of goods is determined on the strike of a hammer relies not simply on the skills of an auctioneer, but on an organisation that enables all those present to participate unproblemmatically in the process. It is interesting to note that while buyers may be unfamiliar with the structure of bidding in terms of the run, the exercise of commissions or the ways in which an auctioneer may take bids against the reserve, they can produce bids and have those bids recognised by the auctioneer. In part, of course, their ability to participate in the auction derives from the ways in which the auctioneer renders visible, witness-able, the contributions of participants and thereby the organisation of the action and interaction that arises. This is not to deny that problems of participation do arise, but more often than not they are associated with experienced auction goers, individuals who, for example, attempt to place bids late, coerce the auctioneer into accepting a different increment or loudly complain about the pace of the auction, rather than those less familiar with the process.

In one sense, the opportunity to bid can be treated as a structural problem: opportunities are created by the auctioneer that enable buyers to volunteer or agree to bid at particular places during the developing course of the proceedings. While the auctioneer may establish an impression of interest to encourage bidding at the beginning of an auction, it is often assumed within both lay and professional models of auctions that buyers have a pre-established idea of the price they are willing to pay with the auctioneer providing a neutral vehicle through which he mediates the contributions of buyers. In practice, however, evidence suggests that, despite hard and fast decisions on prices made in advance of the sale, buyers not infrequently pay significantly more than planned and in some cases get carried away by the competition and the excitement of the occasion. Auctioneers are well aware that buyers, in some cases highly experienced members of the trade, can find themselves bidding far more than planned, and may attempt to facilitate and encourage bidding. In other words, rather than simply mediating the contributions of buyers, auctioneers can encourage, in some cases even cajole, buyers to bid and to bid well in excess of the price they were willing to pay. Indeed, the reputation of auctioneers such as Tobias Meyer of Sotheby's or Christopher Burge of Christie's derives not simply from their ability to create interest and excitement but to encourage bidding and achieve outstanding prices for goods. It is not unusual for the vendors of major works of art and collections to request that a particular auctioneer take the sale in the confidence that he or she is likely to achieve the very best prices.

Before exploring the ways in which auctioneers attempt to encourage, even cajole, people to bid, it is helpful to consider how people ordinarily participate in auctions.

Securing an Opportunity to Bid

The organisation of initial or first bids is very different from those that arise within a run. The following fragment involves the sale of a Berlin plaque. We join the action as the auctioneer alternates the bidding between a commission and a prospective buyer in the room. At £260 the commission is out and the auctioneer looks for a new bidder.

Fragment 5.1

    A: Two fifty with me now:

    A: Two sixty do I <u>hear</u>?<Two fifty

        [B.1]

→A: Two sixty there: (.) Two sixty (.) Taken the commission out. Two sixty your bid. At two sixty

    A: Two seventy <u>now</u> do I hear? (.) Two si:

→   [B.2 raises pen]

    A: Two seventy

        [B.1]

    A: Two eighty: (0.2) two eighty [B.2 bids] Two ninety

    A: Two ninety

With 'At two sixty', the auctioneer turns to the left of the saleroom looking for a willing participant with whom to establish a new run. He continues to gesture towards the buyer who currently holds the increment. No bid is forthcoming. With 'Two seventy <u>now</u> do I hear?' he turns to the centre and then the right of the room. As he begins to repeat the current increment, 'Two si:', a bidder to the far right of the room raises his pen to bid.

B.2 does not attempt to bid at the beginning of the break in the run. He waits until the auctioneer turns from the centre of the room to his right;

At two sixty Two seventy <u>now</u> do I hear? (.) Two si: Two seventy

Fragment 5.1. Image 1, 2 & 3.

as the auctioneer's orientation nears the buyer, he raises his pen. The bid is noticed and successful by virtue of its position, not simply in response to the general invitation to bid following a break in the run, but through the way in which the gesture is sensitive to the projected course of the auctioneer's search for willing participants. The auctioneer immediately announces the bid and establishes a run between the two protagonists with the plaque finally selling at £410. It is worth noting that the buyer's subsequent bids are rather different. No pen is raised or gesture produced; he simply nods in response to the auctioneer's invitation to bid the next increment.

Unlike contributions within the run, first or initial bids are designed to address two interrelated issues: on one hand they draw the attention, catch the eye, of the auctioneer; on the other hand they successfully place a bid and enable the auctioneer to establish a run. The accomplishment of these two interrelated actions, these two duties, is reflected in their interactional location and design and show how they differ from the minimal actions that arise in response to the specific invitations to bid during a run. First bids are positioned to co-occur with the anticipated trajectory of the auctioneer's search so that they are produced just as the auctioneer looks towards the prospective buyer. The gesture has to stand out from, to contrast with, the range of actions and activities others in the vicinity may produce – on occasions of course competing first bids, but more ordinarily the chatting, the scribbling in catalogues, the gestures and the like that occur during an auction irrespective of whether the auctioneer is looking for bids. In a crowded saleroom, where the auctioneer may be at some distance from the buyer, more subtle movements may pass unnoticed, even as the auctioneer looks towards the region in which the buyer is located, and it is not unusual to find people waving or calling out to gain the auctioneer's attention. In an attempt to ameliorate the problems that people face in placing a first bid during the sale of a lot, it is not unusual to find the clerk acting as a bid spotter. Moreover one suspects that the practice adopted by some auction houses in issuing paddles to prospective buyers is in part to facilitate bidding and having bids noticed.

In the following fragment, a prospective buyer, B.2, attempts to bid by raising his paddle at a break in the run. At that moment, the auctioneer is looking to the bank of sale assistants on the left of room. As the auctioneer re-ascribes the bid of $38,000 to the online bidder, he fails to notice that he has a bid in the room.

Fragment 5.2

    A: We have gone th<u>irt</u>y <u>eig</u>ht online. Thirty eight thousand. Tami it's against you.

→   (0.3) [B.2 attempts to bid]

    A: My online bidder is holding at thirty <u>eig</u>ht. Where are you thirty-eight?

        (0.5) [B.2]

    A: <u>It's</u>: <u>you</u> again sir: <u>Forty</u> thank you

As he looks for a bid, the auctioneer fails to notice the raised paddle. The bidder raises his paddle higher, waving it vigorously in the air. It is the clerk standing alongside the rostrum who notices the bid and points it out to the auctioneer. The failure to place the bid successfully arises by virtue of the timing and location of the gesture; the paddle is raised just as the auctioneer's orientation passes by the buyer. When the action is upgraded, it still fails to draw the notice of the auctioneer and it is only noticed by virtue of the clerk who gradually follows the auctioneer's search of the room.

Fragment 5.2. Images 1 & 2.

Sequentially, first or initial bids have a different organisation to bids that arise during a run. Bids within a run are produced in response to the announcement of the current increment. The announcement of the increment bid, coupled with visible orientation towards the underbidder, invites a particular participant to accept or decline the projected next increment. In contrast, first or initial bids are produced in response to a general invitation for anyone to bid, be they in the room, represented by a sale assistant or online. During a run, the auctioneer selects a particular participant to bid, whereas an open invitation provides an opportunity for anyone to volunteer to bid, ordinarily at a specified price, with the participant self-selecting or nominating himself as a bidder. For this reason, we can begin to see why the design of first bids differs from bids that arise within a run.

One further point: auctioneers suggest that they are often able to tell when it is likely that someone in the room will bid before they actually raise their hand. Certain actions foreshadow the production of first bids and provide auctioneers with a sense that a potential buyer is preparing to enter, or attempt to enter, the action. For instance, in the first fragment, 5.1, as the auctioneer repeats the current increment, 'Two sixty there: (.) Two sixty', displaying a break in the run, the prospective bidder looks up from his catalogue and watches the auctioneer. He rearranges his pen in his right hand, with the pen raised a few moments later to bid. In other cases, we find similar patterns of conduct; the prospective bidder watching the auctioneer and preparing to bid by rearranging his or her belongings or simply placing a hand in a position so it can be raised with ease. These preparatory actions enable the buyer to produce a timely gesture or movement that can be noticed by the auctioneer.

The conduct of a prospective buyer in preparing to bid differs from the conduct of others gathered in the room. While one or two others may also prepare to bid at a break in the run, for those not interested in bidding for the goods or at least the goods at their current price, it can be important to display that they are neither preparing to, nor interested, in bidding. The open invitation for anyone to declare interest at the beginning of a sale or during a break in the run renders potentially relevant an action that can or might be treated as a bid, and those in the room are sensitive to conduct that may be inadvertently misconstrued as a contribution. In this regard, as the auctioneer undertakes a search for bids, it is not uncommon to find people becoming distracted, or momentarily engrossed in other activities and minor involvements such as glancing at the catalogue, adjusting their belongings or simply looking down. On occasion, auctioneers, noticing some ambivalent movement, will enquire whether it is indeed a contribution, or even deliberately treat an untoward gesture as a bid – much to the amusement of others in the saleroom. Thomas Hardy gives a delightful illustration of how an auctioneer can turn an innocuous gesture to his or her advantage.

> 'I knowed a' auctioneering feller once – very friendly feller he was too. And so one hot day I was walking down the front street o' Casterbridge, just below the King's Arms, I passed a' open winder and see him, stuck upon his perch, a selling-off. I just nodded to en in a friendly way as I passed, and went my way, and thought no more about it. Well, next day, as I was oilen my boots by fuel-house door, if a letter didn't come wi' a bill charging me with a feather-bed, bolster, and pillars, that I had bid for at Mr Taylor's sale. The slim-faced martel had knocked 'em down to me because I nodded to en in my friendly way; and I had to pay for 'em too. (Thomas Hardy 1872: 54)

First Noticed, First Served

In providing an open opportunity for any prospective buyer to bid, more than one participant may respond to the invitation. The possibility of creating competing bids at the same price is resolved in principle by the auctioneer selecting the participant who bids, or attempts to bid, first, that is first come is first served. In practice, however, which prospective buyer is successful in securing the opportunity to bid will depend in part on the structure of the search undertaken by the auctioneer. For example, in the following fragment, a prospective buyer, B.2, to the rear of the saleroom in the centre, raises his hand at 'twenty eight thousand'. The bid passes unnoticed and he waves more animatedly at 'at twenty eight thousand'.

Fragment 5.3

→A: Twenty eight thousand. *[B.2 bids]* At twenty eight

→   thousand. *[B.2 bids]*

  A: Coming back in? (0.3) >At twenty *[B.2 bids]* (.) eight (.) thousand
         (0.2) *[SA.2 bids]* [B.3]

  A: Thirty thousand I took in the room. At thirty thousand against you on
         the *[SA.2 bids]* telephone (0.5) In the room at thirty thousand

→   (0.2) [B.2]

  A: >Thirty two thousand.

With 'At twenty eight thousand', the auctioneer turns towards the centre of the room looking for a new bidder. He fails to notice the participant's second attempt and turns to one of the sale assistants to ask whether she is 'coming back in', issuing a further bid. Receiving no response, he begins a wide-ranging search of the room, turning to the far right and progressively returning to the left. Once again he fails to notice the prospective buyer, now with his hand held high, and finds a new bidder, B.3, in the centre left – who secures the bid by raising his hand as the auctioneer's orientation nears the locale in which he is seated. In the meantime, a sale assistant raises her hand in advance of the bidder in the centre left of the room and her bid also passes unnoticed. She repeats the bid as the auctioneer announces 'Thirty thousand', and this time, noticing her bid, he turns towards her and adds 'I took in the room'. Once again he looks for a new bidder and turns from the telephones to the right of the room, and finally finds the original bidder, B.2, with his hand raised well above his head. A run is established between the two bidders, raising the price rapidly to £170,000.

Fragment 5.3. Transcript 2

thousand. At Twenty eight thousand…thousand. Thirty…phone…. In the

↑	↑		↑	↑	↑	↑
B.2 bids	B.2 bids		SA.2 bids	B.2 bids	SA.2 bids	B.2 bids
fails	fails		fails	fails	fails	

Whereas auctioneers and prospective buyers orient to the principle of first come first served, in practice who secures the opportunity to bid depends upon the structure of the auctioneer's search. Given that buyers will attempt to produce a bid with regard to the emerging trajectory of the search to maximise the possibility that their bid will be noticed, how the search is structured, its starting point and progression, will favour certain candidate bids over others. Moreover, the very location of people in the saleroom, its ecology – layout, obstructions and the like – and the relative visibility of particular participants and design of their contribution, favours certain attempts to bid over others. Indeed, we find particular participants, by virtue of their location in the room, having to make repeated attempts to attract the auctioneer's attention at successive breaks of runs.

These difficulties can be exacerbated in cases in which we find significant numbers of people attending a sale, many of whom are interested in and willing to buy particular lots. For example, at a sale of Chinese art it was reported:

> The enormous potential of the market for contemporary Chinese art was dramatically underlined by the almost frenzied scenes at Sotheby's eagerly awaited Contemporary Art Asia sale in New York. Numerous multiple-estimate bids were frantically screamed across the packed sale-room at auctioneer Tobias Meyer helping to generate a record breaking total of $13.2m far above the pre-sale valuation of $6–8m. (*Antiques Trade Gazette* 15.4.2008 : 1)

In one sense, it does not matter whether the auctioneer can identify and accept the first bid issued at the onset of a search since subsequent breaks in the run will provide prospective buyers with opportunities to bid until the lot is sold. However, failing to notice or worse still disregarding contributions can cause frustration or irritation and lead to complaints. To address these sensitivities, it is not unusual to find the auctioneer informing persistent individuals that he will 'come to them due course'. Moreover, depending on the way in which the sale is brought to a close, in particular the extent to which participants are provided with an opportunity to bid in the final few moments, buyers may complain they were not provided with an adequate chance to bid during the sale. In turn if a vendor witnesses or hears of these difficulties, it can lead to embarrassment and even claims for retribution against the auction house. The principle of first come first served, therefore, is of some importance to the fairness and the transparency of fairness, that no participant is shown particular favour and that all have an equal opportunity to place a bid during the proceedings if they so wish.

In this regard, it is said that certain auction houses advise their auctioneers when conducting sales in the United States that they should take particular care to accept, or even appear to accept, bids from a range of prospective buyers during the early stages of the sale to avoid complaints from participants who might feel that they were ignored. It is interesting to note that when one sees these seemingly all enveloping series of bids at the beginning of some auctions in the United States it is unclear whether they are sensitive to actual bids or placed against the reserve.

Notwithstanding the avowed commitment of auctioneers to enable buyers in the room to bid before those represented by sale assistants, arguing 'at least they have taken the trouble to turn up', telephone buyers are at some disadvantage when attempting to secure the opportunity to bid. They are dependent on a sale assistant recognising when an opportunity to bid is arising and the value of the next increment. As the opportunity to bid emerges, the sale assistant has to secure the prospective buyer's permission to bid at the next increment and one hears remarks such as – 'it's sixty five thousand would you like to bid', 'forty five shall we bid' or 'do you want to go'. By the time a sale assistant has secured permission, especially when placing a first bid, the opportunity has sometimes passed – the sale assistant raising a hand only to find that another buyer has bid first. These difficulties arise, not simply by virtue of the time it takes to communicate the current increment and secure permission to bid, but also by virtue of the relative lack of constraint on the remote participant to bid with dispatch. Unable to witness the proceedings, the sequential force of the invitation to bid, coupled with the import of the progressive search for contributions, is weakened when mediated through a sale assistant. The significance of co-presence to the constraint placed on prospective buyers to bid and to bid with dispatch cannot be underestimated and plays an important part in the auctioneer's ability to establish a rapid and even pace of bidding. Freed from these constraints, remote participants, including those bidding through the Internet, can inadvertently undermine their opportunity to bid and enter the action, and in some cases threaten the pace at which goods are ordinarily sold at auction – causing some frustration both for the remote participant and those in the room.

Ways of Bidding

It is often thought that those familiar with auctions have various strategies, tricks of the trade, through which they secure goods at a price well below expectations. Perhaps the most well known of these is the 'ring', an informal agreement amongst prospective buyers not to bid against each other. Having secured the lot well below its market price, it is re-auctioned amongst members of the ring, each of whom receives a proportion of the price it then achieves. In Britain, the Auction Bidding Agreements Act of 1927 and 1969 outlawed these informal arrangements and yet in practice it is difficult to police – especially ad hoc arrangements made amongst friends and colleagues who attend particular sales on a regular basis (see Harvey and Meisel 2006). Copies of the Act are displayed by law in British salerooms throughout Britain and they can often be found hanging from the rostrum, though in recent years there have been very few cases brought under the legislation. Less formal but perhaps more pervasive are the nuanced ways of bidding during a sale that some believe can serve to discourage, even disconcert, the opposition, enabling goods to be bought more cheaply.

While bids consist of the most minimal of actions, gaining, at least during a run, their significance by virtue of the sequence in which they arise, they can be produced so as to display certainty and confidence. A buyer may, for example, join the action early and remain in the bidding throughout successive breaks in the run to display his commitment. He may adopt a style and pace of bidding that attempts to force the pace, producing a contribution so that the protagonist is subjected to rapidly repeated demands from the auctioneer and given little time to consider his position. In some cases, for example, rather than responding to each successive invitation from the auctioneer, the buyer will simply hold his raised hand or paddle in the air treating each price rise as if it is of little importance. Through the ways in which they bid, prospective buyers can attempt to display a determination to secure the goods 'whatever the price', a determination revealed through the unequivocal acceptance of each invitation to bid, enabling the auctioneer to subject the underbidder to rapid, repeated demands to go to the next increment.

Buyers can attempt to display their determination and disconcert the opposition by bidding significantly more than the expected next increment. A dramatic example arose at an auction of old masters in central London when a painting by Greuze that had been given a relatively conservative estimate was offered for sale. An opening bid was received at £80,000. A second bid, £300,000, was immediately volunteered from the saleroom, some £210,000 more than the next increment. It is said the manoeuvre helped secure the painting for a major London dealer, a dealer well known for his aggressive tactics in the saleroom.

In fact they attracted international interest before the sale on February 1 and bidding from 22 registered telephones saw proceedings start at £80,000 and jump to £300,000 in a single bid. The winning bid was tended by a "strictly anonymous" buyer thought to be London dealer Richard Green. (*Antiques Trade Gazette* 11.2.2006: 3)

More frequently, however, an attempt to bid significantly more than the next increment arises during a lengthy run when one of the two protagonists attempts to disconcert the opposition. A less dramatic example of the gambit is found during the sale of the Doulton Dinner Service discussed earlier. It will be recalled the catalogue estimate was fifty pounds to eighty pounds. From seventy pounds on, two bidders battled forth at increments of two pounds. At £206, one of the prospective buyers offers significantly more, £220.

Fragment 5.4

    A: Two hundred pounds
        [B.3]
    A: got two two
        (0.2) {B.2]
    A: Two four:
        (.) [B.3]
    A: Two six::
        (0.2)
→B.2 Two twenty [B.2]
    A: er>Two Twenty
        (1.2)
→A: Don't let him put you off: (0.2) At two twenty bid, two twenty,
        [B.3]
    A: Got two two (.7) Are you bidding? (.) At two two on the left here at two two two I've go(t)
  B.2: Four [B.2]
    A: Two two four
        (.) [B.3]
    A: Two two six

The underbidder, B.3, hesitates and for a moment the gambit looks as if it might succeed. The auctioneer is sensitive to the hesitation and attempts to encourage her to bid, characterising the protagonist's move as an 'attempt to put her off'. The tactic fails. A few moments later B.3 withdraws and the dinner service is sold for £240 – some £160 more than the catalogue estimate.

Sniping, placing a last-moment bid, is a familiar strategy in Internet auctions and, though more traditional sales do not have a fixed timescale, sniping is a commonplace tactic in attempting to secure a lot. It is primarily used to disconcert the opposition and not infrequently proves successful. Its success depends, in part, on just how late the 'final' bid is issued, in some cases just as the hammer is about to fall, so a bidder who believes that he is about to secure the goods for a certain price can be disconcerted to find that a new buyer has entered the action.

Not so much to outwit the opposition, but all the same concerned with attempting to secure goods at the lowest possible price, is the split increment. Whereas auctioneers will not infrequently offer split increments to encourage uncertain participants to bid the next increment, prospective buyers who are sensitive to the seeming lack of interest in a lot may offer the auctioneer a reduced price rather than confirming the projected next increment. If they are indeed the only or remaining bidder, securing the auctioneer's agreement to a split increment can significantly reduce the price paid for the goods. Recall, for example, the sale of the 'Hockney' that we discussed in the previous chapter. The potential buyer makes his first bid at $1.6 million, and with increments of $100,000 the auctioneer announces the next bid of $1.7 million and then turns back to the original bidder, inviting a bid at the projected next increment, namely £1.8 million.

Fragment 5.5

    A: At one million <u>five</u> hundred thousand [B.1] <one million six hundred thousand <u>new</u> bi<u>dd</u>er

         (.)

    A: At one million six hundred thousand

         [A.]

    A: One million <u>seven</u> hundred thousand °hh

         (0.2)

    A: At one million seven hundred thousand dollars now,

         (1.2)

→A: At one million (0.5) <eight hundred thousand? <seven fifty:? (0.2) One million seven hundred and <u>fifty</u> <u>thousand</u>

The prospective buyer does not immediately respond to the auctioneer, but turns to one side, appearing to speak on a mobile phone. Bidding is stalled whilst the auctioneer awaits a response. She does not, however, initiate a search for a new bidder. After a second or so, the bidder raises his hand to bid, but rather than simply accepting the projected next increment, mouths an offer to the auctioneer of 'seven fifty'. The auctioneer accepts the bid and the picture sells for $1,750,000 a few seconds later. Splitting the increment saves the buyer more than $65,000 when the buyer's premium and taxes are taken into account.

Whereas splitting the increment is a negotiation with the auctioneer, a number of the tactics and strategies used by buyers involve attempts to discourage bids or further bidding by the opposition. So while on one hand, the principal responsibility of auctioneers is to enable and mediate the contributions of prospective buyers, in practice the very ways in which those contributions are positioned and articulated can have an impact upon the bids and bidding of protagonists. In other words, it is not solely the auctioneer who on his own behalf, might, for example, encourage further contributions from a buyer, but through the way in which participants bid, buyers themselves can have auctioneers announce bids that can discourage the opposition. Within the moment-by-moment escalation of price at auction, we can begin to see how the conduct of both buyers and the auctioneer can create and be sensitive to a range of emerging behavioural contingencies that in turn can have a profound impact on the price that goods achieve.

One further point in this regard. Through committed and eager bidding, buyers may also seek to demonstrate enthusiasm and demand for particular goods in which they themselves might, however indirectly, have an interest. Many were amused, for example, to notice Jay Jopling of the White Cube Gallery eagerly bidding for lots at the Sotheby's sale of works by Damien Hirst, an auction that took place as the banking crisis began to take hold.

> But the first lot set the pace for the sale. Heaven Can Wait, a large triptych with butterflies estimated at £300,000 – £500,000, took £850,000. It was bought by White Cube's Jay Jopling, vigorously chewing gum as proceedings got underway. Perhaps he had more to lose than anyone. (*Antiques Trade Gazette* 27.9.2008: 5)

It is hardly surprising; the importance of the sale both to Hirst's principal dealer and the auction house could hardly be overestimated.

> The auction house (Sotheby's) has contacted clients on its books even those who don't collect Hirst, and urged them to bid at the auction

intimating that the future of the art market depends on its success. This suggests a dire warning "Buy Hirst or watch your own collections lose value". Sotheby's have more than most to fear. Tonight Damien Hirst will attempt to sell 233 new works of art amid damaging revelations that he and his business partners were less than frank about the £50 million sale of his diamond encrusted skull last year when they purchased a controlling stake in the objects themselves and that White Cube, the gallery of Hirst's London dealer Jay Jopling, has £100 million worth of unsold "Damiens" in his store. Bloomberg even reported a fall in Sotheby's share price on Friday – amounting to $188 million – stating that analysts and dealers sited "investor unease" about the sale. (*London Evening Standard* 25.9.2008: 14)

Preserving Anonymity: Surreptitious Bidding

It is not uncommon for buyers to attempt to preserve their anonymity. Following the sale of the Greuze, for example, we find the trade press speculating as to who bought the picture, with both the buyer and auction house attempting to preserve his anonymity. It is becoming increasingly rare for the names of the buyers of major works of art, save for a small number of high-profile collectors such as Andrew Lloyd Weber or major public institutions such as the Met' or National Gallery, to be published, and even then much trouble is taken to conceal the identity of prospective buyers before and during the sale. This is hardly surprising. If it becomes known that a particular buyer is interested, for example, in a particular painting, it can serve to encourage the interest of other buyers. It can also provide a resource for the auctioneer, who may well attempt to exploit the interest of a particular buyer to escalate the price. Moreover, for those in the trade, it is not always advisable to have clients know what was paid for a particular lot and the profit that was accrued.

Commission bids, bidding on the telephone or via the Internet all provide ways in which buyers can attempt to preserve anonymity, and yet, for reasons that we have begun to touch on, buyers are often keen to attend the auction themselves and to bid on their own behalf. There are, however, ways of bidding that can help conceal the buyer's participation in the sale of particular lots.

There are many apocryphal stories of the lengths to which certain buyers will go to preserve their anonymity when bidding at a sale. Perhaps the most renowned example is the sale of Rembrandt's *Titus* at Christie's in 1965. In order to preserve his anonymity, Norton Simon, the multimillionaire founder of the Hunts Food Corporation, insisted on what the auctioneers believed were 'impossible bidding instructions'

> In brief, if Mr Simon was sitting down he would be bidding for Titus; if he
> stood up he would have stopped bidding. If Mr Simon was successful in buy-
> ing the picture it would be knocked down to Autolycus, a nom de vente.
>
> Herbert 1990:104.

For some unknown reason, when the sale of the lot began, Simon actually verbally bid for *Titus* and then withdrew. Believing that Simon's more
explicit participation countered the previous arrangement, the auctioneer
sold the painting to Geoffrey Agnew, one of the leading London dealers.
The fall of the gavel was greeted by applause; the painting achieved an
outstanding price, only to be interrupted to everyone's surprise by Simon
standing up and protesting at the sale of the picture.

There are less contorted ways in which people attempt to preserve their
anonymity during the sale of particular lots. First, where a buyer chooses
to sit or stand in the saleroom during an auction can be crucial to whether
others, aside from the auctioneer, are able to detect their bidding. Second,
the position and timing of bids can enable buyers to preserve their anonymity. For example, joining the action as the lot is about to sell can help
avoid participating in lengthy runs and thereby reduce the chances of others detecting who is actually bidding. Third, the way in which bids are
produced can also be of some importance, not simply in placing the first
bid, but in issuing contributions during a run. So, for example, animated
gestures to attract the attention of the auctioneer to make an initial bid are
bound to be noticed by those nearby, and in turn their noticing will often
draw the attention of others in the room. In contrast, waiting until the
auctioneer happens to glance in your direction during a break in a run can
enable a buyer to place a bid and enter a run with the slightest of movements. It is difficult to show examples in text, but it might be worthwhile
briefly considering the following fragment. Bidding begins at £45,000 and
we join the action at £90,000, when one of the telephone bidders withdraws. With 'against you <u>both</u> on the telephone' the auctioneer turns from
the row of sale assistants on the left-hand side of the room and looks for a
new bidder. No bid is immediately forthcoming, and with 'At↑' it as if the
auctioneer is about to sell the picture.

Fragment 5.6

    A: Up front at ninety thousand pounds

        (0.4)

    A: No? (0.3) In the <u>room</u>: (.) against you <u>both</u> on the telephone (0.3)

    A: At↑

→   (0.3) [B.4]

A: Ninety <u>five</u>↑ thousand.

(0.2) [B.3]

A: One hundred thousand

(0.3) [B.4]

A: One hundred and ten thousand

As the auctioneer's search reaches the centre of the room, a prospective buyer, a few rows back in the central aisle, slightly raises his right hand. It is lowered immediately as the auctioneer begins to announce the new bid – 'Ninety'. The gesture appears to pass unnoticed even to those sitting alongside the bidder and is invisible to those behind or seated in front. As the auctioneer returns to the buyer to invite successive contributions during the run, he produces a hardly discernable upward movement of the head – momentarily raising his eyebrows – movements that are enough to place bids of some significant value, but pass unnoticed by even those seated close by.

The buyer on the right momentarily raises his hand to place a first bid.

Fragment 5.6. Drawings 1 & 2.

Is it interesting to note that as the run develops and the painting begins to reach a price far in excess of the estimate, two or three people sitting to the front of the buyer use the auctioneer's orientation and accompanying gesture to turn and attempt to identify who is bidding. Each attempt is coordinated with the auctioneer turning towards the bidder, B.4, and announcing the increment and yet, by the time they look in the appropriate direction, the bid has been produced and the buyer appears as if he is simply watching the auction. Indeed, at one moment, one of the audience members turns towards the buyer just as he bids; he immediately turns slightly away from the auctioneer – providing no indication that he is actively involved in the proceedings. His declination at £200,000 is produced with the slightest of lateral head shakes as he looks down. Despite the length of the run, it is unlikely that anyone other than the auctioneer is aware that he bid for the picture.

Declining an Opportunity to Bid

Once a run is established, the auctioneer successively invites each of the two bidders to bid the next increment. The invitation establishes two distinct possibilities. The buyer can accept the increment, in which case the opportunity to bid is immediately offered to the underbidder, or he can decline. Both actions are ordinarily produced immediately following or during the invitation to the bid the next increment. Consider the following fragment. We join the action towards the end of a brief run between a buyer 'on the phone', represented by a sale assistant, Julia, and a buyer in the room, B.1. At £20,000, B.1 withdraws.

Fragment 5.7

     [SA.1]

  A: Two: <u>two</u>::: on the phone sir

→   [B.2 shakes his head]

  A: Thank you sir

  A: Two: two: then I've got two two from (.) Julia. At two thousand two hundred↑ (for this)

     [B.3 bids]

  A   <u>Four</u>::(.) new bidder (0.4) At two thousand four

As the auctioneer announces the increment and turns to the underbidder, B.1, he looks down at his catalogue and produces a lateral head shake; the shake fades into a slight wiggle as the auctioneer accepts his refusal with 'thank you sir' and turns away.

    Declining the opportunity to bid has various characteristics. It ordinarily consists of a lateral head movement accompanied by the participant

Begins to shake head   Looks down at catalogue

Fragment 5.7. Image 1 & 2.

turning away, most often looking down. Not infrequently, the eyes are
also momentarily closed. Occasionally, the head nod and reorientation is
accompanied by a minimal utterance such as 'no' or 'no thanks'. In declining the opportunity to bid, participants often become engaged, if only
momentarily, in a different activity, ordinarily looking at or annotating the
sale catalogue – an activity soon abandoned as the auctioneer seeks a bid
elsewhere. In withdrawing, the participant transforms the ways in which he
is engaged in the sale. He no longer participates as a ratified (prospective)
buyer within the emerging proceedings, in mutually coordinated in interaction with the auctioneer and the protagonist, but rather forms part of an
audience, an observer rather than an active participant, within the rapid
escalation of price.

For his part, in receiving the declination, the auctioneer turns from the
underbidder and in some cases after thanking the bidder, re-announces
the current increment. With the re-announcement he begins a search to
see whether anyone else is willing to bid the projected next increment. In
Fragment 5.7, the auctioneer successfully secures a bid from a new buyer,
B.3, 'Fou̲r̲:: (.) new bidder', and returns to the sale assistant, SA.1, to see
whether her buyer wishes to bid the next increment.

Whereas a declination to bid is ordinarily issued with some dispatch,
with or immediately following the invitation to bid, there are occasions
when a buyer does not immediately respond to the invitation. The delay in
response poses a problem for auctioneer: whether to seek bids elsewhere

or wait until the buyer either confirms the bid or declines. Consider the following fragment. The auctioneer has established a run between a bidder in the room and a commission. With 'Fifty here', he turns and invites B.1 to bid the next increment.

Fragment 5.8

      [A. bids]

  A: At six hundred an <u>fifty</u>

      [B.1 bids]

  A: Seven to you sir

      [A. bids]

→A: Fifty here

      (0.4)

→A: Seven fifty one more sir?

      (2.2) [B.1. bids]

  A: <u>Eight</u> <u>hundred</u> thank you

  A: Eight hundred now I've got it in the third row (0.2) <u>Eight</u> (0.4) an sellin(g) against the telephones (.) Eight to you sir

      (0.2 <No where e<u>ls</u>e↑ (0.2) eight hundred (0.2) {knock}

As the auctioneer announces the commission bid 'Fifty here' and turns to the underbidder, B.1, the buyer looks away, turning towards the sale assistants on the left-hand side of the saleroom. No further response is forthcoming – he neither accepts nor declines the invitation. In less than half a second, the auctioneer repeats the current increment and explicitly invites the buyer to bid the next increment but again no response is forthcoming – he continues to look towards the sale assistants and a pause of more than two seconds ensues as the auctioneer awaits a response.

    The auctioneer does not simply wait for the bidder to accept or decline the invitation. He moves bodily towards the bidder as if attempting to encourage a response and begins to tap his fingers loudly on the rostrum. Still no response is forthcoming and the auctioneer, continuing to look at the bidder, rocks his head from side to side recycling his visual orientation to encourage a response. A moment later the buyer turns and looks at the auctioneer. Even then he does not immediately respond. Continuing to tap his finger, the auctioneer raises his eyebrows with a questioning look. The buyer immediately produces a vertical head nod, he bids, and following a

Fragment 5.8. Transcript 2. Images 1, 2, 3, 4 & 5.

search that fails to identify any other interested parties, secures the goods at £800.

Rather than treat the participant's conduct as a candidate declination and initiate a search for a new bidder, the auctioneer produces a series of actions that subject the participant to successive demands to respond and respond with dispatch. Indeed, the very ways in which the auctioneer reaffirms the invitation not only encourages an immediate response but a positive response. The auctioneer succeeds in securing the further bid and thereby one suspects is able to sell the goods that, by virtue of encouraging the buyer to bid the next increment, have now reached their reserve.

In Pursuit of Bids

The way in which a buyer declines the invitation may display uncertainty and lead the auctioneer to believe that the buyer is vulnerable to encouragement to bid the next increment. We join the following fragment action during a run between a buyer in the room and a sale assistant, William.

Fragment 5.9

    A: Twenty thousand

        (.) [B.2 bids]

    A: Twenty two thousand

    A: Twenty two:: thousand (.) to the lady in the room

        (.) [SA bids]

→A: Twenty four:

        (1.0)

    A: Twenty six (0.5) °Twenty five?

        (0.2)

    A: Twenty four:: (.) >back with Will:iam

→B.1 Twenty five

    A: Twenty five thousand now thank you

        (.)

    A: I'll take twenty six. I'll take twenty six if you have it (0.2) Twenty five thousand pounds: (0.4) In the room (0.2) it's with the (young) lady.

With 'Twenty four:', the auctioneer turns towards the 'lady' and invites her to bid the next increment, £26,000. A moment later, he re-announces the increment and almost immediately transforms the figure to £25,000, offering her the split increment: 'Twenty six (0.5) °Twenty five?'. It fails to elicit a bid. The auctioneer turns and attributes the current bid to the sale assistant, William. The way in which the lady declines the invitation would appear to encourage the auctioneer to pursue her for a further contribution.

The lady's response to the initial invitation to bid neither involves a bid nor consists of the lateral head shake coupled with looking away characteristic of a declination. As the auctioneer announces the increment 'Twenty four:' and turns towards her, she momentarily turns to one side and smiles. She produces no declination component and though turning away, remains

| leans back | looks and smiles | reattributes bid |
| ↓ | ↓ | ↓ |

Twenty four: (1.0) (Twenty six) (0.5) °Twenty five (0.2) with Will:iam Twenty

| ↑ | ↑ | ↑ |

| turns to one side & smiles | turns back to A. | agrees to increment |

Fragment 5.9. Transcript 2. Drawings 1, 2, 3, 4, 5 & 6.

partially oriented towards the auctioneer. The auctioneer produces a momentary movement backwards, and coupled with the announcement of '(twenty six)', has the underbidder turning and looking towards him. At this moment, meeting his gaze, she produces a declination component – a head shake coupled with turning away – but as she does, she once again smiles. With the offer of the split increment, '°Twenty five', she turns back to the auctioneer and purses her lips, as if visibly withholding a response. Rather than initiating the search for a new participant, the auctioneer momentarily glances at the sale assistant, 'with Will:iam', attributes the current price, and turns back to the underbidder. She immediately bids.

The qualities of the declination, the way in which it does not immediately occur following the invitation, coupled with slightness of the reorientation and its accompanying smile provide the resources with which to recognise the equivocation of the bidder – her potential vulnerability to pursuit or persuasion. The bidder's hesitancy serves to engender the offer of a split increment from the auctioneer and her continued orientation towards the auctioneer enables him to pursue her for a further bid – albeit at half the increment. Within these few moments that follow the invitation to bid, therefore, we find the auctioneer and bidder negotiating the next increment and agreeing to an increment that advances the price of the lot by half. Sadly it fails. The lady does not secure the large Egyptian bronze cat; the telephone bidder goes the next increment and the figure is sold for £26,000.

Although the way in which a bidder declines the opportunity may enable the auctioneer to believe that she is vulnerable to persuasion, it is by no means the only consideration that might inform his pursuit of a further bid. If, for example, the auctioneer is confident that other prospective buyers wish to enter the fray, then there is little point attempting to encourage a particular individual to go the next increment. Indeed, attempts by an auctioneer to encourage a further bid ordinarily arise when there is little indication that other prospective buyers are interested in entering the action. In this regard, the auctioneer's interest in encouraging a further contribution may not be so much driven by an interest in a small increase in the commission gained by the auction house, but rather in securing actual sale of the goods. We have already noted that the selling rates of auctions are of some concern to the auction houses, not solely as a consequence of the immediate implications for revenue but by virtue of the critical comments they may receive from the trade press. Encouraging an underbidder to agree the next increment can have as much to do with achieving the reserve and 'getting the lot away' as with pursuing an uncertain buyer.

It is worthwhile returning to a fragment discussed a little earlier. It will be recalled that the prospective buyer declines to bid £2,200. The auctioneer accepts the declination. This is not the first occasion on which the bidder declines to bid.

Fragment 5.7. Transcript 2

    A: Eighteen hundred

        (1.6) [B.1.]

→A: Ni<u>nete</u>en °hundred

        (0.5)

→A: Ni<u>ne</u>::teen round it up?

        (1.2)

→B.2 °Alright

    A: <u>Two</u> thou<u>sa</u>nd well done sir. Thank you two thousand

        (0.5)

A: (At) two thousand
      (.) [S.A 1 bids]
A: Two: <u>two</u>:: (on the phone sir)
      [B.2 shakes head]
A: Thank you sir
A: Two: two: then I've got two two
      [B.3 bids]
A: Two thousand four

The bidding involves a run between two buyers in the room, one sitting on the front row, B.2, the other at the rear of the saleroom. At 'nineteen hundred', the auctioneer turns towards B.2 and invites him to bid the next increment, £2,000. As he turns and announces the increment, the underbidder shakes his head and looks down at his catalogue. It is a clear, unambiguous declination of the invitation.

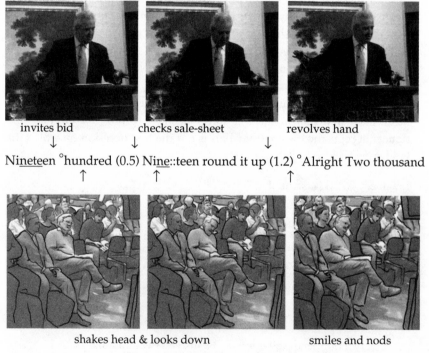

Fragment 5.7. Transcript 3. Image 1, 2, 3, 4, 5, & 6.

The auctioneer turns and momentarily looks at the sale sheets to check whether he has reached the reserve. Rather than accept the declination and look for a new bidder, the auctioneer returns to the underbidder and produces 'Ni<u>ne</u>::teen round it up?' The re-invitation and the ensuing pause are accompanied by two simultaneous gestures. With the right hand the auctioneer points towards the competing bidder at the rear of the sale-room; with the left he slowly revolves his hand towards the underbidder as if stretching the opportunity and invitation to bid. The underbidder looks up, smiles, and a moment later bids with 'alright' and an accompanying head nod; curiously the auctioneer then announces a bid of £2000'.

Even in circumstances, therefore, in which the buyer produces an unambiguous response to an invitation to bid, the auctioneer may successfully encourage a further bid. It is worthwhile mentioning two or three considerations that appear to inform the successful pursuit of a further bid.

In encouraging a further bid, the auctioneer has to re-establish the prospective buyer as the principal recipient, the addressee of the (re)invitation. This is not always unproblematic. As we have suggested, an unambiguous declination to bid is routinely accomplished by the prospective bidder declining the opportunity both by producing a 'negative component' and by turning away from the auctioneer and becoming engaged in an alternative activity. Since the names of prospective buyers are commonly unknown and if known, rarely used, the auctioneer has to rely on other resources with which to secure the bidder's alignment towards any subsequent actions designed to encourage an acceptance of the increment. The announcement of a re-invitation, for example 'Ni<u>ne</u>::teen round it up', can be heard as specifically addressing the particular participant. Address terms are also used as in 'last chance Madam', 'one more Sir?' or 'at the rear of the room?'. They are preceded or accompanied by the auctioneer turning, and in some cases gesturing towards, the underbidder. This shift of visual orientation, coupled with gesture, can successfully secure the realignment of the participant and thereby render him subject to the sequential demands of the re-invitation.

Second, in pursuing the underbidder for a further contribution, auctioneers display the source of the competing bid, pointing, for example, towards a bidder in the room, a sale assistant, or a commission on the book. It is worth mentioning two points in this regard. First, the gestures that accompany the elicitation and acknowledgement of bids frequently serve to display the source of the competing bid and underscore their legitimacy, that it is a genuine bid on behalf of an interested party, a prospective buyer. Second, in displaying the other bid, the auctioneer can attempt to create an impression of competition and encourage the buyer

to believe that a further bid may win the lot. Indeed, we find the auctioneer explicitly appealing to the competitive spirit of the underbidder with
remarks such as – 'don't let him put you off', 'you can win this', and 'one
more and you will knock him out'. Whether such appeals serve to actually
encourage further bids is a moot point, but it is certainly the case that auctioneers attempt to exploit a sense of personal competition to encourage
people to place a further bid.

Third, we can begin to see how the auctioneer's conduct in attempting
to secure a bid from an underbidder may subject the prospective buyer to
successive demands to respond to an invitation. We have noted that the invitation can be recycled, made more explicit, even appeal to the competitive
spirit of the prospective buyer, but the negotiation that emerges between
auctioneer and the bidder is more complex, more subtle. While a silence
or pause may follow the initial invitation, the auctioneer's realignment
of gaze, and in some cases repeated realignment of gaze, can subject the
prospective buyer to successive demands to respond, if only to re-decline
the opportunity to bid. Moreover, gesture and other bodily movements
such as postural movement towards the underbidder can underscore the
invitation, encouraging the participant to respond and indeed bid at the
next increment. The performative impact of these successive attempts to
encourage the prospective buyer to make a further bid derives not simply
through the interaction between the participant and the auctioneer, but the
ways in which their interaction is part of an emerging event that involves
numerous participants – the protagonist, other interested parties and the
audience as whole. In other words, the pursuit of the underbidder is visible and audible to all those present, and subjects the underbidder to public
scrutiny and even, on occasions, humiliation.

One further point: in each of these cases, pursuit is undertaken with
good humour. In returning to the underbidder and if only momentarily
establishing orientation, we find the auctioneer smiling and encouraging
the buyer to smile. Rather than undermine the seriousness of the pursuit,
establishing this personal, light-hearted standpoint enables the auctioneer
to make, in some cases, repeated attempts to elicit a bid without causing
offence or difficulty. It might be considered that the laughter itself under-
mines the sequential import and significance of the various attempts to elicit
the bid. Quite the contrary; it provides the environment that allows the auctioneer to render the underbidder the centre of attention, to maintain their
mutual engagement and to preserve a certain politeness and demeanour
towards the auctioneer; an environment of good that is ruthlessly exploited
to increase the price of the goods in question and have them sold.

Participation in Auctions

> The week that the billionaires of the world arrived in London.... The dominance of private bidding is hardly stop-press news at Impressionist, Modern and Contemporary sales, but what was different about the February series in London was the geographical breadth and depth of private interest. Christie's reported that clients from 55 different countries registered to bid in their London auctions, generating over 2500 telephone bids.(*Antiques Trade Gazette* 25.2.2006: 27–8)

The ability to participate unproblematically in an auction rests in part on the transparency of an organisation that systematically distributes opportunities to bid at particular prices. The organisation is deployed, orchestrated, by the auctioneer, whose actions render visible and coordinate the contributions of particular participants and thereby remove the necessity for individuals to interact directly with other interested parties. Even the vagaries of price that occasionally arise in establishing competition between prospective buyers are replaced by an ordered system of increasing increments that largely determines the price at which people are free to bid. The system not only provides recurrent opportunities for people to participate, so, for example, if you have missed one opportunity another is bound to arise, but selectively orders contributions and juxtaposes the bids of two and no more than two parties. It also enables contributions, bids, to be produced through the most simple of actions, the nod of a head, a gesture or wave of a buyer number. In this way the complexities that might arise by virtue of gathering together numerous buyers who have varying interests and ideas of price – to compete against each other to purchase particular goods of variable quality and type – are resolved by virtue of a seemingly simple organisation that enables the unproblematic participation of the uninitiated. Underlying this form of interaction is a sequential organisation that not only provides a particular participant, namely the auctioneer, to selectively allocate turns to particular individuals, but successively implicates the actions they produce to advance the price of the goods. In this and other ways, an organisation is deployed that provides the resources to enable people to unproblematically participate in the event and enables contributions to consist of no more than a simple bodily movement – be it a nod of the head or gesture. It is hardly surprising that buyers can participate in auctions with little difficulty and even those unfamiliar with auctions or even the language in which they are conducted are able to bid for the goods in question.

The routine operation of auctions, however, relies not just on a transparent and simple organisation but the good and appropriate behaviour of participants. We have noted, for example, that, notwithstanding the highly constrained ways in which people are able to participate in the event, largely producing specific contributions in response to the invitation of the auctioneer, they can shape that participation in an attempt to achieve particular outcomes. We have remarked on the ways in which immediate bidding may be used to display confidence and determination, how prospective buyers may attempt to transform the incremental structure to disconcert the opposition and the ways in which bidders may attempt to preserve their anonymity. Within the framework of this conventional organisation, there are highly variable and contingent ways of accomplishing particular actions that preserve the routine and recognisable characteristics of particular activities. This is not to say that troubles do not emerge, and it is interesting to note that in those few institutions that train their auctioneers, training pays particular attention to managing 'difficult' prospective buyers – buyers, for example, who complain that the auctioneer is selling too slowly or failing to acknowledge their bids, or buyers who attempt to repeatedly challenge the incremental structure or who place bids as the hammer falls – individuals not unfamiliar with the organisation of auctions but rather people who threaten its routine operation for their own advantage.

One further point should be mentioned. The legitimacy of auctions and their ability to determine price and exchange relies upon the transparency of the event, an event that is both witness and witness-able. Relatively little time at auction is spent actually bidding for particular lots. Prospective buyers participate during a run, but much time is spent waiting for lots to come up for sale and for an opportunity to bid. Moreover, it is not unusual for auctions to attract an audience of people unlikely to bid but who have an interest in the proceedings if only to see how particular goods are selling and witness the dispersal of a well-established collection. The participation of an audience is critical to the event and its legitimacy, warranting the determination of price and the exchange of goods by virtue of the sale being witnessed and witness-able.

The auction relies on the good or appropriate behaviour of the audience, that they are willing to cooperate with and preserve the integrity of the event. Occasionally, for example, formal protests will arise at particular events or members of the family will disrupt the proceedings in an attempt to undermine the sale of a particular article. In a recent case, a vendor attempted to stop the hammer falling on the sale of a rare, early ewer, realising apparently that the auction house had severely underestimated its value. Indeed some months later it was sold for many millions of pounds by a different auction house.

The Fatimid rock crystal ewer 'sold' for £220,000 at Lawrence's at Crewkerne will reappear at Christie's next month with an estimate of over £3m. Remarkably it has emerged that the original sale in Somerset had been annulled after doubt emerged regarding the legitimacy of a sale that the vendor reportedly had tried to stop as the bidding soared. (*Antiques Trade Gazette* 20.9.2008: 1)

Notwithstanding these more unusual dramatic cases, the conduct of the audience during an auction is critical to its success, and an unruly audience, even members of an audience who are restless or talk loudly, can disrupt the sale and undermine the auctioneer's ability to engender an appropriate competitive yet orderly atmosphere.

While it is undoubtedly the case that some buyers determine the precise value of goods prior to their sale and do not waiver from the price they are willing to pay, in practice prospective buyers may be more flexible and subject to the contingencies that inevitably arise at auction. The conduct of other buyers, not simply the price they are willing to pay, but the ways in which they bid can have an important impact on the psychology of participation. It is remarkable perhaps, how this most minimal of actions, the bid, can be produced in qualitatively distinct ways in order to display a certain disposition towards the matters at hand, and at least some cases, to have an important impact on the price that goods achieve and their future ownership. In mediating the contributions of buyers, the auctioneer not only voices the bid, but can articulate the bid so as to embody specific characteristics of the ways in which the buyer produces the contribution.

Auctioneers too encourage bidding, not just through the ways in which they create an impression of competition during the early stages of a sale, or how they voice increments to facilitate bidding, but more explicitly by enabling and in some cases, persuading, buyers to change their mind and bid the next increment. One might expect that auctioneers frequently provide underbidders with the opportunity to change their mind, to go the next increment. In practice it is not so common and yet more often than not, it successfully secures a further bid.

To explore these issues a little further, we reviewed the recordings of a range of auctions, undertaken in Britain and abroad, involving different auctioneers selling goods at different price levels in order to examine the frequency of pursuits or return invitations following a declination, and to gain a measure of their success. The cases include examples in which the bidder unambiguously declines the next increment and those in which the declination is more ambivalent, though there were fewer weak declinations than expected. In more than half the cases in which the buyer declines to bid and the auctioneer re-invites a bid, the underbidder agrees to bid the next increment. Only a small number of these cases involved the auctioneer offering a split increment to encourage the prospective buyer to bid. In more than eighty per cent of cases that included a second active participant, that is the auctioneer was neither taking bids from commission nor against the reserve, a further bid was issued by the other party. In other words, in cases in which the auctioneer successfully encourages the buyer to change his mind and bid, the protagonist within the run bids the next but one increment. Successfully pursuing an underbidder for a further contribution therefore more often than not advances the price by two rather than one increment. If the sale consists of goods of a relatively low value, then the revenue implications for the vendor and the auction house of securing two further bids may be relatively insignificant. On the other hand, if the increments are in the thousands or tens of thousands, then securing a further contribution from an underbidder can be of some economic importance.

Given the potential revenue implications of encouraging an underbidder to reconsider their decision to withdraw from the bidding, it may come as some surprise that auctioneers do not routinely attempt to encourage further bids. It is important to bear in mind one or two issues. First, auctioneers have to balance the interest in securing the maximum price for individual goods against the demands of selling a substantial number of lots in one session. Consider, for example, that you may have well in excess of 400 lots to sell in one day and that by attempting to pursue underbidders in numerous cases you would inevitably extend the length of the sale and run the risk of frustrating those sitting through the proceedings waiting for the lots in which they are interested. Even the leading international auction houses, and one suspects their clients, expect their auctioneers to be selling at least 80 lots an hour and in many cases, especially in provincial auction houses, it is not unusual to find lots selling at a rate of 120 or more. Second, encouraging, even persuading, prospective buyers to bid further increments poses questions concerning the role and the neutrality of the auctioneer and 'whose side he is on'. Whereas the auctioneer is selling goods on behalf of the vendor, the auction house relies upon the participation and commitment of prospective buyers, including the trade and regular buyers, and their good will is critical to the success of auctions. More importantly perhaps, the idea that auctioneers principally mediate competition for scarce resources, rather than actively influence demand, is an important feature of the legitimacy of the event. Indeed, in this regard, it is worth contrasting the conduct of auctioneers at more conventional sales with the ways in which they encourage and coerce bidding at charity events. The concerns that can arise with auctioneers more actively pursuing bids have been exacerbated by the introduction of guarantees and certain auction houses having a financial 'interest in property consigned for auction'. For instance:

> On occasion, Christie's has a direct financial interest in lots consigned for sale, which may include guaranteeing a minimum price or making an advance to the consignor that is secured solely by consigned property. (Christie's 14.5.2008: 288)

Whereas it is now conventional to indicate in the sale catalogue the lots in which an auction house may have financial interest, and besides the practice has largely been abandoned since the financial crisis, there is always the danger that the over-rigorous pursuit of bids may irritate buyers and even lead some to suspect the motivations of the auctioneer.

6   Remote Presence and Online Participation

One of the more remarkable developments over the past couple of decades has been the extraordinary success of the Internet auction. It is delightful to find that one of the more widespread applications in e-commerce draws on a seemingly simple mechanism, a social organisation that evolved long before the birth of Christ. The exponential growth of Internet sites such as eBay has had a significant impact on the number and range of goods and services sold through auction, with eBay alone listing some 650 million items, at a total value of $16 billion dollars (U.S. dollars), in the first quarter of 2007. Despite predictions to the contrary, these developments do not seem to have had an adverse effect on the more traditional auction, at least in the fields of art, antiques and objets d'art, with the value of goods sold through live sales increasing alongside the burgeoning growth of the Internet auction. Indeed, the auction houses were quick to recognise the enormous potential of the Internet, and as early as 1999 Sotheby's collaborated with eBay and Amazon to introduce online bidding into the live auction. This initiative proved problematic, costing Sotheby's some millions of dollars, but since then we have witnessed the widespread deployment of systems to support real-time Internet bidding at auctions of art and antiques. These systems enable new forms of participation and have facilitated global access to auctions that hitherto would have remained parochial, largely of interest to the local trade. The introduction of real-time Internet bidding, however, raises questions concerning the coordination and integration of remote bids with live co-present action and the matters of trust and legitimacy that underpin the ability of sales to secure the price and exchange of goods.

The introduction of electronic technologies to enhance auctions is by no means new. The 1960s brought widespread interest in the 'Dutch clock system' that enabled buyers during auctions using the Dutch model to literally stop the clock and place a winning bid by pressing a button, a system said to enable up to 600 transactions an hour to be performed (see Cassady 1967). Some years later, Fuji Electronics developed a more sophisticated technology, primarily for wholesale auctions of fruits and vegetables, that enabled bidders to use a keyboard to select and bid particular prices that in turn were displayed on an electronic board placed to the front of the saleroom. Both systems were principally concerned with enabling bids to be issued with greater speed and reliability. As early as the 1940s, however, a system known charmingly as 'selevision' was developed. Based on tele-type machines, it allowed geographically dispersed buyers to submit bids by wire, and by the 1960s we witnessed the progressive introduction of the telephone to auctions of art and antiques to support remote participation. Television was first used in auctions of art and antiques in the 1960s to enable potential buyers in adjoining rooms and, in some cases, other cities to follow the sale and bid through saleroom assistants who transmitted the contributions to the auctioneer from the remote site. In 1965, the Early Bird satellite was put to service by Parke-Bernet and Sotheby's to enable those in New York to watch the sale in London and bid by telephone. Until now Commission bids and bidding via the telephone remain the principal means through which those unable or unwilling to attend a sale can purchase goods at auctions of art and antiques; however the Internet is of increasing importance, and many sales of art and antiques now provide the opportunity for buyers to bid online during the auction.

Of all the Internet auction sites, eBay (and its precursor AuctionWeb), created by Pierre Omidyar in the early 1990s, has proved the most successful, surviving the burst of the Internet bubble in 2000 and going from strength to strength in terms of the range and number of goods sold online, the international breadth of regular users and the revenue generated through sales. While it is argued that the system was based on Omidyar's commitment to creating a 'perfect global market place that everyone comes to on an equal basis' (Cohen 2002), it is clear that the underlying mechanism is based on the conventional English auction model coupled with a preset period of time for the sale of each lot. Various additional procedures have been put in place over the years to address the problems and issues that arise in selling goods by auction online. Putting to one side matters regarding secure payment, the quality of goods and the legal responsibilities of eBay and other operators, a number of problems have emerged that are ordinarily managed within the interaction itself in more traditional auctions, but that present serious difficulties for the design and management of auction Internet sites.

A growing corpus of research addresses online auctions and the design of auction mechanisms (for an overview, see Ockenfels et al. 2006). This research examines some of the significant issues and problems that arise with online auctions, the impact on outcomes of different methods of auction and their implications for the design of particular mechanisms. Matters of trust, integrity and the coordination of bids are of some importance in this regard. For example, despite the absence of an auctioneer, a problem that pervaded online auctions from the outset was shill bids, bids placed by the vendor or confederates, often through the use of multiple identities, in order to enhance competition and unfairly inflate prices. Service providers, including eBay, have developed software designed to identify and manage shill bids, but it still remains a matter of some concern. Moreover, not unlike the traditional auction, it is common for prospective buyers to place bids late during the sale in attempt to secure the goods in question, especially given that almost all online auctions stipulate a fixed end time. Indeed, irrespective of the time allocated to the online sale, a large proportion of bids are routinely submitted within the final moments of the auction, buyers strategically submitting a last-second final bid to secure the goods (see, for example, Kauffman and Wood 2004; Resnick et al. 2000; Rogers et al. 2007). Software is available to enable buyers to snipe the competition. The problem is so severe that a number of service providers are exploring the possibility of introducing a 'soft close' in which the end of the sale is progressively accomplished and enables flexible late bidding. Integrating online bids into the more traditional auction has raised related problems, but in this case, these problems have not been resolved through the introduction of formal procedures, but by participants themselves in and through the interaction that arises at these sales.

It is worthwhile raising one further issue. Over the last two decades, there has been a burgeoning interest in developing new technologies that enable communication and collaboration amongst individuals located within different physical spaces; technologies primarily concerned with supporting work and organisational activities. Alongside these developments, we have witnessed a growing corpus of research in the social and cognitive sciences concerned with the forms of interaction and 'presence' enabled by these systems and the limitations and difficulties that can arise in mediated communication (see, for example, Finn et al. 1997; Harrison 2009). It has been found, for instance, that technologies designed to support audio-visual communication between remote participants, videoconferencing as well as more sophisticated systems such as media spaces, can undermine the interactional impact and significance of particular actions, both spoken and visible, and thereby render the collaborative accomplishment of certain activities problematic (see, for example, Heath and Luff 2000; Gaver et al. 1993). Whilst online bidding in live auctions is technically less sophisticated than many of the systems developed to support remote collaboration, it raises some interesting issues with regard to 'presence' and the extent to which remote participants are subject to the interactional constraints that enable auctioneers to efficiently elicit and coordinate contributions from prospective buyers in the room or those represented by sale assistants. Unlike systems which support remote collaboration, systems primarily designed to support interaction among small numbers of individuals, auctions pose a particular challenge, since any system is required to enable cooperation among large numbers of participants, both local and remote, who flexibly and contingently engage and disengage within rapidly emerging activities.

Fragile Runs

Throughout the last decade, we have witnessed the widespread introduction of online bidding into auctions of fine art and antiques. It began with leading international houses such as Christie's introducing online bidding into specialist sales, but since then has become a pervasive facility for many auctions of art and antiques. The most common systems for online bidding in the United Kingdom, with variants in mainland Europe, North America, and the Far East, require buyers to register with the service provider, or in some cases the auction house, enabling bids to be placed on any lot as the sale proceeds. In Britain, many auction houses use a system known as 'i.bidder'. It is provided by 'the-saleroom.com', a subsidiary of the principal trade journal, the *Antique Trade Gazette*. As the sale proceeds, the remote participant receives information concerning each lot, normally accompanied by a picture, and can listen to the live auction. The current increment appears on screen and the remote participant is invited to bid at the next increment by clicking on a button on screen. If the bid is successful, then the button changes colour and informs the buyer that he or she has the current bid. A sign of 'fair warning' is used to enable the remote participant to know that the lot is about to be sold and to invite further bids. The system also informs the buyer whether he or she has been successful in purchasing the lot. One important addition to this standard system, a feature available on 'Christie's.live' since its introduction in 2005, is a video image that enables the remote participant to see as well as hear the auctioneer. Not all auction houses provide video as well as audio access for their sales

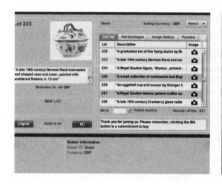

i.bidder without the video image   Christie's.live

Figures 6.1 & 6.2.
i.bidder without the video image. (By kind permission of thesaleroom.com)
Christie's.live. (By kind permission of Christie's)

at the current time. The following screen shots show 'i.bidder' without the video link and Christie's.live with its video access to the auctioneer (Figures 6.1 and 6.2).

In the saleroom, the system is operated by an Internet administrator responsible for entering data into the system and in many cases informing the auctioneer of online bids. At Christie's and a number of other auction houses, the auctioneer also has a display that allows him to see online bids as they appear on screen. The Internet administrator enters the lot number and sets the incremental scale at the onset of the sale of each lot; he then simply clicks on a button to advance the increments. The remote participant is invited to bid through a message that appears on screen that specifies the next increment – the price required to make a bid. The operation of the system relies, therefore, upon the efficiency of the Internet administrator, who has to follow the sale, make adjustments to the increments where necessary and anticipate when the goods are about to be sold so that the message of 'fair warning' can be issued in a timely manner. The system also relies on the clarity with which the auctioneer takes the auction, in particular the pace and orderliness with which he structures and announces increments. Indeed, the *Antiques Trade Gazette* recently offered a prize to the auctioneer who best integrates online bidding into the live auction. The Internet administrator is normally positioned alongside the rostrum. The following is a shot of the administrator's screen for 'thesaleroom.com' (Figures 6.3 and 6.4).

Over the last five years, there has been a rapid increase both in the number of auction houses that offer online bidding and the range of sales

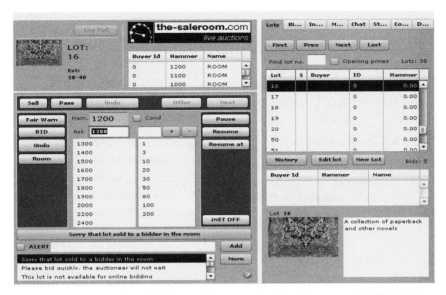

Figures 6.3 & 6.4. the administrator's screen for 'thesaleroom.com'. (By kind permission of thesaleroom.com)

in which the systems are used. There is significant variation in the number of lots sold to online bidders at auctions, and different types of sale and lot have proved particularly attractive to those bidding online. For example, certain types of collectables, including coins, toys, cameras and books, are more likely to sell to online bidders, as are watches, porcelain and silver, whereas furniture and pictures not infrequently receive significantly fewer online bids. Initially, it was the cheaper goods that sold to online bidders, but in the past few years we have witnessed an increasing number of more expensive items, in some cases selling for tens of thousands of pounds, bought by buyers through the Internet. The growing number of prospective buyers bidding through the Internet is beginning to have an important impact on the activity that arises at some auctions. Surprising, perhaps, requests to bid by telephone do not seem to have had a corresponding decrease over the same period; whether this is due to its appeal to a different cohort of prospective buyer or the fact that online bidders have to pay a small percentage to the service provider to bid remains unknown.

It is worthwhile considering two sales that include online contributions. In the first case, the remote participant can hear the auctioneer with bids communicated through the Internet administrator. In the second fragment, the remote participant can see as well as hear the auction, and the auctioneer has direct access to a screen that displays online bids. IA refers to Internet Administrator. OL refers to the Online Bidder, OL.1, numbered in the order in which they enter the bidding.

Fragment 6.1

    A: Two forty, two sixty on the Internet?

    IA: Yes sir [OL.1]

    A: Two sixty two eighty now?

        (0.3) [B.1]

    A: Two eighty three hundred on the Internet? (0.2) At three hundred we're <u>waiting</u>. On the Internet?

    IA: Yes sir [OL.1]

    A: Three hundred bid an twenty?

        (0.3) [B.1]

    A: Three twenty three forty on the Internet? Three forty? (0.4) Three forty on the Internet?

    IA: Yes sir [OL.1]

    A: Three forty

        [B.1]

    A: Three sixty now three eighty on the Internet (.) Three eighty on the Internet we are waiting at three eighty (0.3) At three eighty waiting for a bid for the Internet

    IA: Yes sir [OL.1]

    A: Four hundred

        [B.1]

    A: Four twenty

Fragment 6.2

    A: At twelve hundred thousand it's back in the room (0.4) Against you online (0.2) twelve hundred

        (0.2) [OL.1]

    A: Thirteen hundred online (0.6) Thirteen hundred

        (1.4) {SA.2]

    A: Fourteen hundred (0.8) Fourteen still in the room (1.0) It's against you I'm afraid online (0.6) Fourteen selling to the room bidder (0.6) One more online if you want it. (0.2) At fourteen

        (0.2) [OL.1]

A: Thank you (0.2) Fifteen hundred Online goes fifteen

(1.8) {SA.3 bids}

A: Sixteen new telephone bidder comes in (0.4) Sixteen hundred (0.8) Still underbidding online go seventeen if you want it (0.2) Sixteen at the moment (0.8) Any advance?

(0.5) [OL.1]

A: Seventeen online thank you (1.0) Seventeen hundred pounds

(0.6) {SA.3 bids}

A: Eighteen hundred (0.5) Eighteen back in the room at eighteen (0.3) Online if you want it gotta go to nineteen I've got eighteen already (1.0) Eighteen hundred

(0.6)

A: No more online? It's at eighteen (0.4) Going to lose it online (0.5) It's going to the room (0.6) Eighteen hundred pounds

(1.9)

A: {Knock} Sold

The first fragment consists of a run between a bidder in the room and a buyer online, with the picture finally selling for £420. In the second fragment there are two runs, both involving a sale assistant and a buyer bidding online. In both cases, the auctioneer establishes runs between the online bidder and buyers or their representatives in the room. There are however, significant differences between runs involving online buyers and those that arise between participants in the saleroom.

First, there are severe delays in bids received from online participants, with bids often taking some seconds before they are issued even once the run is established. Second, there is significant variation in the time it takes for an online bid to be issued and we find little of the rhythm or evenness of pace that ordinarily emerges within a run. Third, in contrast to the ways in which the announcement of a bid coupled with a reorientation to an underbidder serves to invite the next contribution, the auctioneer has to make successive attempts to have the online buyer confirm the next increment. Indeed, we find auctioneers making successive attempts to have online buyers confirm the next increment – even in cases in which they subsequently bid far in excess of the current price.

If we consider just one of the Internet bids, we can begin to see the difficulties that can arise in having the online bidder confirm the next increment.

Fragment 6.2. Transcript 2

   A: Fourteen hundred
      (0.8)
→A: Fourteen still in the room
      (1.0)
→A: It's against you I'm afraid online
      (0.6)
→A: Fourteen selling to the room bidder
      (0.6)
→A: One more online if you want it.
      (0.2)
→A: At fourteen
      (0.2) [OL.1]

The auctioneer announces the current increment and invites a contribution from the online buyer. No bid is issued. He repeats the increment, attributes it to the 'room', and waits for a response. Neither an acceptance nor a declination is forthcoming. He then explicitly announces that the bid is against the online bidder, still receives no response and declares he is about to sell to the room. No response is forthcoming. He then specifically invites the online participant to bid, and once again repeats the increment. Following five attempts, the auctioneer finally receives a bid.

In the first fragment, online bids are issued more rapidly. Even there, however, it is worth noting that the auctioneer has to make successive attempts to have the online bidder confirm the next increment prior to the contribution being issued.

Fragment 6.1. Transcript 2

→A: Two eighty three hundred on the Internet?
      (0.2)
→A: At three hundred we're <u>waiting</u> on the Internet
  IA: Yes, sir [OL.1]

Delays in the issue of online bids are not a consequence of data entry by Internet administrators. In reviewing a series of online sales using different service providers, we found little delay between the voicing of an increment and the opportunity to bid appearing on screen. Indeed we often find the invitation appears on screen during the announcement of the increment and if not, it rarely takes more than three-tenths of a second following the announcement. We have little evidence to suggest that transmission time causes anything more than a split-second delay in the remote participant hearing the sale and receiving the invitation to bid.

The delay of online contributions can threaten their efficacy as well as pose problems for their coordination and management of bids. It is not unusual, for example, to find that at a break in a run, delays in the issue of online bids favour contributions from the room as the auctioneer accepts first come first served. For the online bidder, it can be unclear why his or her bid has not been accepted.

Fragment 6.3

    A: At >twenty four°twenty thousand dollars:

        (0.2)

    A: At twenty four thousand [B.3] <twenty six thousand.

→A: Ahead of you online

        (.) [B.2]

    A: Twenty eight- an against you

Where the system does not provide a video link, the lack of visual access to the auctioneer can undermine the remote participant's ability to see why his or her attempt to bid has been unsuccessful. It is not unusual to find online buyers making successive attempts to bid during a run in cases where they fail to secure acceptance of their first at a break in the run. Even in cases in which the remote participant can see the auctioneer, limited access to the rest of the saleroom can undermine his or her ability to know why the contribution failed to be acknowledged. It is not simply that he or she is unable to see competing bidders within the room, but rather the remote participant is unable to determine the import and implication of the auctioneer's bodily alignment and gestures that routinely accompany the announcement of bids.

The delays that arise in the issue of online bids can not only undermine the remote buyer's ability to enter a run, but also his or her participation during the run. For example, following successive attempts to encourage an online participant to bid the next increment, an auctioneer may accept a bid from the room or a sale assistant even though the remote buyer re-enters the bidding some time later, and, in some cases, even secures the lot. In other words, the delays that arise in the issue of online bids *render the run fragile*, with the auctioneer, often in frustration, taking bids from new prospective buyers before the Internet bidder has actually withdrawn. In turn, these delays engender difficulties for the Internet administrator as he looks at the screen waiting for a bid to be issued whilst the auctioneer looks at him demanding a response.

The delay in the issue of online contributions also creates difficulties for the close of sale. In Fragment 6.2, for example, the auctioneer makes successive attempts to determine whether the online bidder will place a further bid before finalising the sale. More difficult still, it is not unusual for online participants to produce a bid in response to the screen message of 'fair warning', the message issued by the Internet administrator as the goods are about to be sold. Delays in the production of the online contribution can result in bids being received following the strike of the hammer, causing difficulties for the auctioneer and frustration to the competition. In both the following cases, the auctioneer reopens the bidding following the issue of a late online bid.

Fragment 6.4 (abbreviated)

    A: At one sixty is all that I'm bid, one eighty now? One eighty now, then sixty all and done now. At a hundred and sixty

→   {Knock}

    IA: [points to screen]

→A: Oh (.) I can <u>do</u> one eighty is that a one eighty bid <u>yes</u>?

    IA: <u>Yes</u>

    A: One eighty is the bid. One eighty is on the Internet one eighty one eighty one eighty one eighty (.) with the <u>Internet now</u> (.) at a hundred and eighty pound, the next bid is two hundred (.) if anyone is interested? (.) At one eighty on the Internet

       {Knock}

Fragment 6.5 (abbreviated)

    A: Seventeen:: anywhere else? (0.2)

    A: Going to sell at seventeen hundred

       (0.3)

→A: {Knock} [B.2 raises his buyer's number]

→A: Online eig<u>hteen</u>, online sir I'm afraid

       (.)

    A: Nineteen sir? … Nineteeen thank you sir. (.) Nineteen: back in the room nineteen (0.2) ag<u>ainst</u> the online bidder.

Surprising, perhaps, we rarely find complaints arising from a lot having been 'sold' and the auctioneer then reopening the sale. In both cases, the auctioneer provides little opportunity for objection and immediately following the online contribution invites the co-participant, or anyone else for that matter, to bid the projected next increment. Towards the rear of sale catalogues, in the small print, the auction houses attempt to defend themselves from the possibility of dispute or litigation that might arise from having 'sold' a lot and then reopening the sale.

> The maker of the highest bidder accepted by the Auctioneer conducting the sale shall be the buyer at the Hammer Price "the buyer" and any dispute about a bid shall be settled at the Auctioneer's absolute discretion by reoffering the Lot during the course of the auction or otherwise. (Peter Wilson Fine Art 8 and 9.7.2009: 139)

Managing Online Participation

It is not uncommon for auctioneers to seek to postpone accepting online contributions until only one prospective buyer remains in the room or on the telephone. However, given there may be little interest in the lot or interested parties may withhold bids, it can prove necessary to accept contributions through the Internet earlier in the sale. Even if online contributions are resisted until the final moments of a sale, it is likely that they will require the auctioneer to establish a run and more often or not, a run between a participant in the room (be they a prospective buyer or a sale assistant) and the remote bidder. The auctioneer has to encourage the online buyer to bid and to bid with dispatch – not only so the sale can be brought to a rapid and efficient completion, but to avoid frustrating other buyers and the audience and undermining the atmosphere of the sale.

It was noted earlier that it is not unusual for auctioneers to make repeated attempts to have the online buyer confirm an invitation to bid throughout the course of a run. Consider the following instance. We join a run between an online buyer and a sale assistant with the small nineteenth-century watercolour selling to the telephone buyer at £260.

Fragment 6.6

    A: Two two on the Internet. Two two, two three now?

       [SA.1]Two three.

→A: Two four:? (0.4) Two four:. (.) Two four on the Internet? Do I hear two four:?

    (1.2)

IA: Yes sir [OL.1]

A: Two four on the Internet, yes?

A: Two four

A: [SA.1] Two five

→A: Two six on the Internet we're waiting

A: Two six.

→A: Bid quickly on the Internet if you would please. Two six and we're waiting.

      (0.4)

A: At two six. Two six? Two five:: (0.3) There two five Am I bid two six anywhere else? At two thousand five hundred pounds going to be sold. At two five only. All out at two five::

A: {Knock}

In this and previous examples, we can begin to see the contrast between the ways in which auctioneers invite bids from prospective buyers or their representatives in the room or represented by sale assistants with the ways in which they invite bids from those bidding via the Internet. In the case of online participants, the auctioneer announces the current bid and turns to the Internet administrator or the screen. As the current increment is announced, the Internet administrator sends a message to the online bidder inviting a bid and stipulating the bid price – the next increment. With no response forthcoming, we find the auctioneer not only repeating the increment with a questioning intonation, but also explicitly identifying the recipient namely the 'Internet' or 'online bidder'. In other words, the auctioneer attempts to underscore the sequential import of the invitation and the necessity to respond with dispatch by repeating the increment following a delay and reaffirming that it is the responsibility of that particular participant to respond. Despite attempts to secure the next bid and secure the bid with dispatch, we find the auctioneer producing repeated invitations for the online buyer to bid and indeed in this case issuing a general request for the remote participant to 'bid quickly'.

The problem of delay and its resolution points to some interesting aspects of the ways in which visible conduct features in the production of bids and the ability of auctioneers to establish a rapid pace and rhythm of bidding. It is worthwhile considering a fragment in a little more detail. It is drawn from the sale of a portrait attributed to Kneller. In this example, the auctioneer can see online bids on a transparent screen to the right of the rostrum. A camera, attached to the ceiling, enables online participants to see the auctioneer. We join the action during a run between a sale assistant and an online buyer.

Fragment 6.7

> A: Thir:teen (0.2) online
>
> (0.2) [SA.1]
>
> A: Fourteen in (the room) (0.4) Fourteen hundred. Against you online [OL.1]
>
> A: <u>Fifteen</u> online (0.3) Fifteen hundred here:
>
> A: Fifteen.
>
> [SA.1]
>
> →A: Sixteen hundred (0.2) back of the room at sixteen
>
> A: Against you online [OL.1]
>
> A: Back to seventeen the online bidder goes

The auctioneer receives a bid from the sale assistant and announces 'Sixteen hundred'. With the announcement, the auctioneer turns from the sale assistant to the screen that displays the online contribution.

The screen stands as surrogate participant. The announcement of the increment, coupled with the bodily and visible realignment of the auctioneer, not only serves to invite a participant, namely the online buyer, to bid the projected next increment, but displays to all those present that it is the turn of the online buyer to accept or decline the invitation. The announcement is also accompanied by an electronic invitation. No response is forthcoming. The auctioneer turns from the screen and towards the sale assistant, reattributing the source of the current bid. He then once again turns to the screen and re-invites the online participant to go to the next increment. Again, no response is forthcoming.

The embodied announcement, coupled with the online request, does not appear to have the sequential import or interactional significance of an invitation addressed to a participant in the room or an invitation mediated through a sale assistant to a telephone buyer. Neither the auctioneer's announcement nor his visible and bodily orientation towards the screen underscore the immediacy of the request for the remote participant to bid. The sequential organisation of the run and import of the temporal characteristics of the actions of both the auctioneer and co-participants appears undermined; they fail to encourage, even constrain, the online bidder to issue a timely contribution.

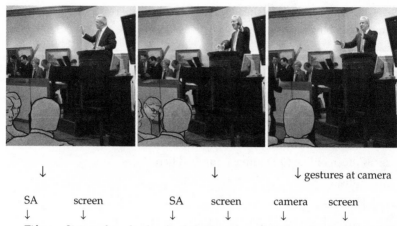

    ↓   ↓   ↓ gestures at camera

SA   screen   SA   screen   camera   screen
↓   ↓   ↓   ↓   ↓   ↓
Fifteen. Sixteen hundred - - back in the room at sixteen Against you online

Fragment 6.7. Transcript 2. Image 1, 2 & 3.

In the case at hand, it is interesting to note how the auctioneer attempts to address the problem. After failing to secure a bid in response to the announcement of the increment and the reattribution of the current bid, he turns from the screen and looks directly at the camera. As he turns towards the camera, he raises his right hand and gestures towards the online bidder, announcing 'against you online'. Whether it is the auctioneer's attempt to personally address, both vocally and visibly, the remote participant we cannot know, but the online bidder immediately issues a bid and the run continues in this awkward fashion for a further few increments. The auctioneer appears to believe that his visible actions, visual alignment and gestures, directed towards the online buyer's viewpoint through the camera, can underscore the invitation to bid and the urgency with which the remote participant should respond.

There is a further difficulty. Participants in the saleroom, be they buyers or their representatives, accept or decline the opportunity to bid during a run in response to an invitation. The acceptance or declination is typically issued with, or immediately following, the invitation and is visible to the auctioneer and in principle to anyone who happens to have visible access to the participant. Even if a delay in issuing a response emerges following the invitation, the participant's conduct is visible to the auctioneer and frequently provides an account for the delay. In contrast, those bidding online do not have the opportunity to inform the auctioneer or administrator that they are declining the opportunity to bid, nor is their conduct immediately following the invitation accessible to those in the saleroom. Internet auction systems provide no decline button and there is no action that online bidders may deploy, other than not bidding, that allows the auctioneer, let alone anyone else in the saleroom, to know whether the bidder has withdrawn or not. For the auctioneer, the difficulty is exacerbated by the fact that online bids are frequently issued with some delay and during that delay neither the auctioneer nor anyone else knows whether the absence of a response is a delayed acceptance or whether the prospective buyer has withdrawn from the bidding. Moreover, unlike a run that arises between participants within the saleroom, where the auctioneer can often anticipate the likelihood of a buyer withdrawing from a run by virtue of the way in which he bids, there are few resources with which to infer the likely import of a delayed response following an invitation to bid. In other words, the very resources that the auctioneer relies on to create smooth and unproblematic transitions in runs are unavailable when managing the participation of prospective buyers online. These difficulties are reflected in the following fragment:

Fragment 6.8

    A: Three sixty do I hear

    A: [OL.1] Yes

    A: Three sixty (0.2) [A.] Three eighty on commission

        (0.3)

→A: Four hundred now on the Internet? Four hundred only bid. (0.2) At four hundred yes or no on the Internet? (0.3) At three eighty the bid's with me. (0.3) At three eighty I'm bid. On commission at three eighty. Four hundred on the Internet if there is still bidding?

        (0.3)

→A: Four hundred pounds on the Internet yes or no? Three eighty if they are all finished^

        (.)

    A: {Knock}

As for the online bidder, however sympathetic he may be to the auctioneer's difficulties, he has no independent way of confirming his withdrawal from the bidding.

The Attribution and Integrity of Online Bids

Online bids raise questions concerning the integrity of contributions – whether they are indeed contributions from genuine buyers or, for example, placed by vendors or their confederates to increase the price of goods. They also raise a related issue for auctioneers: Given that neither online participants nor their contributions are directly accessible to other buyers, what are the ways in which their integrity, at least for the practical purposes at hand, is established and sustained during the auction?

Unlike bids issued by participants, be they buyers or their representatives, auctioneers routinely announce the source of online contributions. So, for example, in the fragment discussed earlier, note that the auctioneer attributes the bids from the Internet to the online bidder, for instance 'Online goes fifteen'. It is worth adding that in inviting bids from the remote participant, the auctioneer frequently names the source from which he is seeking the bid – 'It's against you I'm afraid online' – though the naming of sources often arises following the failure of initial attempts to have the online buyer bid.

Fragment 6.2. Transcript 2

→A: Thirteen hundred online (0.6) thirteen hundred

(1.4) [SA.2]

A: Fourteen hundred (0.8) Fourteen still in the room (1.0) It's against you I'm afraid online (0.6) Fourteen selling to the room bidder (0.6) One more online if you want it at (0.2) at fourteen

(0.2) [OL.1]

→A: Thank you (0.2) Fifteen hundred. Online goes fifteen

(1.8) {SA.3 bids}

A: Sixteen new telephone bidder comes in (0.4) Sixteen hundred (0.8) Still underbidding online go seventeen if you want it (0.2) Sixteen at the moment (0.8) Any advance?

(0.5) [OL.1]

→A: Seventeen online thank you (1.0) Seventeen hundred pounds

(0.6) [SA.3 bids}

A: Eighteen hundred

In circumstances in which the Internet administrator bids on behalf of the remote participant by signalling or voicing the bid to the auctioneer, the announcement of the bid is not necessarily accompanied with reference to the source of the bid. In the first fragment we discussed (6.1), it is interesting to note that each online bid arises in response to an invitation that announces the potential source of the bid, for example, 'At three hundred we're <u>waiting</u> on the Internet'. Moreover, in informing the auctioneer of each online bid, the actions of the Internet administrator are visible and in some cases audible to those gathered within the saleroom – not dissimilar to a sale assistant bidding on behalf of a telephone buyer. The presence of the Internet administrator in the saleroom and the visibility of his or her actions, not simply in bidding but operating the system during the sale, provides access, albeit limited, to the activity and the auctioneer's dealings with the remote participant through the workstation. Ironically perhaps, the more sophisticated systems through which auctioneers directly receive bids from the Internet pose more questions concerning the transparency and integrity of remote participation.

The visible conduct of the auctioneer when inviting contributions from the Internet and in some, if not many, cases pursuing a response, also serves to display the source of the (potential) contribution. On receiving a bid from the principal protagonist, the auctioneer routinely announces the increment and turns towards the screen or Internet administrator to invite a bid from the online buyer. The reorientation of the auctioneer that accompanies the announcement of the bid enables all those present to see and to witness for themselves the source of the relevant next contribution. Moreover, it is not unusual for auctioneers to gesture towards the screen that displays Internet bids when inviting and acknowledging contributions from an online bidder – the screen serving as surrogate for the actual buyer. In the following fragment, the auctioneer gestures towards the screen as she invites the bid and then transforms the gesture, flipping the hand up and down to acknowledge and display its receipt.

In each of these cases, the remote participant has visual access to the auctioneer through the camera positioned in the saleroom. There are small variations in the location of the camera, but typically it is focused on the head and shoulders of the auctioneer. With little access to the auctioneer's surroundings and the actions that arise within the saleroom, it is not necessarily the case that the remote participant can determine the significance of the auctioneer's visual orientation and gestures. In consequence, the sequential and interactional import of the auctioneer's bodily conduct for the remote participant is questionable. Its relevance, however, to the organisation of action within the saleroom may be of some importance. It enables all those present, including the principal protagonist(s) to know who is being invited to bid and to await their response. It also serves to

gestures towards display   flips hand up and down
↓   ↓

We've gone thirty eight <u>on</u> <u>line</u>. (.) Forty online

Fragment 6.9. Images 1 & 2.

display the source of the bid(s) and the independence of particular contributions, the announcement by the auctioneer and its accompanying bodily alignment demonstrating that the bid is a bid in response to the action of a prospective buyer, even if that buyer is online and inaccessible to those gathered within the saleroom. The auctioneer's actions therefore serve to reveal, at least to those within the saleroom, his interaction with the remote participant and thereby give online contributions a presence and legitimacy they might not otherwise have.

While auctioneers may orient to the remote participant and look at and gesture towards the camera, they have no 'vanity monitor' and are unable to see how they and their actions are seen even whether they are being watched at all. All the same, they believe, and it may well be the case, that online buyers are sensitive to the visible conduct of the auctioneer, and one suspects that as a way of attempting to bolster the sequential and performative import of an invitation to bid the next increment, the alignment of visual and bodily orientation towards the camera, coupled with a re-announcement of an increment or even a more explicit request to bid, may serve to encourage a response from the remote participant. It is difficult to provide evidence either way for the impact or significance of the ways in which bodily comportment serves to encourage, even engender, response; however, once again, it may well be of some importance to the organisation of local action and the impression of the auction's process. It can enable the protagonist and others, in particular those awaiting an opportune moment to enter the bidding, to make sense of delays in the issue of bids and to coordinate their contributions with opportunities that arise within the developing course of the auction.

One further point; the integration of online contributions to the live auction raises one or two issues with regard to how a bid is characterised both for the audience of the sale and the principal protagonists. It will be recalled that auctioneers may describe prospective buyers, in particular when they first enter the run with regard to their location within the saleroom – 'in the front row', standing at the back', 'on the right-hand side'. This way of describing a participant serves to reveal the source of the contribution whilst preserving the anonymity of the bidder. Sale assistants, who, of course, bid on behalf of buyers who remain anonymous, are not infrequently referred to by first name, 'with Vicki', 'against you, Ami', 'I'm waiting, Sarah'. The reference to the location of the buyer or the name of the representative, coupled with the visible and bodily orientation of the auctioneer, serve to reveal to all present the source of the bid. With online participation, we find a marked shift in the way in which the auctioneer characterises the prospective buyers in the room. Sale assistants are rarely referred to by their name, but rather the source of their bids is described in terms of a 'telephone bid', 'new telephone bidder', and the like. The alternative characterisation enables the Internet bidder to know the general source of the contribution rather than person's Christian name, a name that would not necessarily enable a remote participant to distinguish between a buyer in the room and someone bidding via the telephone. Similarly, descriptions that characterise the location of a prospective buyer in the saleroom are rarely used – the online bidder would have little sense of the geography of the space or the respective distribution of the participants. For the remote participant, as well as those gathered in the saleroom, 'in the room' serves to differentiate the contributions of the remote participant, the 'online bidder' from those issued from within the immediate setting, the characterisation enabling the source of bids within the run to be contrastively determined. In other words, the integration of Internet bidding into the live, co-present auction demands significant changes in the ways in which the participants and their contributions are described, identified and rendered 'visible'.

An 'Intelligent' Gavel: A Small Experiment

Despite the widespread deployment of systems to enable remote bidding at live auctions, there remain some important challenges, challenges that reflect both matters of trust and coordination with the introduction of online contributions into sales of art and antiques. To address one or two of these challenges, with colleagues from a leading engineering laboratory at the University of Tsukuba, Hideaki Kuzuoka and Jun Yamashita, we developed a system designed to enhance the presence of remote participants within the saleroom and to provide auctioneers with resources with which to more flexibly integrate online contributions into the live auction (Heath et al. 2009). We were fortunate to receive support from two auctioneers, namely Robert Stones and Nicholas Allsopp, from one of the leading auction houses in northwest England (*Antiques Trade Gazette* 29.4.2008). In designing the system, we were keen to preserve the integrity of the traditional auction, including the typical layout of the saleroom, and to enable participants to use familiar objects and artefacts.

There are three key elements to the system – first, an 'intelligent' gavel that enables auctioneers to point to and take bids from remote participants, allowing more direct interaction with people bidding online; second, an 'intelligent' paddle that enables online participants to efficiently bid at the correct increment rather than using a conventional keyboard; and third, two large screens placed within the 'saleroom' to one side of and visible to the audience. Each screen displays an avatar, a simple graphical figure representing one of two online bidders to represent the two parties to a run. We use avatars rather than live video images in order to preserve the anonymity of the remote participants. When the remote participant raises his or her bidding paddle to bid, the hand of the avatar is raised displaying the action to all those within the saleroom. In an actual system, we could include in principle any number of avatars to represent different online bidders registered to bid at the sale, though it would be necessary to use alternative display technologies to project, for example, a large-scale image of the wall of the saleroom.

The gavel is the conventional wooden hammer used by the auctioneers, but in this case it is augmented by a small magnetic Polhemus 120Hz FASTRAK sensor. The sensor allows us to track the position (X, Y and Z Cartesian coordinates) and orientation (azimuth, elevation and roll) of the gavel. A magnetic emitter placed on the rostrum allows us to detect the orientation of the gavel. We developed software that computes orientation

Figure 6.5. The experiment showing online bidder, OL.1, on the left bidding. OL.2 is on the screen to the right. The 'intelligent gavel' is being held in the right hand of the auctioneer.

even if the auctioneer holds the gavel by its head and points with its base (as in Figure 1.2). When an online bid is accepted by the auctioneer, he or she presses a small button on the handle and the background to the avatar turns from green to red. In this way a successful bid by an online bidder is displayed to all those within the room.

The 'intelligent paddle' is equipped with a one-axis accelerometer that detects when it is raised to bid. A unidirectional video and audio connection from the saleroom to the remote site allows the online participants to observe and hear the auctioneer; the cameras are placed close to the avatar display to present the appropriate view for the remote participant. Like conventional systems, we provided remote participants with software displaying a description of the present lot and the current price. In the experiment, we used two displays (of different sizes), one for each avatar, and adjusted the scale of the image so that it was almost life sized. These screens were on the right side of the auctioneer along the wall not dissimilar to the position of sale assistants in some auction houses. Participants in the saleroom sat to the left of the auctioneer so that they could observe both auctioneer and the avatars.

We recognised it would be premature to introduce the system into an actual live auction. However, we were keen to test the technology in a

challenging situation that would enable us to explore matters of coordination, trust and presence. With our two professional auctioneers, we recruited
thirty potential buyers: members of staff, postgraduate and undergraduate
students. We prepared the appropriate materials for the auction: a detailed
catalogue listing lots of various types and their estimates (based on recent
sales of art and antiques) and salesheets for the auctioneers documenting
lot numbers, estimates and commission bids. We allocated each buyer a
fixed sum of £1,500 to spend on lots of their choosing. We also secured the
services of a saleroom assistant, who issued bids from the telephone.

We recorded the event using several cameras and microphones, enabling
us to analyse the conduct of both bidders and the auctioneers. Immediately
after the event, we also undertook a series of debriefings and interviews
with the bidders (room and online) and the auctioneers to explore their
reactions to the experiment and the system. For the analysis, we tran-
scribed a proportion of the data and identified various actions, sequences of
action and events such as runs. We also counted the frequency of particular
actions, action sequences and events including, for example, the relative
numbers of bids received from different participants, the number of bids
that arose within runs, the time it took for local and online bids to be issued
and so on. Both the auctioneers and the prospective buyers reported they
found the auction realistic.

Orders of Remote and Local Bidding

The system enabled the auctioneer efficiently and flexibly to take remote
bids at any stage during the sale of particular lots. The auctioneers established runs among participants in the room, between participants in the
room and online and between the online bidders. We found that thirty-two
of the forty lots involved an online participant and eleven of those involved
runs between the two online buyers. Runs that only involve online buyers
are rarely found within real auctions of art and antiques. In the following
fragment, after a late contribution from an online bidder, OL.1, the auctioneer establishes a run between the remote participant and a buyer in the
room.

Fragment 6.10 (experiment)

  A: It's eight hundred pounds. The bids the:re at eight hundred pounds. (.)
    Last chance (.) at eight hundred pounds. Being sold then at eight

→   [OL.1]

→A: Eight hundred Eight fifty is it now? Eight hundred, eight hundred and fifty pounds. It's eight fifty on the Internet, eight [B.2]) Nine hundred pounds. [OL.1] Nine fifty on the Internet (0.4) [B.2] One thousand pounds [OL.1] One fifty.

In Fragment 6.10, bidding that appeared to reach near completion after thirty seconds following successive runs between participants in the room is eventually brought to completion some seventy-three seconds later following a lengthy run involving a buyer in the room and a participant on the Internet. In the following fragment, a run emerges between the two online buyers. One of the two online buyers withdraws and a buyer in the room then enters the fray.

Fragment 6.11 (experiment)

A: [OL.1] Seven fifty. [OL.2] Eight hundred (.3) [B.2] Eight fifty [OL.2] Nine hundred (.5) nine hundred on Screen B. [OL.1] Nine fifty, nine fifty on screen A, at nine fifty (.3) [OL.2] One thousand one thousand on Screen B.

A: At one thousand pounds on screen B. [B.2] One thousand and fifty. (0.3) One thousand and fifty [OL.1] Eleven hundred thank you (.3) eleven hundred pounds. [B.3] Eleven fifty. Eleven fifty's the lady's bid in the room. [OL.1] Twelve hundred on the Internet. [B.3] Twelve fifty.

Auctioneers were able to use the system to alternate seamlessly between online buyers and buyers in the saleroom, and the ease with which they were able to identify and select online bids allowed remote contributions to be juxtaposed with those from buyers in the room at any stage during the proceedings. It was not unusual for the auctioneer to return to the room for bids following a run involving remote participants, and there were frequent runs involving online bidders alone.

The system enabled smooth transitions between bidders, both those in the room and online, in a way that can be relatively rare in real auctions of art and antiques. In the first place, the acceptance of an online bid by the auctioneer is highlighted for the participants in the room by virtue of the auctioneer having to gesture towards the screen and press the button on the gavel. Second, and perhaps more significantly, buyers in the room could see, on screen, when online participants were bidding or attempting to bid, and could coordinate their contributions appropriately. For instance, in preparing to bid, a participant in the room would see an online contribution and withhold an attempt to bid at that stage, allowing the auctioneer to establish a run with the remote participant. Therefore, the ability to see both the actions of the online buyer and the auctioneer with regard to the remote participant enhanced the participants' abilities to produce smooth transitions in the run.

It is less clear why the system appears to enable a pace and evenness of online bidding uncharacteristic of real auctions of art and antiques. It may simply be a consequence of the experimental situation, but there are two issues worth considering. The intelligent gavel requires a more formal, for want of a better term, selection and acceptance of online bids, with the auctioneer having to point towards the avatar and press a button. It may be the case that these explicit actions on each and every occasion of an Internet contribution, with their visibility to the remote participant, facilitated timely contributions. Second, remote participants knew that their bids would only be accepted if they raised their paddle, in turn raising the hand of the avatar, and were aware that the avatar's actions were visible both to the auctioneer and other buyers. One speculates that the public visibility of the remote participants' actions, rather than simply being transmitted to the auctioneer, might serve to encourage timely contributions.

The Transparency of Online Contributions

The way in which the gavel requires the auctioneer to point to and register bids, coupled with the two screens that show the presence and action of online bidders, albeit represented by an avatar, contributes to both the coordination of bids and the transparency of remote participation. Whereas online contributions are typically only accessible to the Internet administrator and sometimes directly to the auctioneer, with the intelligent gavel, buyers in the room have independent access to the actions of the remote participant, and indeed those in the room have exactly the same access to the online buyer as the auctioneer. Mutual access to the remote participant, coupled with the visibility of the auctioneer's actions with regard to the avatar, enabled buyers as well as all those within saleroom to see and to witness the conduct and interaction of the auctioneer and the local and remote participants. In principle, this arrangement does not exclude the possibility that in practice, the remote participant might, for example, serve as a confederate of the vendor or auction house. However, the mutual visibility of contributions did seem to contribute to the coordination of action as well as the integrity of online contributions.

For the remote participants, the situation is rather different. In the experimental configuration they have limited access to the event. As with the systems currently used in many salerooms, they could hear as well as see the auctioneer and his or her invitations to bid online. They did not have visual access to those in the saleroom other than the auction-eer. During the debriefing following the experiment, the remote partici-pants reported that the lack of access to the saleroom caused difficulties and frustration, in particular the inability to know why an attempted bid was ignored. Disregarded first bids often led to successive attempts by the remote participant to place a bid, only to find that they too were ignored. These difficulties are not unique to the experimental system, and online buyers at conventional auctions often report difficulties placing bids and frustration in not knowing why they remain unacknowledged. One sus-pects that these difficulties might be ameliorated both in the experimental situation as well as more conventional auctions by repositioning and focus-sing a camera to enable remote participants to see at least part of the sale-room, including buyers and sale assistants as well as the auctioneer. In this way remote participants will be able to gain a sense of the ways in which the auctioneer's conduct is sensitive to and coordinated with actions that arise within the saleroom.

Co-presence and Remote Participation

It is perhaps remarkable that the traditional auction, at least in the area of art and antiques, has remained so resilient in face of the challenge posed by the widespread introduction and success of the Internet auction over the past decade. It is increasingly recognised however, that online partic-ipation provides important opportunities for the traditional auction, both in attracting new clients for whom attending the event would be difficult and prohibitively expensive and in providing a method of remote partic-ipation that avoids the demands on staff and resources posed by buyers bidding on the telephone. Indeed, one only has to see the rows of sale assistants manning the phones at high-end sales to realise that the state of affairs is costly and untenable. Despite the challenges posed by introducing online bidding to the traditional auction, it has met with some success, and while the banks of sale assistants manning telephones remain, participation through the Internet is making an increasing contribution to overall sales of many auctions of art and antiques. However, there remain difficulties that in one sense may appear relatively trivial, not just the delay in the issue of online contributions, but difficulties that can threaten the integrity, the atmosphere and even the success of the live event and people's willingness to continue to attend traditional auctions.

The difficulties that arise with the introduction of Internet participation are problems that derive through the interaction that arises at auctions and its routine characteristics and organisation. We have seen, for instance, how the remote participant's access to live auction can undermine the placement of first bids and fail to provide a relevant account for the disregarded contribution. We have also seen how the sequential organisation that underpins the efficient, alternating production of bids during a run does not serve to secure the timely issue of online contributions, the auctioneer's conduct seeming to lose its performative, interactional force when mediated through the Internet in contrast to co-presence. In turn, the inaccessibility of the online buyer or a representative to those within the room can threaten the transparency and efficacy of Internet participation and undermine the witness-ability of auctions so critical to their legitimacy. Indeed, the analysis of remote participation in the live auction helps illuminate and underscore the criticalness of the seemingly simple social interactional organisation that enables the efficient accomplishment of the traditional auction. It also points to an issue of increasing importance to those concerned with the development of advanced technologies to support remote participation and collaboration and the requirement to support the resources on which people rely, ordinarily, when they are in each other's presence, to accomplish particular activities.

Notwithstanding these issues and difficulties, some of which will undoubtedly be resolved in the near future through advances in the design of systems used for online participation, the introduction of the Internet to bid at live auctions has met with some success and within a few years become widely used in sales in the United Kingdom, mainland Europe, North America. Its success demonstrates, if demonstration is needed, the extraordinary resilience, yet flexibility of the interactional organisation of auctions. Here we have an organisation that enables actions to be performed through technologies, technologies that emerged some hundreds if not thousands of years after it first became instantiated, even routine, to be integrated into the interactional structure it provides. Rather than replace or transform human society, we find these impressive technological innovations are exploited and made to operate through our long-standing, conventional forms of social and interactional organisation. Indeed, it is the very ways in which we organise our activities that provide the resources that enable us to encompass these extraordinary developments into our ordinary lives, our routine ways of doing what we do. Perhaps this speaks more to human ingenuity than many of the impressive innovations that attract our attention. As Sacks happened to mention during one of his lectures:

> That's a funny kind of thing, in which each new object becomes the occasion for seeing again what we see anywhere; seeing people's nastinesses or goodnesses and all the rest, when they do this initially technical job of talking over the phone. The technical apparatus is, then, being made at home with the rest of our world. And that's a thing that's routinely being done, and it's the source for the failures of technocratic dreams that if only we introduced some fantastic new communication machine the world will be transformed. Where what happens is that the object is made at home in the world that has whatever organisation it already has. (Sacks, 1992 (1972): 548)

7   On the Strike of the Hammer

> The dynamism of performance is arguably reflected in the performative inclination to think of law not as things but as acts, not as rules or agreements, but as processes constituting rule or agreement. A performative contract, for instance is not an object, but a routine of words and gestures.... At the same time, the ephemerality of performance cultures, encourages members of the performance cultures to maximise the memorability and minimise the likelihood of change.... Performance is publicized by being presented in front of many people, the theory being that in such a setting more people are likely to remember it.
>
> Hibbitts 1992: 61

In a series of essays concerned with legal expression in performative cultures – preliterate and early societies – Hibbitts (1992) discusses the ways in which contracts and quasi-legal contracts are accomplished through gesture, touch, oral proclamation and even loud, piercing noises. He describes, for example, how land transfers in central Africa required the discharge of three gunshots to convey property, the ways in which contracts in feudal France were concluded with a buyer striking the palm of the vendor's hand and how, in the early Middle Ages, 'straws, gloves, arrows, and staffs were exchanged to form pledges'. Hibbitts explores how we find traces, remnants, of these conventions within contemporary society, but argues that they 'frequently operate as a mere ceremonial reflection of an agreement made and communicated by other means, that is by writing' (Hibbitts 1992: 12). Auctions are remarkable in this regard. The valuation and exchange of goods is achieved by virtue of a hammer being struck on a wooden surface. The strike of the hammer marks the sale and exchange of goods and establishes a contract between the buyer and the seller.

Striking a wooden hammer on the surface of a rostrum might seem a crude way in which to secure the transfer of ownership of goods that in some cases sell for many millions of pounds. This simple action, however, provides a practical solution to the difficulties that might arise when finalising the sale of goods that involve the rapid competition of numerous buyers. First, unlike other ways in which a sale might be brought to completion, for example, by announcing the sale of the goods, the sound and gesture of striking a hammer on a hard surface is a momentary action, lasting less than a tenth of a second. It is not a sound that can be sustained and serves to mark the precise moment at which the contract is concluded. Second, the sound and gesture are very different from the many other sounds and gestures that arise when people are gathered in each other's company, unlikely to be confused with other actions that may arise within the local environment. Third, it is a sound and gesture, especially when performed on a rostrum, which is audible and visible to all those attending the event, including the protagonists and other prospective buyers. Indeed, even those participating remotely in the auction via the telephone or Internet are able to hear, and in some cases see, the gavel striking the rostrum. While perhaps crude, the strike of a hammer enables the auctioneer to unambiguously mark and display the sale of goods and to render that action transparent to all those who might have an interest in the transaction or just happen to witness the proceedings.

Auction catalogues typically include a statement referring to the strike of the hammer, or the gavel as it is commonly known, concluding the sale of goods.

> Subject to the auctioneer's reasonable discretion, the highest bidder accepted by the auctioneer will be the buyer and the striking of the hammer marks the acceptance of the highest bid and the conclusion of a contract between the seller and buyer. (Christie's 2006: 181)

In contemporary society, the strike of the hammer that concludes the contract between seller and buyer at auction is supported by written documentation. Buyers are required to register with the auction house before bidding and registration requires personal information including, in some cases, details of a bank account. Following the strike of the hammer, the auctioneer records details of the contract, in particular the price and the bidder's number (or name) on the sale sheets alongside the particular lot. The sales sheets are later passed to the accounts department. They form the basis of the invoice for the buyer and determine the monies received by the vendor. The strike of the hammer establishes a contract between two independent parties; the auction house mediating the transaction between seller and buyer.

The auctioneer looks and gestures at the buyer and strikes the hammer

Fragment 7.1. Images 1 & 2.

Bringing the valuation and exchange of goods to a satisfactory and legitimate conclusion poses an organisational 'problem' that has to be resolved in and through the interaction of the participants. The problem is analogous to the question posed by Schegloff and Sacks in their seminal paper on closings in conversation:

> How to organise the simultaneous arrival of the co-conversationalists at a point where one speaker's completion will not occasion another speaker's talk, and that will not be heard as some speaker's silence. (1973/4: 237)

The problem is exacerbated in the case of auctions by virtue of the importance of maximising the opportunity for any interested party to declare interest while bringing the sale of each lot to a rapid and satisfactory conclusion. To make matters worse, buyers may strategically withhold bids until the last moment, and yet, if contributions pass unnoticed then disputes can arise that may cause the auction house some difficulties and even undermine its ability to secure goods in the future. The strike of the hammer, therefore, forms part of a 'properly initiated closing' section through which the auctioneer enables prospective buyers to express their demand – the maximum price they are willing to pay – a price that may evolve during the course of the proceedings. In this way, the price that goods achieve during a transaction, is, and can be seen as, the outcome of unfettered demand and competition.

The matter of bringing a sale to a satisfactory completion has been a long-standing issue for those interested in the design of auction mechanisms. It is interesting to note, for example, that one of the avowed advantages of the Dutch or declining bid model of auctions is that the first and only bid finalises the sale. As suggested, in the English or Roman ascending price model, the problem of completion was sometimes resolved through the practice of lighting a candle at the beginning of the sale of a lot – when it burnt out, whoever has the bid and price at that moment secures the lot (see, for example, Pepys 1660; Learmount 1985). eBay and other Internet auction sites employ a related model by prescribing a set period for the auction of, say, five days, marking the point at which the goods are sold to the highest bidder. In practice, this solution simply results in the majority of bids being submitted in the last few moments. Each of these solutions presents two interrelated issues: on one hand enabling interested parties to express their demand while on the other delimiting the time and thereby the opportunity for bids to be received for particular goods and services. Contemporary auctions in the English manner rarely invoke a formal system for demarcating the end of bidding in advance of the auction. Rather, bringing the sale of a lot to a satisfactory completion rests upon a social and interactional organisation through which the auctioneer maximises the opportunity for interested parties to bid while progressively bringing the sale to an orderly and efficient conclusion.

The End of a Run

The opportunity of bringing the auction to a satisfactory completion arises when a run comes to an end – one of the two protagonists declines the invitation to bid the next increment. The auctioneer undertakes a search for remaining buyers and if no one volunteers a bid then the auctioneer can, if the goods have met their reserve, sell the lot to the outstanding bidder at the current price. Bringing the sale to a satisfactory and legitimate conclusion requires an outstanding bid that achieves the reserve and enables all those who might have an interest in the goods to know where they stand with regard to the sale of the goods and the price at which the lot is likely to sell. We join the following fragment, the sale of a nineteenth-century watercolour, as one of the two protagonists declines to bid the next increment.

| ↑ | ↑ | ↑ |

Three eighty your bid   if you've all <u>finish</u>:ed   {Knock}

Fragment 7.2. Image 1, 2 & 3.

Fragment 7.2

    A: No (.) three twenty with the lady.

    A: Three twenty, Three twenty, Three fifty anywhere else. <u>At</u> three↑ twenty (.) [B.3] Three fifty [B.1] Three eighty now:: (.) Three eighty. Four <u>hun</u>:dred?

→   (0.7) [B.3 declines]

    A: Three eighty your bid. Three eighty. Three eighty.

    A: Going to be sold.

    A: <u>At</u> <u>three</u> hund↑red and <u>eighty</u> pounds then if you've all <u>finish</u>:ed

        (0.2)

    A: {Knock}

On the underbidder declining the invitation to bid, the auctioneer re-announces the current price and attributes the bid to a particular participant in the saleroom – the eventual buyer of the picture. As he re-announces the current price, 'Three eighty. Three eighty', the auctioneer undertakes a search for any further bids turning from the far right to the left of the saleroom. No bids are forthcoming and there is little indication that anyone is preparing to bid. The auctioneer announces that the lot is 'Going to be sold'. He glances momentarily at the outstanding bidder as he announces the current price, £380, and once again turns from the right to the left of the room asking, 'if you've all <u>finish</u>:ed'. A moment later, the gavel is brought down and the goods sold.

    Each break in a run establishes the possibility that the auction may be brought to completion with the outstanding bidder purchasing the lot at

The auctioneer searches the sale-room for bids

Fragment 7.3. Image 1 & 2.

the current price. In some cases, we find auctioneers undertaking a more extensive search at a break in the run before progressing to the close of sale. So, for instance, in the case of the Carracci, following the withdrawal of B.4, the auctioneer reiterates the current increment, 'six million, six hundred thousand pounds' four times before finally bringing the hammer down. As he reiterates the increment, he turns from the far right, to the centre, and then to left-hand side of the sale room a number of times to see whether anyone is willing or preparing to bid.

Fragment 7.3

    A: Six million four hundred thousand

        (0.2) [B.5]

    A: Six million six hundred thousand

→   (5.6) [B.4 declines]

    A: At six million, six hundred thousand pounds (2.3) At six million, six hundred (0.2) <thousand pounds (2.3) At <u>six</u> <u>million</u> (0.8) six (0.5) h:undred (0.5) <thousand pounds

        (2.3)

    A: Last chance (0.6) Anywhere (0.5) at six million (0.2) six (.) hundred (0.2) thousand pounds (0.2) {Knock}

The extent to which the auctioneer will look for, even encourage, bids following a break in the run is sensitive to a range of contingencies and considerations. It is not unusual for a more prolonged search to arise when the price is near, but has not yet reached, the reserve. By creating a more extended opportunity for buyers to show their hand, the auctioneer facilitates further bids and secures the sale of a lot that might otherwise remain unsold. Whether the search for further bids is protracted or relatively attenuated is also sensitive to the number of runs that have arisen during the sale and the remaining interest as the sale proceeds. Since each break in the run provides an opportunity for interested parties to declare their interest, the auctioneer is able to gain a measure of the interest in a particular lot. So, for example, finding a number of prospective buyers attempting to bid at a break in the run might encourage a more extensive search for new bidders at a subsequent break – just to make sure that people have had an opportunity to bid if they so wish – whereas lacklustre interest may lead the auctioneer to foreshorten the search at a later break in the run, believing it is unlikely that new bidders will enter the fray. The auctioneer has to strike a balance between maximising the opportunity to bid while avoiding a protracted and unsuccessful search for further bids that can even depress bidding on subsequent lots. There is an auctioneer's saying to the effect 'never chase the bid', a saying that captures the danger of trying too hard and being seen to try too hard to encourage bids.

The Declaration to Sell

A break in the run may foreshadow the immediate sale of a lot, but more often than not it serves to secure a further bid and re-establish competitive bidding. In moving towards the close of sale, the auctioneer has to differentiate the opportunity for anyone to bid that arises following a break of the run from the upcoming close of sale. Clearly differentiating the transition is of some importance when one considers that buyers may receive successive opportunities to bid following breaks in runs and in some cases, strategically withhold bids until the final moments of a sale. The auctioneer has to enable participants to recognise unambiguously the upcoming sale of the lot unless a further bid is issued.

The strike of the hammer is routinely preceded by an announcement that declares that the lot is about to be sold, a declaration to sell.

Fragment 7.1
→A: An(d) selling
         (0.5)
   A: If we are all though
         (.)

A: For one million (.) two hundred thousand dollars

(0.7)

{Knock}

Fragment 7.2

→A: Going to be sold.

A: <u>At</u> <u>three</u> hund↑red and <u>eighty</u> pounds then if you've all <u>finish</u>:ed

(0.2)

A: {Knock}

Fragment 7.3

→A: Last chance

(0.6)

A: Anywhere (0.5) at six million (0.2) six (.) hundred (0.2) thousand pounds

(0.2)

{Knock}

The declaration to sell stands in marked contrast to the preceding actions. It consists of an announcement that the goods are about to be sold and provides participants with a final opportunity to bid. The declaration to sell projects the end of the auction on condition that no further bids are issued. It operates both retrospectively and prospectively and serves to re-display that no further bids have been received and to project the close of sale. It stands as the pivotal action in the concerted accomplishment of the auction's legitimate and satisfactory completion.

A range of expressions is used to declare the upcoming sale of goods. They include announcements that make explicit reference to the immediacy of the sale including, for example, 'gonna sell it now', 'going to be sold', and 'make no mistake I'm selling now'. They also include the expression 'fair warning', a phrase often used to forewarn the end of the auction when the lot has failed to reach its reserve and will remain unsold.

The declaration to sell is also accomplished through an announcement that does not necessarily make explicit reference to the finality of the auction or the upcoming sale of the goods but has a characteristic, almost formulaic, prosodic pattern. It consists of a sharp rise and fall of intonation that serves to project the end of the auction. The pattern can be produced through an announcement of the increment, the attribution of the outstanding bid, or coupled with an explicit reference to the upcoming sale of the lot. It projects the upcoming sale of the lot and differentiates this announcement, typically of the current price, from the previous statements of the current increment. In the following fragments we find for example;

Fragment 7.4

→A: At seven↑ hundred↓ an eigh:ty pounds:
       It's: <seven hundred an eighty: pounds:
       (.)
   A: {Knock}

Fragment 7.5

→A: <u>Twentyfive</u>: with↑Tina↓
       (0.2)
   A: Twenty five thousand dollars:::::s:::
       (0.3)
   A: {Knock}

The declaration to sell seemingly provides a final opportunity for any interested party to bid for the goods in question and declares that if no bids are forthcoming the goods will be sold to the outstanding bidder at the current price. It declares 'show now, or forever hold your peace' and differentiates this opportunity from previous opportunities to bid that have arisen during the sale. It stands as an invitation for anyone to declare an interest 'here and now' before the lot is sold. It implicates the end of the sale on condition that no further bids are issued.

If no further bids are forthcoming, the declaration to sell is routinely followed by a restatement of price, the current increment. The restatement of price serves to display to the potential buyer, the principal protagonists and all those present the price at which the goods are to be sold. It also provides a final opportunity for people to respond to the declaration to sell by issuing a bid. It is accompanied by the auctioneer undertaking a search of the room in order to see if anyone is willing or preparing to bid. If no bid is forthcoming, then the hammer is struck, the contract established and the episode of interaction brought to completion. The overall structure of the close of sale reflects the well-worn phrase 'going, going, gone' and like three part lists used in other conversational and institutional environments progressively projects its emergent completion (see, for example, Jefferson 1991; Atkinson 1984).

Figure 7.1.

i.	Going	Declaration to sell
		[no further bid issued]
ii.	Going	Statement of the selling price
		[no further bid issued]
iii.	Gone	Strike of the hammer

The strike of the hammer, therefore, is foreshadowed by a sequence of actions through which prospective buyers are provided with the opportunity to bid if they so wish. If no bids are forthcoming, then the sale is finalised at the current price. The declaration to sell *conditionally projects* the strike of the hammer with the reiteration and attribution of the increment serving to confirm the selling price and the (prospective) buyer. The statement of price preserves the relevance and immediacy of the strike of the hammer while sustaining the opportunity for anyone to show their hand. The clarity and performative force with which the declaration to sell projects the strike of the hammer is critical to the satisfactory conclusion of the auction. It projects the upcoming sale of the goods whilst providing a final opportunity for any interested party to show their hand – the strike of the hammer and the sale of the goods legitimised by virtue of no further interest being declared. It serves to demonstrate that the price the goods have achieved is the outcome of fair and open competition in which interested parties have had, for all practical purposes, the opportunity to bid for the goods in question and that the person willing to pay the highest price has secured the lot. Failure to project properly the close of the sale and provide an opportunity for final bids before the hammer is struck can lead to complaint, with prospective buyers, in some cases, calling for the auction to be reopened and goods put back up for sale.

Occasioned Bids

It is not unusual for the declaration to occasion further bids. These bids may be issued by the underbidder or from others who until then have not declared an interest. Consider the following fragment. We join the action towards the end of a sale of a picture by Robert Motherwell; B.3 declines the invitation to bid the next increment of $240,000. The auctioneer undertakes an extensive search for anyone willing to bid, and with 'Are we all through then', turns and looks at the underbidder. The underbidder looks away, and once again declines the opportunity to bid. The auctioneer produces the declaration to sell with the phrase 'an selling' and momentarily returns to the underbidder, who raises his hand and mouths 'two fifty' – offering to bid at a split increment. The auctioneer accepts, announces the bid and immediately invites the protagonist, B.4, to bid $260,000.

Fragment 7.6

    A: Two hundred an forty thousand

→   (1.0) [B.3 declines]

    A: You're out (.) At two hundred an <u>forty</u> th<u>ou</u>sand dollars now it's this side the lady's bid for two↑hundred↓an forty thousand

        (0.4)

→A: Are we all through then, [B.3 declines] At two hundred an forty thousand dollars

        (0.2)

→A: Last chance then an selling

→A: [B.3 mouths 'two fifty']

    A: <Up to <u>fifty</u> thousand I'll take sixty from you madam

        (0.7) [B.4]

    A: Two hundred and sixty thousand

→   (0.5) [B.3 declines]

→A: You've said that b<u>efo</u>re (0.2) At two hundred an sixty thousand dollars: (0.2) Against you this side

        (.)

→A: An selling to you Madam

  an forty thousand   <Up to <u>fifty</u> thousand   and sixty thousand

Fragment 7.6. Images 1, 2 & 3.

Even in cases in which a lot is selling well in excess of expectations and a number of breaks in the run have already arisen during the auction, we find the declaration can serve to provoke bids from buyers who, until then, have shown little inclination to participate. There has been intense bidding on the following picture, a portrait attributed to the studio of van Dyck. Bidding began at £15,000 and rapidly rose through a series of runs to £140,000 – more than four times the upper estimate.

Fragment 7.7

A:	One hundred and thirty thousand
	(2.3) [B.3]
A:	°One hundred an forty thousand
	(4.2) [B.4 declines]
A:	°t one hun<u>dred</u> an forty thousand
	(2.3)
A:	One hundred, an forty (0.5) <<u>thou</u>sand pounds:
	(3.4)
→A:	<u>In</u> the <u>room</u> (0.5) and <u>selling</u> it
→	(0.2) [SA.3]
→A:	One hundred an fifty thousand
	(13.5) [B.3 declines]
A:	To Diana now (0.7) At <u>one</u> (0.2) <u>hun</u>dred (0.2) an fifty (0.3) <<u>thou</u>sand pounds:
	(0.3)
A:	Against you in the doorway
	(0.3)
A:	At one (.) hundred (.) an↑ fifty↓ (0.2) ><u>thou</u>sand pounds
	(0.2)
	{Knock}

Diana, a sale assistant, raises her hand to bid at the word 'it' of '<u>selling</u> it'. One suspects that the bid is positioned strategically – the buyer having refrained from entering the fray until the painting is about to be sold. The underbidder declines to go a further increment and the picture is sold to the buyer's maiden bid for £150,000. It is worth noting that once again the subsequent search for new bidders is relatively abbreviated and the final declaration of sale produced through the announcement of the selling price combined with the characteristic prosodic pattern used to prefigure and project the strike of the hammer.

The declaration to sell, therefore, is critical to the satisfactory close of sale. It is not unusual for the declaration of sale to provoke bids, and assuming that a declaration to sell will foreshadow the end of the auction, prospective buyers can delay, even withhold, bids in the confidence that there will indeed be a final opportunity to declare their interest. The ability of auctions to establish the price and value of goods within a highly circumscribed temporal framework is accomplished through a sequence of actions that unambiguously projects the close while providing an opportunity for interested parties to show their hand.

Auctioneers are well aware that prospective buyers may withhold bids until the final moments of the sale. Indeed, it is not uncommon to find auctioneers appearing to fabricate the close of sale to provoke bids in the face of lacklustre bidding. It is interesting to note that in many cases these pretences do not quite have the characteristics of a routine declaration to sell; for example, they may not follow an extended search for new bidders or include words such as 'selling', 'going now' and so forth – more often than not relying on prosody to project the close of sale. For instance, in the sale of the picture in Fragment 7.7 where the auctioneer and many in the room believed the painting to be a sleeper, the bidding stalls following a series of runs at £90,000. Following a relatively abbreviated search for new bidders, the auctioneer announces the increment using the intonation pattern characteristic of a declaration to sell. It proves successful; at least four people in the room immediately raise their hands to bid, with the auctioneer announcing – 'coming in lots of places'.

Fragment 7.7. Transcript 2

    A: Eighty five thousand

        (1.2) [B.3]

    A: Ninety thousand

        (1.2) [B.1 withdraws]

    A: At <u>nin</u>ety thousand now::. On my right

        (.)

    A: At ninety thousand on my right.

        (0.2)

→A: At ninety↑thou↑sand↓ pounds

        (0.5)

→A: Coming in lots of places.

    (0.2)

A: Ninety five thousand (.) with Alice

People in the room are sensitive to the opportunity created by the declaration to sell and the auctioneer's search for any new and final bids, and,
for example, may take care not to produce an action that could inadvertently be treated as a bid. As suggested it is not unusual to find members
of the audience turning away as the auctioneer looks for any further bids
or beginning to write the anticipated selling price in their catalogues. For
the auctioneer, it is critical not to miss any further bids. Auctioneers are
sensitive to movements that arise in the saleroom following the declaration of sale that may constitute bids. In this regard, it is not unusual to find
the auctioneer expanding the opportunity for people to bid following the
declaration to sell in the light of conduct that suggests that a further contribution might be forthcoming from a buyer.

    In the following fragment, for example, as the auctioneer produces 'An
selling' a sale assistant who is holding the phone to her ear raises her hand.

Fragment 7.8

A: Eight hundred thank you

A: Eight hundred now I've got it in the third row

    (0.2)

A: Eight

    (0.4)

→A: An:↑ selling↓

→A: Against the telephones

    (.)

→A: Eight to you sir

    (0.2)

→A: No where else↑

      (0.2)

A: Eight hundred

    (0.2)

    {Knock}

She does not issue a bid. Rather 'than' progress to the statement of price,
the auctioneer follows the declaration with an announcement that not only

Auctioneer notices the sale-assistant raise her hand

Fragment 7.8. Images 1 & 2.

serves to extend the opportunity to bid, but identifies a potential source of a bid 'Against the telephones'. Indeed, as the hand is raised, the auctioneer turns and looks at the sale assistant. As she speaks on the phone, her hand is held in mid-air, and rather than bringing the sale to a close, the auctioneer preserves the opportunity to bid by re-ascribing the current price. Whereas 'No where else↑' might be seen as a general invitation for anyone to bid, it is accompanied by the auctioneer turning and looking at the sale assistant to see whether she is planning to bid and to encourage an immediate response. At that moment she shakes her head and the auctioneer immediately states the selling price and strikes the hammer.

Encouraging the Underbidder

Bids may be issued at any place during the declaration of sale and the statement of price until the gavel strikes the rostrum. Consider the following fragment, the sale of a picture by Greuze. It has generated little interest despite successive attempts by the auctioneer to encourage people to bid. The sale is being drawn to a close at £60,000, some £10,000 less than the lower estimate. The auctioneer declares 'fair warning'. He slowly articulates the statement of price 'At sixty (0.5) thousand pounds' he turns from the far right to the left of the room.

Fragment 7.9

    A: At sixty (0.3) thousand pounds

        (0.2)

→A: Fair warning

        (0.5)

    A: At sixty (0.5) thousand pounds

→B.3:   ᴸ°Sixty two (thousand)

    A: Sixty two thousand I'll take

        (0.2)

    A: At sixty two thousand in the room Not yours Paul nor your Alice.

→A: At sixty↑ (0.3) <u>tw</u>o thousand↓

   B.4:   ᴸ (snaps fingers)

    A: Sixty five thousand

        (2.3)

    A: Eight?

The production of the statement of price, its pace, the pause within the course of its production and the auctioneer's progressive search of the room serve to invite and enable bids – projecting, yet delaying, the close of sale. As his visual orientation nears the centre of the room, a buyer on the front row looks up and whispers '°Sixty two (thousand)'. The bid is accepted. The auctioneer produces a second declaration to sell: 'At sixty↑ (0.3) <u>tw</u>o thousand↓'. Immediately, a new buyer on the far left of the room snaps his fingers. He bids and secures the painting for £65,000, still some £5,000 less than the lower estimate. One suspects that the first, if not the second bid, is opportunistic, members of the trade attempting to buy a picture well under estimate, a picture for which it is said there is a reasonable market within continental Europe – at least at the right price.

It is not unusual to receive late bids following the declaration of sale from buyers who until then have failed to declare an interest. However, it is the underbidder who most commonly places a further bid having declined the opportunity moments before. Auctioneers are sensitive to the possibility that underbidders may have a change of heart during the final moments of a sale and that the underbidder may be vulnerable to encouragement, if not persuasion. So while the final moments of the auction are designed to provide a general invitation for anyone to bid if they so wish, the auctioneer may go to some trouble to create an opportunity, even successive opportunities, for the underbidder to make a further contribution.

Consider for example the following fragment involving the sale of an early aniconic figure. With 'No more sir?' the auctioneer attempts to encourage the underbidder to go to the next increment, £1,300. It proves unsuccessful. He produces the declaration to sell – 'Twelve then, it's on the far↓asle'.

Fragment 7.10

    A: At eleven (0.6) Eleven anywhere else
       [B.2]
    A: Twe:lve: <u>behin:d</u>↑
       (0.6)
    A: No more sir?
       (0.2) [B.1 declines]
    A: Twelve: hundred (.) Thirteen sir? (.) you look lucky
       (0.3)
    A: <u>Twelve</u>: hundred °You never know sir
       (.)
→A: Twelve then, <u>it's</u> on↑ the far↓ aisle
    A: Twelve (.) hundred pounds:
       (1.2)
    A: {Knock}

As he begins the final statement of price, the auctioneer raises his right hand and slowly turns from the right to the far left of the saleroom where the buyer and the underbidder are standing.

The sweep of gaze and gesture progressively differentiate the audience, subjecting people gathered in different regions of the room to a specific opportunity to bid if they so wish. While this general invitation for anyone to bid is progressively differentiated with regard to successive regions of the room, one particular participant is subject to a specific invitation from the auctioneer. As the auctioneer turns from the far right of the saleroom to the outstanding bidder on the far left, he momentarily arrests his movement and orientation and looks at the underbidder. The underbidder looks

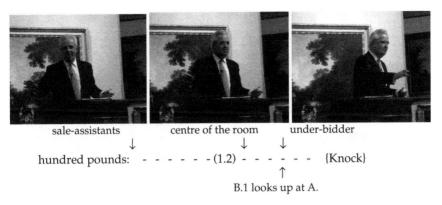

sale-assistants   centre of the room   under-bidder
   ↓   ↓ ↓
hundred pounds: - - - - - - (1.2) - - - - - - {Knock}
            ↑
        B.1 looks up at A.

Fragment 7.10. Images 1, 2 & 3.

up. The auctioneer raises his eyebrows as if questioning whether he wishes to bid. The underbidder immediately looks down, shakes his head, declining the invitation to bid. A moment later the figure is sold.

While providing an opportunity for anyone to produce a further bid, therefore, the auctioneer can differentiate participants and even address the invitation to a particular participant to have him or her accept or decline. The import of this specific action does not undermine the opportunity for anyone to show their hand, but rather, while enabling all those present to bid if they so wish, subjects a particular participant to the invitation. In consequence, the particular participant is obliged to respond to the auctioneer – if only by turning away, to decline the invitation, whereas others can simply disregard the opportunity to bid.

An underbidder can be subject to some encouragement, if not persuasion, to bid the next increment. In the following fragment, the auctioneer announces 'selling now make no mistake' and follows with the statement of price 'on the last cou:n:t two four two:::'. The hammer is brought down a second later. As the auctioneer produces the statement of price, he turns towards the underbidder. He raises the gavel and adopts a facial expression in which he firmly grips his mouth – as if withholding what he is about to do.

The gavel is held mid-flight and with the facial expression serves to subject the underbidder to a sustained invitation to bid the next increment. It fails. No further contribution is forthcoming, and a second or so later the gavel is brought down on the rostrum with some force.

The declaration to sell, therefore, conditionally projects the close of sale while creating an opportunity for anyone present, including the

make no mistake on the last cou:n:t > two four two::: --------- {Knock}

Fragment 7.11. Images 1 & 2.

underbidder, to make a further contribution. The opportunity to produce
a further contribution is preserved by the (re)statement of price and any
subsequent pause until the hammer is struck. The sequential import of the
declaration and the conditional relevance of the hammer's strike provide an
interactional environment in which the auctioneer's visible and bodily orientation can differentiate the audience and encourage particular individuals to respond to the opportunity to bid. In other words, the final moments
of an auction can be built to encourage, even engender, action from particular participants, while simultaneously preserving an open opportunity
for anyone present to contribute to the proceedings and thereby arrest
progression to the close of sale.

Consider the (re)statement of price. It repeats the current increment
but by virtue of its location, immediately following the declaration to
sell, serves to announce the likely selling price of the goods, conditional
on no further contributions being issued. The statement of price can be
announced with some brevity and serve to satisfy the necessity to announce
the selling value of the goods and provide an opportunity for a further bid
to be issued but rapidly foreshadow the strike of the hammer. On the other
hand, the statement of price may be produced so as to expand the opportunity for further bids and in some cases encourage particular participants
to declare their interest or further interest. We can begin to consider how
tension is created within the final moments of the sale: on one hand the
auction's completion is projected as a conditionally relevant next action; on

```
A.              repeatedly turns to under-bidder and then away
                 ↓   ↓      ↓    ↓       ↓    ↓      ↓       ↓
A:    At nine - - hundred - - an eighty - - thousand pounds - - Last chance - - {Knock}
                 ↑              ↑              ↑              ↑
UB:           lowers eyes    closes eyes    closes eyes    negative head nod
                 ↑                             ↑
```

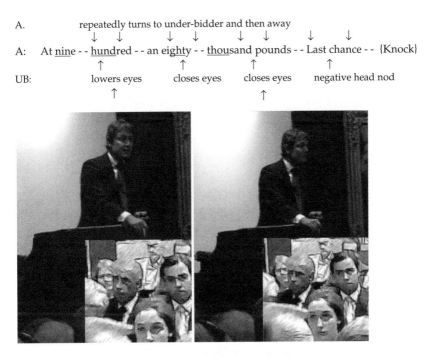

The auctioneer turns to the under-bidder who closes his eyes.

Fragment 7.12. Transcript 2. Images 1, 2, 3 & 4.

the other, the close of sale can be temporally delayed through the ways in which the statement of price is articulated.

The following fragment involves the sale of a charming picture, a Dutch genre scene by Gerrit Dou. As the break arises in the run, the current price of the picture is announced as 'ni:ne hundred an eighty thousand pounds'. A few moments later, following the declaration to sell, produced through 'Any↑more↓', the statement of price is produced as 'nine (0.2) hundred (0.2) an eighty (0.2) thousand pounds'. It is spoken more slowly, with pauses before each figure is announced and with each figure emphasised.

Fragment 7.12

    A: Nine hundred and fifty thousand

        (1.2) [B.4]

    A: Nine hundred and eighty thousand

        (2.6) [B.5 declines]

A: At <u>ni:ne</u> hundred an <u>eighty</u> thousand pounds

(2.2)

A: Any↑more↓

(1.0)

→A: At <u>nine</u> (0.2) <u>hund</u>red (0.2) an <u>eighty</u> (0.2) <u>thous</u>and pounds (0.2) Last
chance

(0.3)

A: {Knock}

While the announcement, immediately following the declaration to sell, provides an open opportunity for anyone to issue a bid, the way in which the turn is produced serves to segment the utterance into a number of distinct actions, actions that project the close of sale, whilst delaying the strike of the hammer. Anyone present may indeed respond to the opportunities created by the auctioneer to place a bid within these final few moments of the sale, but the way in which the statement is articulated, vocally and bodily, attempts to encourage, if not cajole, a bid from a particular participant, namely the underbidder. During the articulation of the utterance, the auctioneer looks towards different regions of, and individuals in, the saleroom, but principally addresses distinct components of the announcement to the underbidder. He is seated to the left with a colleague to his right.

The underbidder is sensitive to the successive glances of the auctioneer. As the auctioneer turns and looks at the underbidder with the word 'hundred', the underbidder lowers his eyes, averting his gaze. The auctioneer turns away and looks to the right of the saleroom. With 'an eighty' he once again turns and looks at the underbidder. The underbidder closes his eyes. The auctioneer looks up, glancing to the left of the room, and then again turns and looks at the underbidder with the word 'thousand'. The underbidder looks down and closes his eyes – almost cowering in response to the gaze of the auctioneer. The auctioneer continues to look at the underbidder and while 'last chance' provides all those present with an opportunity to bid, it is bodily and visually addressed to the underbidder, who produces a negative head nod. A moment later the painting is sold.

We can begin to see how a turn at talk, in this case the statement of price, is produced so as to accomplish successive actions during the course of its articulation, actions that place distinct demands on particular participants. In this way, the auctioneer renders the turn's progression vulnerable to incursion or interruption, seeking to encourage action that will prematurely undermine its projected course and establish an alternative trajectory of action, namely a run. In contrast to the practice that entitles a speaker to have a turn at talk that consists of the unit type that has been employed where 'the first possible completion of a first such unit constitutes a transition-relevance place' (Sacks et al. 1973/4: 12), in the case at hand we find the turn produced to enable and encourage its own incursion through the production of a bid prior to its projected completion. The statement of price is produced so as to encourage and render a turn vulnerable to interruption.

In this regard, it is worthwhile briefly considering an earlier moment of the sale, when the underbidder declines to bid the next increment, namely £1 million, leading to the sale of the lot. The auctioneer announces the current increment, 'nine hundred and eighty thousand', and turns from the bidder to the underbidder at the beginning of the word 'hundred'.

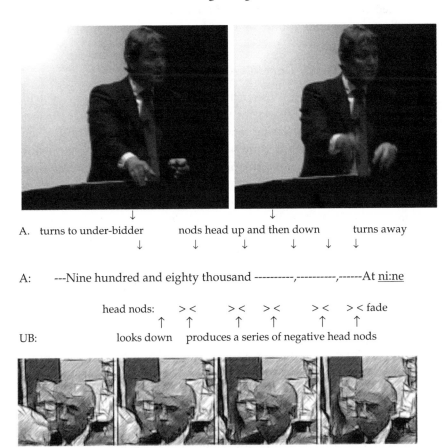

```
            ↓                      ↓
A.  turns to under-bidder    nods head up and then down      turns away
        ↓          ↓         ↓            ↓        ↓        ↓

A:    ---Nine hundred and eighty thousand ----------,----------,------At ni:ne

            head nods:      > <      > <   > <      > <    > < fade
                            ↑        ↑     ↑   ↑    ↑      ↑
UB:                     looks down   produces a series of negative head nods
```

Fragment 7.12. Transcript 2. Image 5, 6, 7, 8, & 10.

On the beginning of the word 'eighty', the figure that specifically voices the competing increment, the underbidder looks down. As he looks down, he produces a lateral, negative head nod. The auctioneer nods up and down in response, as if accepting the withdrawal from the run. Rather than turn away and look for a new buyer, the auctioneer leans over the rostrum and looks at the underbidder. On 'thousand', the underbidder, still subject to the auctioneer's gaze, produces a second negative head shake, right and then left, declining the invitation to bid, and then a third, and then fourth, and then begins a fifth. As the fifth negative shake begins, the auctioneer finally turns away and at that moment, the underbidder ceases his lateral head movement – his declination is brought to completion. By virtue of the continued orientation towards the underbidder, the prospective buyer is subject to repeated demands to bid, and has to successively decline the recycled invitations. In other words, the auctioneer transforms a single turn at talk into a series of distinct actions addressed to a particular participant.

Handling the Gavel: Unresolved Gestures

The actual strike of the hammer is the final moment in an evolving sequence of action that marks the valuation and exchange of the goods in question. Within this evolving sequence of action, the strike of the hammer, at its simplest, is the third and final part of a three-part structure that brings the particular episode of interaction to satisfactory completion. While the strike of the hammer can be conceived as a distinct action that serves to mark the close of sale, this simple action consists of a series of components. These may include, for example, grasping the gavel, raising the gavel to a particular height, cocking the head of the gavel and striking the gavel on the surface below. This action can be accomplished with some economy, taking little more than two-tenths of a second, or can be undertaken slowly, even dramatically, over some seconds. Once begun, the action and the movements of which it consists progressively project its unfolding completion. The initial grasping and raising of the gavel enables those present to see that the auctioneer is about to strike the hammer, and as successive components of the action are issued, they are able to anticipate and predict its final strike. How this seemingly simple action is accomplished can be of some interactional significance.

Whereas the three-part structure of the auction's close would suggest that the strike of the hammer forms the third and final action, the action may be produced to both complete the sale and co-occur with the

cocks gavel   lifts and   strikes gavel
↓   ↓   ↓

Last chance   at <u>six</u> million--<u>six</u> hundred--<u>thousa</u>nd pounds---{Knock}

Fragment 7.3. Transcript 2. Images 3, 4 & 5.

movement towards closure. The onset of the action does not necessarily await the completion of the statement of price, but may begin as the closing sequence evolves. It is worthwhile returning to Fragment 7.3. With 'Last chance', the declaration to sell, the auctioneer begins two distinct actions, one with his right hand, and the other with his left. With the right he raises his hand, his arm outstretched encompassing the right-hand side of the saleroom, including one of the two banks of telephones. With his left hand, the auctioneer raises the gavel and as he begins to announce the statement of price, flips the gavel backwards, holding and presenting the hammer's head to the saleroom. The two gestures accompanying the statement of price serve to project, with the declaration of sale, the close of sale, while displaying the continuing opportunity for anyone present to issue a bid. The auctioneer turns from the telephones on his left to the far right of the saleroom looking for further bids. He finally arrests his gaze on the underbidder. Receiving no further bids, he looks at the buyer, re-raises the gavel and strikes it with some force on the rostrum. The audience bursts into spontaneous applause.

While the strike of the hammer on the rostrum delivers a sharp, loud, momentary sound lasting for less than a tenth of a second, and the preparation for the final action, the grasping and raising of the gavel, can take little more than three-tenths of a second, in this case the action takes nearly five seconds. Two parts of the action, the rise and fall of the gavel, are fragmented into two distinct components, the first action foreshadowing and projecting the second, whilst delaying the strike of

the hammer. With 'Last chance (0.6) Anywhere', the raised gavel underscores and projects the close of sale – its cocking and arrest forewarning
completion whilst providing and being seen to provide a final opportunity to bid. The statement price 'at <u>six</u> million (0.2) <u>six</u> hundred (0.2)
<u>thous</u>and pounds' coupled with the unresolved gesture projects but
delays the close and the sale. In this way, the articulation of the gavel
implicates, yet withholds, an action not only relevant, but expected to
occur here and now.

The manipulation of the gavel may not only be used to display the
imminent sale of the lot but to encourage prospective buyers to bid and
to bid with dispatch. In the following fragment, involving the sale of an
eighteenth-century Genoese bureau, the auctioneer creates successive
opportunities for prospective buyers to bid following the break in the run.
As he produces the declaration to sell, he raises the gavel above his shoulders, with the head of the hammer facing the small crowd gathered to the
front of the rostrum.

Fragment 7.13

    A: Fourteen thousand (2.3) Fourteen thousand pounds (.) in the room
        at fourteen thousand pounds (0.4) in the room at fourteen thousands
        (0.4) in the room at fourteen thousand pounds (0.4) back of the room
        at fourteen thousand

        (.)

→A: For the last time

        (0.3)

    A: Selling in the room at fourteen thousand::

        (1.6)

        {Knock}

With the word 'selling', the auctioneer turns and looks at the sale assistant
bidding on behalf of the likely buyer. He clasps the gavel and begins to
bring it down onto the rostrum to complete the sale. As the gavel is about
to hit the surface, it is raised once again and held mid-flight, the auctioneer
pointing the head at the audience in front of the rostrum. For nearly two
seconds, the gavel is held still, ready to be struck, while the final component of the action is withheld. The auctioneer turns from the right to the
left of the saleroom, looking for a prospective buyer whose bid might be
provoked by the imminent close of sale. No bid is forthcoming and the
gavel is struck on the rostrum with some force.

selling in the room at fourteen thousand::----------,-------{Knock}

The unresolved action with the gavel held, momentarily, mid-flight.

Fragment 7.13. Images 1, 2, 3, 4, 5 & 6.

The unresolved gesture, with the gavel held mid-flight above the rostrum, preceded by an action that implies the hammer is about to be struck but is then withheld, coupled with an announcement that projects the upcoming completion of the sale, serves to create tension, through which those present are subject to the shifting gaze of the auctioneer. The orientation of the gavel, the unresolved gesture, coupled with looking at specific regions of the room, places those in the room, perhaps specific individuals, under some pressure to bid and to bid with dispatch. The gavel held mid-fight oriented towards the room, coupled with the shifting gaze of the auctioneer, not only creates a general invitation if not encouragement for anyone present to bid, but subtly differentiates participants, placing particular individuals or small gatherings of individuals at certain moments under specific, localised pressure to bid. The gavel's manipulation and its sequential and interactional significance therefore is not just built through the talk and the ways in which the trajectory of the hammer's action is transformed and stalled, but by virtue of the auctioneer's ability to differentiate the sequential import of these actions for different people through his shifting visual alignment during these final moments of the sale.

It is perhaps interesting to consider one further fragment to reflect on the ways in which auctioneers may use both gesturing hands to differentiate participants and encourage a particular individual to bid in the final moments of the sale. The fragment in question is drawn from a sale in which a picture by Lucio Fontana achieves a record price, £1,900,000, invoking spontaneous applause from the audience. The auctioneer has attempted to cajole the underbidder to bid the next increment, even suggesting that a further bid would 'knock out' the principal protagonist. Receiving no further bid, he appears to accept his refusal 'Definitely no: (0.2) Thank you for your bidding'.

Fragment 7.14.

    A: Give me two million and it'll knock him out

    A: One million nine hundred thousand (it's) the gentleman's bid on the phone (.) for the Fontana

         (0.2)

    A: At one million nine hundred thousand

         (2.3)

    A: Definitely no: (0.2) Thank you for your bidding

→A: At <u>one</u> <u>million</u> (.) nine: (0.2) <u>hun</u>↑dred <u>thou</u>↑sand↓ pounds

         (.)

    A: Now <u>selling</u>

         (0.7)

    A: Last chance

→   (5.0)

    A: {Knock} Sold One million nine hundred thousand

            ⌐(applause)

    A: Well done thank you.

With 'At <u>one million</u> (.) nine: (0.2) <u>hun</u>↑dred <u>thou</u>↑sand↓ pounds', the auctioneer looks at and gestures towards the likely buyer located to the left of the room. Towards the end of the declaration, he turns towards the underbidder and thrusts his pointing hand at the outstanding bidder with 'now selling'. Continuing to look at the underbidder, with 'last chance', the auctioneer raises the gavel. He directs the head of the gavel at the underbidder, holds it mid-flight, arresting its progression to the strike.

right hand gestures towards buyer   gavel oriented towards under-bidder

   gavel raised: fingers cocked   finally strikes gavel
 ↓   ↓
                              (5.0)
A: Last chance ----------,----------,----------,----------,--------- {Knock}

Fragment 7.14. Images 1 & 2.

He raises his index and middle finger, pointing upwards, in readiness to clutch and strike the hammer on the rostrum, displaying that the projected action is momentarily stalled, awaiting the underbidder's response.

While the right hand displays to all those present, including the outstanding bidder and his protagonist, who has the current increment, the left hand is directed specifically at the underbidder. The raised gavel, the cocked fingers and the visual and bodily orientation of the auctioneer serve to encourage, perhaps demand, a response from the underbidder, in particular to bid the next increment, some £2 million. Indeed, far from abandoning his attempt to secure a further bid, in the last few moments of the sale the auctioneer subjects the underbidder to extraordinary pressure; pressure that arises not simply by virtue of projecting the end of the sale through the invitation and unresolved gesture and temporarily withholding the sequentially relevant next action, but by virtue of the way in which he draws attention to the underbidder, rendering him and his response visible, noticeable, to all those present. The two gestures serve to demarcate and differentiate the principal protagonists; the one hand displays the source of the current bid pointing towards the buyer, while the other provides one further opportunity for the underbidder to bid a further increment. The gestures animate the competition between the two, dramatically displaying their relative standing with regard to the purchase of the picture.

Witnessing the Close of Sale and the 'Winner's Curse'

Christie's have launched a multi-million dollar lawsuit against Minor (US Internet entrepreneur Halsey Minor) for breach of contract after he failed to pay for three major works he bid for successfully at auction. Including premium, the three works – a van Dyck, a Stubbs and a Stringer – should have cost Minor more than $7m. but Christie's have accused him of bidding when he knew he did not have the wherewithal to pay for them.... They are suing him for $17m saying he failed to pay for a number of works of art including a Peaceable Kingdom by Edward Hicks. (*Antiques Trade Gazette* 13.6.2009: 4)

Given the thousands of works of art and antique sold through auction almost every day of the working week, there are remarkably few disputes concerning the transactions that arise. Occasionally a prospective buyer may complain that he or she was not given the opportunity to bid but such difficulties are rare indeed. When disputes do arise, they ordinarily involve buyers who attempt to pass dud cheques or credit cards or those who do not have the wherewithal to actually cover the cost of particular goods. There are many splendid stories, some undoubtedly apocryphal, of members of the trade bidding substantial prices for major works of art only to find that they are unable to pay for goods – typically unable to convince their clients to pay the extraordinary price they have bid. Recall, for example, the sad tale of a London dealer paying a record price for a Reynolds, the wonderful portrait of Omai. The picture languished for many months in the stores of Sotheby's while the unfortunate purchaser tried to raise some £10.3 million. The very absence of disputes and difficulties demonstrates the reliability and robustness of the close of the sale and the ways in which it is able to secure, unproblematically, 'the conclusion of a contract between the seller and buyer' (Christie's 2006: 181).

While the strike of the hammer concludes the contract, its articulation forms part of an unfolding trajectory of action that progressively foreshadows and demarcates the close of sale and the moment at which it is likely to occur. The declaration to sell is critical in this regard. It serves to unambiguously display the potential transformation of the proceedings and conditionally project the upcoming close of sale while simultaneously inviting further contributions. In consequence, the statement of price and the manipulation of the gavel serve to progressively project the close of sale, the finality of the proceedings, whilst preserving throughout, until the moment the hammer strikes, an opportunity to bid. This unfolding trajectory rests upon architecture of action in which an overall structure projects the close of sale and within which distinct components project their own course and completion. It has been noted, for instance, how the statement of price or the handling of the gavel implicate, in the course of their production, their satisfactory completion, and in turn preserve and project the final close of sale. The unfolding trajectory of action that foreshadows the close of sale, and its component actions, can be shaped and designed to create, even animate, tension yet forestall the anticipated progression of action. It encourages a particular response and expands the opportunity for that response, namely a bid, to be issued. This trajectory of action, therefore, allows auctions to be brought to a satisfactory completion while providing participants with successive opportunities to declare an interest before the hammer finally falls. It enables and encourages competition, it facilitates the maximisation of price and it formally allocates the goods to the party willing to pay the highest price.

The close of sale and the transaction it secures are built not only to provide successive opportunities for buyers to express their demand but to delineate the standing of participants with regard to the likely transaction. The statement of price enables the buyer to know the price he will pay for the goods in question, just as the declaration of sale underscores for the underbidder that he is out of the running. The evolving trajectory of action that arises to enable the close of sale is designed, however, not just for those implicated in the current upcoming transaction but for all those present, represented or connected to the event, to allow anyone with an interest to know how the sale stands both before its completion and as the gavel strikes the rostrum. Indeed, on the close of sale the auctioneer once again re-announces the price, now the price at which the goods have sold, and the number or name of the fortunate buyer. The strike of the hammer therefore, the sound and visibility of the action, like the trajectory of action that enables its production, is witnessed and witness-able, legitimized by virtue of the ways in which all those with an interest in the goods, indeed all those within perceptual range of the event, are able to see and hear for themselves the progressive, concerted accomplishment of the transaction, the contract between seller and buyer.

In his remarkable treatise on contract and law in early and preliterate society, Hibbitts suggests that it is more appropriate to think of law 'not as things but acts, not as rules or agreements but as processes constituting the law or agreement' (1992:61). His argument resonates with Durkheim's (1911) discussion of the 'pre-contractual' element of social arrangements and the presuppositions and conventions that underlie the integrity and determinate character of formal agreements (also see Seligman 1997). The case at hand points to perhaps the most pervasive feature of a contract's accomplishment: the process, the forms of interaction and participation that underpin and enable the contract's concerted production and serve to establish the character and legitimacy of the agreement and the various rights and responsibilities it entails. In particular it demonstrates, even within contemporary society, the importance of an audience to a contract established through words and gestures, and how the interactional structure of the close of sale is organised to maximize the visibility and memorability of the event.

There is one feature of the traditional English auction that one might suspect could lead to negotiation and even dispute as the lot is about to be sold. It is a feature that has received some attention within economics and is commonly known as the 'winner's curse'. Put simply the problem is this: in placing the highest bid, in particular against 'well-informed bidders', a bidder 'has to be cognizant that the others' unwillingness to bid higher is unfavourable information about the value of the item' (Milgrom 2004: 188). In other words, by paying the price associated with the highest increment bid, a buyer is paying more than anyone else judges the item to be worth. The problem can be exacerbated by the incremental structure of a conventional auction. By bidding the next increment, the buyer pays approximately ten per cent more than the value placed on the goods by the underbidder. If the value of the goods is a few dollars or pounds, then the winning bid might well make little difference to the overall cost. However, if the increments are £100,000 or £500,000, then by bidding the next increment, you may well pay significantly more than others believe to be the value of the goods. It is hardly surprising that it is not unusual to find prospective buyers attempting to split the increment to secure a lot, though this strategy appears to arise more frequently where the goods are highly contested. One solution to this problem that is occasionally applied in some specialist auctions, though not as far as I am aware in sales of auctions of fine art and antiques, is that the highest bidder secures the lot but pays the price bid by the second highest bidder.

Whilst price negotiations with prospective buyers may arise following an auction where a lot has failed to sell, hence the importance in some cases of 'buying in high' it is rare to find a prospective buyer attempting to re-negotiate the price during the sale. The following, however, is one such instance. It arose at an important sale of old master pictures in London. A prospective buyer on the telephone bids the next increment of £100,000 bringing the price of the picture to £1,100,000. It is accepted and the underbidder declines to bid the next increment. As the auctioneer repeats the outstanding increment, the prospective buyer has the sale assistant attempt to reduce the increment she has just bid to £75,000. In one sense it is rational move, but it is interesting to note the outrage it causes. The auctioneer dismisses the request, and the underbidder, B.3, secures the lot, even though as a consequence the vendor receives £75,000 less for the picture than he would if the auctioneer had accepted the price.

Fragment 7.15

        [SA.3 bids the increment: £1,100,000]

    A: One million one hundred thousand pounds

        (0.6) [B.3 declines to bid]

    A: At one million one hundred thousand pounds now

        (0.6) to the telephone

→SA3:   °Seventy five (thousand)

    A: At one million (0.3) One hundred

  SA3:   °Seventy five?

  →A: No (.) it's unfair that's unfair. It's a million <u>here</u>

        (2.3)

    A: It's unfair that

        (0.3)

    A: So it's a million in the room, back to you sir a million

        (1.2)

    A: No?

    A: At one million (1.0) on the isle (.) not here [to SA.3]

        (2.3)

  →A: Selling it for one million. (.) {Knock}

8   Embodied Action and the Order of Markets

In recent years there has been an exponential growth of the auction and
the diversity of property and services valued and sold through competitive bidding. These developments have emerged in part through the
widespread deployment of the Internet that has facilitated participation
in a form of exchange that hitherto was largely used by specialists and the
trade. Alongside these technological developments, we have seen the creation of new services and the emergence of highly ambitious marketing
strategies by service providers and auction houses, all of which contribute
to the increasing presence and popularity of the auction amongst buyers
and sellers. These developments undoubtedly resonate with a number of
interesting issues concerning contemporary economies, the globalisation
of markets and the growing uncertainties of the value of goods and services. In the light of these developments it is perhaps surprising to find that
the more traditional sale, in which people gather in each other's presence
to compete for goods through a process of bidding, remains of some economic importance and in the case of art and antiques, serves as a principal
vehicle for the valuation and exchange of goods.

The resilience of the auction and its importance to the market of art
and antiques reflects in part the characteristics of the merchandise, the
transience of taste and the influence of particular buyers. There is significant variation in the quality and qualities of particular works of art and
antiques, even, for example, works of art by the same artist, qualities that
have a profound impact on the demand for and the price that people are
willing to pay for the property. For example, if you take a trade 'standard' such as an early nineteenth-century mahogany breakfast table, its
colour, patination, the shape of its columnar base and legs, the presence
or absence of boxwood stringing or reeding along the edge of the table,
even the shape and colour of its brass castors can make a difference of

hundreds, and in some cases, thousands of pounds. Or consider, for example, a late nineteenth-century cityscape by a popular artist such as Atkinson Grimshaw – whether the painting contains figures, horse-drawn carriages, recognisable buildings and the like, putting to one side questions of condition and provenance, can make the difference between buyers battling for the piece or the unfortunate painting struggling to make its reserve. Indeed, it is not unusual to find the slightest detail, in some cases indistinguishable to the untrained eye, having a profound effect on the price that a particular antique or work of art will achieve at auction. Traditional sales provide an organisational arrangement through which these seeming idiosyncrasies of taste can be subject to close scrutiny and rendered accountable through the price that goods achieve.

These differences in quality and qualities do not stand independently of the fads and fashion of demand, of contemporary desire and desirables and developments in national and global economies, including, for example, the availability of liquid capital and changes in taxation systems. Consider, for example, the substantial funds paid for eighteenth-century English portraits in the 1890s, or even engravings of those portraits, and the ways in which pictures now considered second-rate gained pride of place within the homes of East Coast industrial magnates. Or consider the rise of Russian picture prices during the 1990s, works by 'young' British artists, the burgeoning demand for Chinese porcelain or the 'discovery' of modern pictures from India, trends that in different ways reflect national economies and disposable capital as well as the search for highly rewarding investments. As Reitlinger (1982) points out, the growing interest since the 1960s in treating art as investment, coupled with the increasing availability of substantial liquid capital, has introduced a volatility into the market that in turn has rendered sales by auction as the primordial mechanism for transactions and a principal source of information and data concerning the price and value of particular works of art and antiques.

It is important not to underestimate the influence particular individuals and institutions may have on the value of works of art and antiques, not just the value of work by a particular artist, but even for a movement, a school or a type of furniture. One only needs to consider individual collectors such as the Prince Regent, Lord Hertford, Andrew Lloyd Weber and Charles Saatchi, dealers such as Duveen, Jopling and Green, the investment strategies of pension funds, or the creation of new museums, to gain a sense of the ways in which the whim and resources of particular individuals and organisations can have a profound impact on the value of particular works of art and antiques. Indeed, in recent years, we have all been witness to the ways in which particular collectors, dealers or institutions can transform the standing of particular works of art and in some cases turn little-known artists, schools or genres into household names and radically transform the price that people are willing to pay (see, for example, Herbert 1990; Reitlinger 1982; Secrest 2003; Towner 1971).

The 'economics of taste' has a fragility, a volatility in contemporary society to which auctions are both the solution and the catalyst. They enable the legitimate pricing and exchange of a diverse range of goods of different quality and qualities, while facilitating fluctuations and change in values. In other words, *auctions provide both stability and instability to the market*, an instability that rapidly comes to the fore in times of swift economic change and uncertainty.

As an institutional solution to a social problem, auction houses and auctioneers mediate exchange between vendors and buyers, providing a neutral mechanism that does not favour particular interests and enables demand to be transparently revealed and price escalated until sold to the highest bidder. As Smith suggests, 'the need to establish the legitimacy of price and allocation informs auctions from top to bottom' (1989: 90). Whilst the reputation of particular houses, the ways in which they organise and promote sales and the limited legislation that applies to the sale of goods at auction undoubtedly contribute to the legitimacy of sales, auctions rely upon a body of socially organised practice that produces fair and transparent transactions through brief, recurrent, yet highly contingent episodes of interaction. The seeming simplicity, yet robustness, of this social organisation is remarkable – the ways in which it provides a system that supports the legitimate production of price and exchange whilst remaining sensitive to the range of contingencies that arise on each and every occasion, not least of which are the vagaries of supply, demand, the characteristics and qualities of goods and critically, the occasioned participation of buyers and prospective buyers.

The analysis of particular auction models, their efficiencies and inefficiencies, found within economics and econometrics is not intended to address the ways in which a particular model relies upon, and is embedded within, a social organisation that provides participants with systematic ways in which they can 'deploy' the model and produce reliable and legitimate outcomes. At their most basic, auctions of art and antiques like other auctions in the English or Roman manner rely upon a characteristic turn organisation that selectively distributes opportunities to bid and juxtaposes the contributions of prospective buyers through an orderly sequence of action that serves to invite and receive bids from particular participants.

This organisation systematically distributes opportunities to participate in the auction and specifies the position and the form of action that interested parties produce at particular moments during the developing course of the proceedings. It structures and enables the orderly production of economic action through the projection of a series of standard prices or increments and the allocation of particular turns to certain individuals. It provides an ordering principle for transitions in participation, in particular the exit and entry of prospective buyers and gives rights to particular buyers to remain in the bidding until they reach their maximum price. The organisation provides opportunities at transitions in the bidding for prospective buyers to bid and to express their demand by agreeing to the projected next increment. The close of sale, the final determination of price, legitimately arises by virtue of an organisation that provides successive opportunities for participants to declare an interest, and when only one interested party remains, goods are sold at the current price if they have achieved their reserve. This organisation, the procedures and practices that inform the interactional production of the auction, is the auction 'model'; a model that enables the systematic expression and management of demand and ameliorates the potential conflict that may, in principle, arise through competition for scarce goods.

Whereas we might assume that interested parties establish the price they are willing to pay for goods prior to the sale and then expose their demand until they purchase the lot in question or are outbid, it is interesting to note that the ways in which auctions operate encourages a rather different conception of the buyers and their participation. In the first place, it is not necessarily the case that prospective buyers will receive the opportunity to declare their interest at the beginning of the sale or even wish to bid at that stage. Second, during the course of a run, prospective buyers are provided with successive opportunities to decide whether they wish to bid or decline – irrespective of the price that they may have formulated in advance. The operation of the system provides successive 'decision places' as bidding alternates between two principal protagonists. In this respect, the English model can be thought to contrast with the Dutch auction in which the price descends until a single bid is received; the first bidder secures the goods, Third, the close of sale is designed to provide further opportunities for all those present or participating in the event to issue a bid if they wish. The auctioneer's declaration of sale projects the end of the auction whilst encouraging further contributions – and in some cases provides successive opportunities for particular individuals to issue a bid. Value or price decisions therefore are enabled and engendered through the interactional organisation of the event, an organisation that is sensitive to and incorporates the contingencies that inevitably arise during the sale. In turn it informs the ways prospective buyers participate in the auction, including the price that they may be able and willing to pay for particular works of art or antiques.

Auctions have long been subject to doubt and debate, reflected in the anti-auction movements of the nineteenth century, the price-fixing scandals of the 1990s, the attitude of the popular press towards the seeming idiosyncrasies of the system and more recently public protests at the excesses of sales of contemporary art. It is hardly surprising that people may be fearful of buying at auction, concerned not so much that they will 'lose their head' though undoubtedly that can happen, but that auctioneers will use various techniques to fabricate interest to sell the goods at a price that bears little relationship to actual demand. The relative absence of formal regulation of auctions or auctioneering, at least in Britain, exacerbates these concerns. There may well be a few unscrupulous auctioneers, and some scepticism concerning the practice of bidding on behalf of the vendor, yet notwithstanding these concerns and reservations, many thousands of lots are sold at sales of art and antiques every week with little evidence of problem, difficulty or dispute. Belief and trust in these transactions does not derive from the standing of the auction house, though its reputation may well provide a certain confidence to the proceedings, nor from the simple application of a particular mechanism. Rather, trust is accomplished in and through the interaction that arises at sales by auction and the ways in which the respective contributions of buyers and auctioneers are produced with regard to routine, socially organised and recognisable practice.

We have touched on the ways in which the use of standard increments, the structure of the run and its transitions and the ways in which auctioneers invite and attribute bids contribute to transparency of bidding and the legitimacy of the auction and its outcomes. As Jarvenpa (2003), Smith (1989) and others suggest, the communities of auction participants are critical to establishing the legitimacy of the auction process and the outcomes it produces, not simply by virtue of their involvement as buyers, but through the ways in which they witness the proceedings. Auctioneers selectively render visible the contributions of particular participants, the auction is not just done, but seen to be done in a routine and transparent fashion – witnessed and witness-able by all those who happen to participate in the event. The event is both taken on trust and serves to establish trust; the reliable and trustworthy transactions that arise in auctions rest upon this fleeting interactional and situated accomplishment, that is, the auction. The organisation that informs the concerted and occasioned accomplishment of an auction reflexively constitutes the legitimacy of price and exchange.

In this regard, it is not surprising that the performance of auctioneers and the theatre of the event have drawn analytic interest (Kuiper 1994; Smith 1990), as well as popular comment (Herbert 1990; Towner 1971). While for many, auctions of art and antiques would be a disappointment if they attended to experience the drama of the event, the idea of performance and theatricality draws attention to an important aspect of an auction's accomplishment. Consider, for example, the announcement of bids and the ways in which auctioneers invite and acknowledge contributions. The announcement, the talk and bodily comportment through which it is accomplished, is not just designed to enable a particular individual to know that it is indeed his or her opportunity to bid, but to enable all those present – the principal protagonist, other interested parties and all those attending the auction – to know the location and source of the bid. The actions of the auctioneer serve to reveal the contributions, the actions, of others and enable all those present to see and to witness the concerted production of price and transaction. The ways in which auctioneers invite and attribute bids, reveal the entry and exit of bidders and create successive opportunities for any interested party to show their hand serve to create an interaction that produces and coordinates action whilst simultaneously rendering that interaction selectively visible to those gathered within the saleroom. It is hardly surprising that people remark on the performance of the auctioneer and theatricality of the event, since the very design of the actions that enable the expression and exposure of demand reveals, for the practical purposes at hand, the real-time contributions of particular participants that might otherwise remain inaccessible.

Competition at auction does not simply arise by virtue of the pre-established demand that certain individuals may hold for particular goods, but is exposed, organised, encouraged and created through interaction. The reticence of prospective buyers to declare their hand early in a sale, the variability of attendance at auctions, fluctuations in taste, high reserves, nuances of distinction and qualities, informal agreements between buyers and the like render competition unpredictable and problematic – hardly a matter of simply coordinating the expressed demand of particular individuals. The price at which bidding is initiated and the incremental structure that is adopted can have an important impact on who has the opportunity to bid and at what price, just as the deployment of commission bids or bids on behalf of the vendor can facilitate competition and impact people's willingness to bid and the price they are prepared to pay. Irrespective of a run's contribution to the transparency and efficiency of the auction and the ability to advance the price of goods through the most minimal of actions, juxtaposing successive contributions from two principal protagonists at any one time enables the auctioneer to enhance and animate competition between particular individuals. While interested parties undoubtedly have preconceptions of the value of a lot and even a determination to pay a price and no more, in practice there is a great deal more flexibility in what people are willing to pay than certain auction theories might have us believe. Auctioneers are able to exploit these uncertainties and in various ways, enhance and engender competition, allowing goods to sell for a price they might well not otherwise have achieved. Demand and competition, and the impression of demand and competition, are not independent of the situated accomplishment of the auction; the social and interactional organisation of the sale enables the expression of demand and serves to provide, even facilitate, the very forms of participation that render price contingent on the circumstances at hand.

One of the most remarkable features of the auction and its interactional organisation is the ways in which it can encompass the range of contingencies that may arise on a particular occasion, and more generally historical changes in demand, supply, fashion, market, medium and technology. Since the 1950s we have witnessed the introduction of new media to support remote participation in auctions, initially through the introduction of telephone bidding and increasingly, over the past ten years, the Internet. Despite the difficulties that emerge by virtue of the use of these technologies, including, for example, the delays that can emerge in issuing bids, these forms of remote participation have been integrated into the interactional organisation of the auction. These media and the rise of the new emerging economies in the East and Far East have had a profound impact on the market for art and antiques, introducing new buyers from countries hitherto unrepresented at auctions. In turn these buyers with access to substantial liquid capital are transforming the demand for certain types of art and antique. The leading auction houses boast of their global network of clients, but even smaller provincial houses find that they are now regularly selling to buyers from regions, even countries, that in some cases they hardly knew existed let alone included collectors with an interest in particular works of art or antiques. This social and interactional arrangement, the auction, an arrangement that has for many centuries enabled buyers to gather together to bid on and to purchase particular goods increasingly provides a global market place for art and antiques – allowing people, irrespective of nationality, culture or geography, to participate in live auctions undertaken in salerooms, both large and small, provincial and national, in towns and cities throughout the world.

Social Interaction and the Operation of Markets

It has long been recognised that social interaction lies at the heart of economic action and market activity. Beckert, for example, argues that markets consist of 'arenas of social interaction' and goes on to suggest.

> They provide a social structure and institutional order for the voluntary exchange of rights in goods and services, which allow actors to evaluate, purchase and sell these rights ... the coordination problem faced by market actors in the complex uncertain situations in which they make decisions are at the heart of a sociological approach to markets. How is it possible to integrate interaction in a social arena populated by actors with highly diverse backgrounds and conflicting interests? The notion of the "order of markets" expresses in abstract terms the explanandum of the sociology of markets. (2007: 7, 13)

The interactional foundations of market activities are characterised in very different ways throughout a range of contemporary research in economic sociology and the sociology of markets. Its explication poses the principal conceptual and methodological challenge for studies of markets and the ways in which the problem of order is resolved analytically. They reflect important methodological assumptions and presuppositions concerning the character of social action and human agency. Notwithstanding the pervasive concern with developing a critique of neoclassical economics, the problem posed by attempts to examine and conceptualise the social order of markets rests on developing at least an implicit theory or model of the forms of interaction or coordination through which economic action and its institutional environments are produced and sustained (for different approaches to the problem see, for example, Beckert 2002; Thevenot 2007; and Preda 2009). Markets are particularly interesting in this regard since they rely upon, at least as is traditionally conceived, people pursuing their own self-interests in competition with others, while simultaneously relying upon mechanisms that underpin coordination and cooperation.

Notwithstanding the widespread recognition that social interaction lies at the heart of the operation and organisation of economic action, the ways in which the problem of order is conceptualised throughout a broad range of research on markets draws analytic attention from the situated production of everyday transactions and the forms of interaction in and through which they are produced. Take, for example, the long-standing commitment to analyse markets in terms of institutional forms, inter- and intra-organisational relations; the implications for our understanding of the structure and pattern of action render analysis of the socially situated, interactional accomplishment of market activities unnecessary. The problem of order is largely resolved by virtue of a model of action that presupposes participants' compliance with various forms of rules, norms and, in some cases, practices. There is little theoretical necessity or empirical requirement to address the forms of interaction that arise within transactions and the agency that people exercise is ordinary, everyday practical situations of choice. In consequence, how people in concert and collaboration with others manage competition and exhibit agency, in and through interaction remains epiphenomenal.

There is, however, a growing corpus of, very broadly defined, ethnographic studies of economic action and markets. While there are significant variations in the methodological and analytic commitments found within this work, a principal contribution has been to draw attention to and explore the cultures, communities and networks that underpin and enable market activities and inform the production and coordination of economic action (see, for example, Abolafia 1996; Alexander and Alexander 1987, 1991; Aspers 2001; Bestor 2004; Caliskan 2007; Garcia 1986; Geismar 2004; Ho 2009; Muniesca 2005; de la Pradelle 2006; Smith 1989; Velthuis 2005; Woolgar 2004). The analytic thrust of these and cognate studies stands in marked contrast to more traditional, macro-oriented studies of economic behaviour and the social organisation of markets with their emphasis on institutional forms and inter- and intra-organisational relations. And while it is sometimes suggested (Fligstein 2001) that this growing sociology of markets should 'connect to a broader vision of society' to clarify and extend its theoretical contribution, it is increasingly recognised that these studies are providing highly distinctive insights into the characteristics and social organisation of everyday economic activities including the processes of valuation and exchange – aspects of social life that save for a few important exceptions remain surprisingly neglected by naturalistic sociologies.

Notwithstanding these initiatives, few studies are concerned with addressing the situated production of market transactions and the social interaction through which many economic actions are accomplished. One suspects this relative disregard for the situated production of economic action derives more from the conceptual and methodological commitments that underpin contemporary studies of markets than the belief that the practices, practicalities and nuances of the 'interaction order', to use Goffman's (1983) term, are unimportant to understanding the organisation of market activity. Take for example, 'embeddedness', a concept that has had a profound influence on the studies of markets, and notwithstanding the debates and developments it has occasioned, a concept that has helped drive analytic attention towards the networks, interpersonal ties, social relations, cultures and communities that inform and enable market activity. It has served to enrich our understanding of the ways in which market activities, including the valuation and marketing of goods, is dependent upon and sustained through interpersonal relations, close and loose ties, amongst varieties of participants, producers, dealers, clients and the like. Despite its substantial contribution, the concept of embeddedness, and its implications for understanding economic action in terms of networks and communities, does not encourage analysis of the situated production of everyday transactions and the contingent forms of interaction that enable their accomplishment; indeed quite the contrary. More radical attempts to refashion the notion of network to encompass and conceptualise the inter-dependencies of action, actor and object, while creating a highly distinctive approach to the interdependencies of people and the material, rarely prior-itise analysis of the concerted production of economic actions in ordinary everyday situations. Moreover, recommendations that such studies adopt a 'broader' approach to embeddedness and the structures of social networks (Beckert 2002) – that encompass, for instance, norms and institutions, habitual action and power – would seem unlikely to facilitate analysis of 'action situations in economic contexts' and their social interaction foun-dations (Beckert 2002: 293).

Underlying studies of networks and the cultures and communities that enable market activities is a conception of social order and agency that places particular emphasis on shared cognition and understanding. It is well reflected in Abolafia's discussion of markets as cultures and the wide-spread commitment to conceptualising the order and organisation of mar-kets with regard to mutual understandings that become 'institutionalised'.

> Markets as cultures is meant to denote that as loci of repeated/transaction, markets exhibit their own distinct set of mutual understandings. These under-standings are both enabling and restraining.... These understandings emerge in interaction but become institutionalised. (Abolafia 1988/1998: 69)

The idea of mutual understandings and their institutionalisation, how-ever, does not necessarily resolve the problem of order, and, as Abolafia (1988) suggests, points to the importance of interaction in and through how they emerge and presumably are sustained. How these mutual understandings are accomplished through interaction, and the organisation that informs their accomplishment, remains largely neglected, and yet it would seem that this organisation, the methods, practices and reasoning it might include, underpins the collaborative production of market activities like any other form of social action for that matter (for a related discussion, see Garfinkel 1967; Heritage 1984). In other words, rather than resolve the problem of order, or account for coordinated action, such concepts can hinder analysis of the occasioned production of action and the agency that participants exercise in ordinary practical situations of choice.

The concepts and substantive commitments that pervade the growing corpus of ethnographic studies of markets have methodological consequences that can draw attention from the situated accomplishment of market activities. If, for example, the order of economic action rests with, and is embedded in, social relations and interpersonal ties, then in-depth interviews, augmented by fieldwork, provide the most immediate ways in which the characteristics and qualities of these networks can be explored. Given, however, the transitory, occasioned character of the daily economic actions in which we engage, coupled with the intensity and demands of the interaction through which they are accomplished, it is unlikely that interviews or even field observation, however careful, can provide any more than the most fleeting characterisation and insights into the concerted accomplishment of particular transactions. In this regard, perhaps, it is not surprising that, notwithstanding the growing corpus of ethnographic studies of markets, relatively little attention has been directed to the forms of interaction that enable many market activities, since conventional data and methods of field research provide limited access to the complex, situated and emergent conduct that arises within even mundane transactions – let alone the highly complex economic activities which arise in certain institutional environments.

The growing corpus of studies of the cultures of markets reflects a wide-ranging commitment to prioritising the ways in which participants themselves engage in, organise and give sense to their activities. Despite the diversity of these studies, there is a key concern with placing agency, or as Callon suggests 'agencement', at the heart of the agenda; indeed Callon argues that 'the exploration and description of different forms of agency, as well as the analysis of their (possible) diffusion, constitute an immense project ahead of us' (2005: 4). A distinctive development in this regard that attempts to break with the conventional critical standpoint towards economics is the growing interest in the performative impact of economic devices and models on market activity (see, for instance, Callon 1998; Callon et al. 2007; Mackenzie 2009; Mackenzie and Milo 2003). It seeks to examine how economic devices, models and calculative process, or aspects of those devices, are deployed, enabled and evolve within particular circumstances, and in some cases how such devices may come to be counter-performative. It is not surprising that the empirical programme that has emerged with regard to performativity has been more concerned with developing historical analyses – consider, for example, Mackenzie and Milo's (2003) study of the Black-Scholes-Merton formula and the emergence of the derivatives market – rather than with addressing the ways in which formalisms, models and the like feature in the situated production of specific contemporary transactions. All the same, the analytic commitments that underpin performativity resonate with a number of the considerations that have informed ethnomethodological studies of the use of concepts and rules in everyday life (see, for example, Bittner 1965; Garfinkel 1967; Wieder 1975) and provide an opportunity for a distinctive approach to the analysis of the situated, interactional accomplishment of economic transactions.

The emerging debates within economic sociology have some interesting parallels with developments elsewhere in the social sciences, in particular studies of work and organisation. It is interesting to note that Fligstein's argument that the 'modern sociology of markets rarely connects its theoretical ideas to a broader vision of society or societal change' (2001: 8) is included in a chapter entitled 'bringing the sociology back in', a title reminiscent of Barley and Kunda's (2001) seminal paper 'bringing the work back in'. It is there that the similarity between the two ends. Barley and Kunda suggest the conceptual developments that have emerged in organisation analysis over the past couple of decades have become increasingly out of step with the character of work on contemporary society – theories that are more often than not driven by popular images of social institutions such as the 'network organisation' rather than grounded in empirical analysis. They continue by suggesting that the shortcomings of organisational analysis do not derive from an absence of theory – indeed there is a surfeit models and concepts – but rather the relative absence of research, in particular naturalistic research, that examines the practicalities and characteristics of work in the contemporary workplace. While Barley and Kunda's critique is primarily concerned with drawing out the analytic implications of the relative absence of empirical and ethnographic studies of work for theories of organising and organisation, it reflects challenges and debates arising within research on economic action and the operation of markets. The problem at hand may not be so much an absence of macro-level theory, or a lack of resonance between the micro-analytic studies and the macro, but rather, notwithstanding the growing corpus of broadly ethnographic studies of markets and market devices, the relative paucity of studies of the practical and situated organisation of economic action within everyday settings. This is not to deny the important contribution of recent studies of the 'cultures of markets' but rather that if we are to come to understand the social order of markets and develop insightful and enriching theory as Coulter (2001) and others suggest, it may well be necessary to reconsider, even re-specify, our macro-order concepts with regard to the situated character of economic action in contemporary societies.

There is a growing recognition that alongside the emerging corpus of ethnographic studies of markets, and the diverse commitments being brought to bear upon the analysis of economic action, the social and interactional organisation of transactions requires analytic attention. In their insightful discussion of cambist markets, Knorr Cetina and Bruegger (2002, 2004) demonstrate the significance of interaction to the practical accomplishment of the brief, episodic transactions that arise in such domains, suggesting 'these sequences of utterances (and in this case gestures, bodily actions and the like) do not just convey information, but perform economic actions'. And in his introduction to the sociology of markets, Preda underscores the centrality of social interaction to understanding economic action, suggesting:

> Interactions are constitutive of transactions: the particular sequences in which interactions unfold shape the reciprocal expectation and understandings of participants, their perceptions and definitions of the process and, with that, the outcomes of transactions. (2009: 27)

We have begun to witness the emergence of a small number of empirical studies of the details of embodied action and interaction through which transactions are accomplished, including, for example, Clarke, Pinch and Drew's (Clark and Pinch 1995; Clark, Drew and Pinch, 1994, 2003; Pinch and Clark 1986) wide-ranging analyses of market traders, Llewelyn and Burrow (2009) on street vendors, Vargha (2011) on financial demonstrations, and, in a different vein, Preda's (2009) analysis of electronic trading. The matter at hand, however, is not solely an issue of foregrounding social interaction in the analysis of economic action, but in turning to address the situated and interactional accomplishment of transactions. The distinctive focus of this methodological commitment is sometimes characterised with Goffman's (1983) phrase the 'interaction order', but this might be misleading; the interest may not be so much in identifying generic features of social interaction, but in explicating the resources, practices and reasoning that enable the interactional and ordered accomplishment of particular forms of economic activity.

It is sometimes implied that the coordination of action in markets is theoretically, if not empirically, distinct from matters of value, trust and competition. Indeed, the very terms 'coordination' and 'problems of coordination' that arise in debates in economic sociology, can suggest, perhaps inadvertently, a distinct order and organisation of action. One suspects that Callon is developing a critique of this distinction when he suggests:

> Why not consider that one solution to the question of coordination, in a situation of radical uncertainty, is to admit that beneath the contracts and the rules there is a "primitive" reality without which coordination would not be possible? An understanding of this ultimate basis is the purpose of the notion of social network or, more broadly, the notion of embeddedness as initially formulated by Polanyi and later refined by Granovetter. (1998: 7)

The organisation that informs the concerted accomplishment of, for example, an auction, enables the production and intelligibility of economic actions. The organisation is not just a coordinating mechanism, but part of the very fabric through which transactions are accomplished. These practices, this organisation, are the vehicle through which participants exercise their agency and contingently accomplish economic actions within the developing course of the interaction. This organisation and its deployment reflexively produce transactions and their outcomes – and in turn enable analysis of the market, its stability, changes, influences and the like.

It is worthwhile touching on one further point: while there remain a substantial number of economic transactions undertaken within traditional settings, through the interaction of participants within the same immediate environment, the widespread deployment of digital technology and the Internet has had a profound impact on the operation of many markets. These developments pose significant methodological challenges to research concerned with the situated and occasioned accomplishment of economic transactions, and in some cases demand a very different conception of interaction and communicative action. In many cases, these challenges are far from being identified let alone resolved. Notwithstanding these developments, and the important impact of certain technological innovations on market activity, the circumstances and organisational environments through which people in collaboration with others perform transactions can be critical to understanding their concerted accomplishment. We have noted already, for example, how real-time Internet contributions are integrated into the live auction and how certain forms of Internet auction rely upon an interactional organisation that may be subject to the analytic commitments that have been briefly discussed here. Moreover, if we turn to more complex technological environments such as financial trading rooms and cambist markets, we can begin to see how the participants' activities, including their use of highly complex systems, can be sensitive to and coordinated with the real-time contributions of others, both those within and those connected remotely to particular domains (see, for example, Knorr Cetina 2009; Knorr Cetina and Bruegger 2002, 2004 and Heath et al. 1995). Indeed, there is a burgeoning corpus of studies that examine and demonstrate the inter-dependencies of local and remote action and interaction and address the ways in which the use of tools and technologies and the information and resources they provide informs the interactional accomplishment of complex, collaborative tasks (see, for example, Goodwin and Goodwin 1996; Mondada 2007; Suchman 1996; Whalen and Vinkhuzen 2000; Heath and Luff 2000; Luff and Heath 2000). It may be a misnomer to draw too sharp a distinction, at least a priori, between the natural and synthetic, the situated and the remote, the material and digital, since for many activities it is these occasioned interdependencies that are critical to the interactional and accountable accomplishment of the transaction.

Normal Prices

Stories of record prices achieved at auction for art and antiques pervade the news media and give the impression that the value of works of particular artists or outstanding pieces of furniture, jewellery, porcelain and the like are highly volatile and subject to the influence of particular buyers and rapid changes in fad and fashion. The idea that auctions can establish unpredictable, and in some cases unstable, prices for works of art and antiques is further fuelled by the growing number of television programmes, in particular in Britain, in which householders are encouraged to believe 'finds' at car-boot sales, charity shops and even at home in the attic may engender unexpected competition in the saleroom and lead to extraordinary prices for seemingly mundane objects and artefacts. Auctions do indeed, on occasion, achieve extraordinary prices for works of art and antiques, prices that in turn can serve as a benchmark for the sale of similar pieces, works by a particular artist, or in the same genre. To a large extent, however, auctions produce few surprises, and the prices that goods achieve are at values that one would roughly expect for the work of art or antique in question. Unlike, for example, the motor trade, where auction and used retail prices are dominated, almost governed, by price guides only available to the trade – in Britain 'Glass's Guide' – variations in the supply, qualities and quality of art and antiques disallows precise valuations for many goods, and yet the price that goods achieve at auction is largely and routinely predictable within a limited price range.

The organisation of auctions contributes to the predictability of price and the normalisation of values. In the first instance, many auctions of art and antiques are accompanied by a catalogue which includes pre-sale estimates of price for almost all the lots that are sold. These estimates typically consist of an upper and lower figure, ordinarily within a range of between ten per cent and twenty per cent. The estimates frequently reflect the reserve that the auction house has agreed to with the vendor, estimates that in turn can arise through a subtle negotiation in which expert and seller arrive at an agreed minimal price acceptable for the goods in question. In practice, the considerations that come into play in determining price are often quite complex, with, for example, in some cases realistic reserves and in consequence low estimates used to tempt and encourage buyers, known as 'come hither estimates', when it is expected the selling price will be substantially more than documented in the catalogue. All the same, auction houses are keen that pre-sale estimates are not regularly out of kilter with the price that goods achieve – otherwise doubt can be cast on the knowledge and competence of their experts. Pre-sale estimates are not inconsequential to the price that people pay or are willing to pay at auctions. It is not unusual for private buyers and even members of the trade to use the estimate as a guideline when bidding, and while buyers may be prepared to go one or two increments over the higher estimate, in our data corpus we find that well in excess of eighty per cent of goods sold at auction are sold at a price that falls between the high and low estimate. This predictability of price undoubtedly derives in part from the experts' ability to predict prices for particular works of art and antiques; one suspects it also derives from the ways in which buyers themselves rely upon estimates as resource in bidding. It is hardly surprising that research has found a correspondence between selling prices and pre-sale estimates since pre-sale estimates are oriented to both by auctioneers and buyers during the sale of particular lots.

Second, the conduct of the auctioneer has a significant impact on the production of expected prices at auction and the preservation of certain values for particular works of art and antique. It is not uncommon to find that the lower estimate is priced a little above the reserve – often one increment. As we suggested earlier, the principal concern for an auctioneer in selling a substantial number of lots during a lengthy auction is not to achieve, or expect to achieve, outstanding prices for particular goods, but rather to achieve a reasonable overall selling rate. In consequence, auctioneers go to some trouble to facilitate and encourage bidding to enable particular lots to achieve their reserve and thereby secure a price at least equivalent to, and preferably in excess of, the lower estimate. If an auctioneer can escalate the price well in excess of the estimate then all very good, but in most cases it is neither expected nor critical – an auction with a reasonable selling rate satisfies demands for revenue, keeps vendors satisfied and avoids the detrimental press that can arise from a sale where a large proportion of goods fail to sell. Indeed, a low selling rate from even a single auction can not only lead to bad press but can place an auction house in severe financial difficulties.

The tale of the decline of the Phillips auction house is apocryphal in this regard. Bought by Bernard Arnault, the ambitious head of the LVMH luxury goods conglomerate in 1999, it was sold within a few years following two disastrous auctions where, to secure the consignments, Phillips had agreed to high reserves backed by guarantees. Phillips accounted for a $150 million loss at LVMH in 2001.

> Things looked promising for a while: Phillips won some major consignments. Last May it sold a high-calibre collection that belonged to Heinz Berggruen, an art dealer in Berlin. In November, it sold the much-coveted Smooke collection of 20th-century art. Even so, Mr Arnault's aggressive tactics to buy market share were risky and expensive. He gave much higher guarantees (fixed amounts granted to the seller) than his competitors and handed out more generous loans to buyers. Phillips lost several million dollars when the sale of the Berggruen pictures failed to cover the guarantee; its guarantee for the Smooke collection cost it an estimated $80m. (*Economist* 21.2.2002: 22)

Third, there are substantial price data available for those with an interest in the sale or purchase of art and antiques. The records of sale prices of the leading auction houses are readily accessible; there are an increasing number of lay and professional price guides and the Internet has further facilitated access to results from auctions throughout the world. In consequence, it takes no more than a few moments to find prices of work by particular artists or numerous examples, often well illustrated, of dining room chairs, miniatures, tea services, overmantels, candlesticks, figurines and the prices they achieved at auction. Ready access to data by auctioneers, buyers and sellers from anywhere within the world has had an important impact upon the normalisation and predictability of values, not only informing the price that buyers may be willing to pay for particular goods within certain parameters, but also in the ways in which the auction houses and experts establish reserves and pre-sale estimates and seek to achieve those prices within the auction itself. Notwithstanding, therefore, the uncertainty of the values of works of art and antiques and the contingencies that arise at auction, not least of which is who is able and willing to participate, the prices achieved are in large part unsurprising and unremarkable. They reflect, and serve to reflexively preserve, a normal state of affairs and in turn inform the assessments and prices that form the basis to subsequent auctions and bear upon the prices at which the trade retails goods.

In turn, the normal prices produced at auction inform the updating of price guides and indexes and are increasingly used to direct investment and underpin the prices sought by the retail trade, a trade increasingly sensitive to the public's access to both the auction and auction price records. Although those dealing in the work of living artists go to some trouble to differentiate retail prices from the prices that particular goods achieve, or might achieve, at auction (see Coslor 2009; Velthuis 2005), the ability to preserve a substantial price distinction between auctions and retail is becoming increasingly problematic for many works of art and antiques. The success of the auction houses in encouraging private buyers to buy at auction, coupled with the growing accessibility of auction results and even the forays of one or two of the leading houses into establishing their own retail outlets, has had a profound impact on the ability of the trade to sustain sharply differentiated prices from the values that works might be expected to achieve at auction. These difficulties are exacerbated by the growing number of auctions that involve the sale of the trading stock of former dealers. Moreover, when, for example, at a recent stock sale of controversial London dealer John Hobbs, a member of the highly regarded British Antique Dealers Association, a commode priced in his central London shop at £145,000 sells at auction for £4,000, the publicity does little to encourage the private buyer to purchase from the trade or to trust the prices that members of the trade may attempt to secure.

Thirty years ago, a reasonable living could be had by purchasing particular works of art or antiques in one area of a country and selling in another. In Britain, for example, eighteenth-century oak dressers might be bought in the southwest or southeast of England and sold for a good profit a few weeks later in Cheshire or Shropshire, or good quality Scottish silver bought cheaply south of the border and sold in Edinburgh with little difficulty. In turn, the international trade became increasingly important, with, for example, container loads of nineteenth-century English furniture being shipped for sale to North America through vast warehouses found on the outskirts of major cities. There is still some profit to be had by selling goods such as long-case clocks in a town or region in which they have been made, if they have been bought cheaply elsewhere, but over the last couple of decades regional, and increasingly, international, price differences which were the stalwart of the art and antiques trade for many years have rapidly eroded. Chinese collectors of porcelain for example, do not have to rely on the English trade to buy cheap at a provincial auction and sell high in Hong Kong or Beijing; they can discover with ease what is coming for sale at auctions in Britain, France, Germany and the United States and participate in the live auction. In consequence, it has become increasingly difficult to preserve regional price differentials or to maintain a clear distinction between the prices demanded retail from those achieved at auction. It is hardly surprising that the trade, especially the high-end trade, is increasingly helping collectors to purchase goods rather than, as traditionally, buying stock at auction to sell on. Notwithstanding changes in taste and the like, the inability to sustain a clear distinction between retail and auctions, sometimes characterised as the 'primary and secondary market', is perhaps one of the reasons for the declining numbers of art and antique shops in Britain, mainland Europe and North America.

Despite the normalisation of the prices of art and antiques at auction, there remain significant variation and fluctuations in the price that goods of a same or similar type achieve at auction – be they early Delft tiles, Lalique bowls or Fragonard drawings. As suggested, seemingly slight differences in the type, quality and qualities of particular goods, the theme and focus of the sale, the number and type of similar goods that appeared on the market recently and who participates in the sale can have an important impact on the price that goods achieve and indeed the overall revenue generated by the auction. Even during a single auction, it has long been recognised that the same type of lot, in some cases precisely the same goods, will achieve different prices – indeed the 'declining price anomaly' has drawn much analytic attention in economics. These variations, however small in comparison to the extraordinary prices achieved on occasions for particular works of art, demonstrate the emergent, the accomplished, character of auctions and the ways in which the contingent participation of buyers and auctioneer is critical to the legitimate and concerted production of transactions. The variation of price at auction is not simply explained by differences in the quality or qualities of goods, nor one suspects by predetermined preferences or conceptions of value. Both are important, but how they come to feature in and inform the price that goods achieve arises through the contingent forms of participation that evolve within the developing course of the sale of a particular lot and the auction itself.

The relationship between price and value at auction is more complicated and contingent than sometimes thought. Auctions do indeed constitute the price of goods and enable their exchange and yet the price that goods achieve is not necessarily believed to reflect their value. People can buy cheap at auction, or on occasion goods will sell for significantly more than people believe they are worth. Moreover, a significant fall or rise in the price of, say, the work of a particular artist at an auction will not necessarily reflect, or be seen as representing, a marked change in the value of those goods or goods of a particular type. It is not unusual for buyers, experts and auctioneers to invoke various accounts for incongruous or surprising prices, accounts that for example appeal to the circumstances of the auction, the chance absence of particular buyers, the contingencies of bidding, and of course the qualities of a particular pieces. It is not assumed that there is a correspondence between an auction price and the value of goods, and yet the prices at which goods sell at auction are used as a resource with which to determine the current value of works of art and antiques. In other words, while auction prices stand as a principal resource for determining the value of particular goods, and the price at which certain works of art or antiques sell at auction enables the identification of trends and price movements, a whole range of contingencies and considerations come into play that undermine drawing any necessary conclusions concerning the relationship between a particular selling price and the value of the goods in question.

On the one hand, therefore, auctions can normalise prices and establish a stable market for goods of uncertain value; on the other hand, they provide a vehicle through which remarkable changes arise within the market for art and antiques. They can establish and preserve a stable price for particular goods over many years, even decades, or radically change the fortunes of certain works of art or antiques within moments. With the increasing volatility of Western economies and the emerging influence of the East, one suspects that it will be the auction that will primarily determine the rapidly changing values of art and antiques and help establish and chart shifting patterns of desire and investment. It will be recalled that we began by discussing the remarkable sale in a small auction house in West London of a Chinese *yang-cai* or double-walled vase that achieved a record price of £43 million. Less than a year later, while, for example, the English antique furniture index is showing its biggest ever annual fall, we find leading provincial auction rooms and international houses posting record sales. It will come as little surprise to learn that the very mainstay of the antiques trade for nearly 100 years has been rapidly replaced by the extraordinary demand for Chinese works of art – a demand that has allowed some auction houses to increase the value of their annual sales by fifty per cent. These developments have been accompanied by a significant increase in the registration of new clients, especially the East and Far East, and the rapid growth of live bidding though the Internet. More than 300 years since auctions of second-hand goods and household effects became institutionalised in Europe, we find this seemingly simple form of social interaction underpinning remarkable developments in the markets for art and antiques, developments that mark a profound shift in the economics of taste and in the ways in which people from different regions of the globe participate in auctions.

Appendix I. Glossary

Some Common Terms and Expressions used at Auctions of Art, Antiques and Household Effects

Auctioneer's Book The 'auctioneer's book', also known as the 'sale sheets', list the lots and lot numbers of the goods to be sold during the auction. They include a brief description of the lot, often an abbreviated description of that found within the sale catalogue, details of the estimate and the reserve. They also include the name of the vendor and details of commission bids, ordinarily listing no more than the three highest commissions. On selling the lot, the auctioneer enters the hammer price and the name or number of the buyer. Information from the book or the sale sheets are then passed to the accounts department.

Auctioneer's Clerk Traditionally, auctioneers are accompanied by a clerk who may sit or stand alongside the auctioneer near the rostrum. The responsibilities of the clerk vary between auction houses, but they include, documenting sale prices and the buyers' names or numbers. They also help to spot bidders and issue commissions received too late to enter in the auctioneer's book or sale sheets. They are increasingly responsible for operating the Internet bidding system and announcing bids received online.

Buying Goods In When goods fail to sell, in particular when they fail to achieve their reserve, they are referred to as having been bought in. At what price they are bought in can be of some importance to subsequent negotiations with the vendor and any potential buyers.

Brown Furniture An unfortunate expression that is used to characterise English mahogany furniture of the late eighteenth and nineteenth century, a staple of the antique trade for many decades. It is an expression that has become increasingly common with the fall of furniture prices during the late twentieth and early twenty-first century.

Buyers Premium It is common for the buyer to pay a premium normally a percentage of the 'Hammer Price' for example seventeen and a half per cent of the Hammer Price. The Buyers Premium varies according to the auction house and in some cases the selling price of the goods. In many cases, the buyer's premium is also subject to tax, such as the Value Added Tax (VAT). The buyer's premium generates significant revenue for auction houses.

Commission Auction houses normally charge the vendor a commission to sell their goods at auction. The commission can vary between ten per cent to twenty-five per cent of the selling price, depending upon the particular auction house and the value of the goods. Many auction houses reduce the commission as the selling price of goods increase. For more valuable items or for more important collections, it is not uncommon for the auction houses to offer a reduced rate of commission, in some cases taking no commission at all, in order to sell the goods in question.

Commission Bids Bids left with the auction house by buyers unable or unwilling to attend the sale. Commission bids normally consist of the maximum price a buyer is willing to pay for the goods in question excluding the buyer's premium and taxes.

Conflicting Bids As in 'I have here conflicting bids' is used to announce, at the start of the sale of a lot, that the auctioneer has two or more commission bids at the same maximum value.

Cross-over buyers Established collectors or investors who normally purchase particular works of art or antique who are prepared to purchase in a very different area or field. For example, following the financial crisis, some collectors switched from buying contemporary art to old masters.

Fair Warning An expression used to forewarn the end of the auction of a particular lot, often in cases in which the lot has failed to reach its reserve and will be bought in unless further bids are received.

Financial Interest Until the banking crisis in 2008, it was not uncommon for auction houses to take a financial interest in some goods they sold in auction. This 'interest' might include advancing the vendor funds in advance of the sale or selling lots which were in part, or wholly owned, by the auction house. It became conventional to declare in the sale catalogue the lots in which the auction house had a financial interest. Not surprising, there is much debate concerning the conflict of interest that arises in cases in which the auction house is selling goods in which it has an interest.

Gavel The name of the hammer used by the auctioneer to end the auction of a particular lot.

Guarantee In some cases, in particular when attempting to secure important works of art and antique to sell at auction, the auction houses may offer the vendor a guaranteed price. Since the financial crisis of 2008, this practice has grown increasingly rare and in some cases led to severe loses for the auction houses.

Hammer Price The highest price that a buyer is willing to pay for a particular lot at an auction; the price at which the goods have achieved at the strike of the hammer. In addition to the hammer price, the buyer will normally pay the 'Buyers Premium', which in turn is subject to taxes such as VAT.

Incredibly Solid An expression used to describe the demand for a particular type of goods sold at the auction as for example in 'incredibly solid demand for early oak at the sale'.

Increment The amount by which the auctioneer increases the bidding. Some auction houses detail the incremental structure that will be used between certain vales in the sale catalogue. The increments used are approximately ten per cent of the current price of the lot during the auction.

Interest Here The expression 'interest here' normally precedes the announcement of a starting price and refers to commissions that enable the auctioneer to bid and begin bidding at particular price.

Lot An individual object or collection of objects offered for sale at auction as a single unit.

Maiden Bid The first actual bid for a lot an auction. The expression is commonly used when describing the sale of lot that sells on the first and only bid made by a prospective buyer.

Fresh to Market An expression ordinarily applied to more important works of art or antique that have not been traded or sold in auction for some years, if ever. Such goods will often generate significant interest by virtue of the market 'freshness' and in many cases as a consequence of their not having been over-restored or subject to extensive repair and tampering.

Online Bids Bidding at live auctions via the Internet has significantly increased in recent years. The auctioneer receives the bids, either directly on screen or through an Internet administrator based in the saleroom, not infrequently the auctioneer's clerk. The bids are integrated into the flow of bids received from absentee buyers, participants in the room or those represented by sale assistants.

Paddle In some auction houses bidders are issued with a small wooden paddle on which their buyer number is inscribed. Less sophisticated versions consist of a white card detailing the buyer number. It is not unusual for prospective buyers to use the paddle or card to bid.

Pass When a lot fails to achieve its reserve the auctioneer announces 'pass' on bringing the hammer down.

Pre-Sale Estimate The price range within which an auction lot is expected to sell. Pre-sale estimates are generally published in the catalogue. Substantial interest in a lot in advance of the sale may result in estimates changing before the sale date. The pre-sale estimate provides prospective buyers with a guide to the selling price of the lot. It often reflects the reserve price that is not uncommonly one or two increments below the lower estimate.

Reserve The lowest price that a vendor is willing to receive for goods excluding the monies subtracted by the auction house for commission and associated taxes. Some auction houses encourage vendors to agree to say, leeway of ten per cent so that if necessary the lot can be sold for less than the reserve.

Right Foot The starting price that enables an auctioneer to achieve the reserve and avoid having more than one final bid at the same price. 'Getting off on the right foot' can prove a highly demanding calculation and is said to be one of the matters new or trainee auctioneers can find particularly challenging.

Run Auctioneers ordinarily establish bidding between two and no more than two bidders at any one time. When one bidder withdraws, they seek to replace that bidder with a new bidder and establish a new run.

Sale Assistant The term is used in this book primarily to describe saleroom personnel who represent prospective buyers who bid by telephone. Sale assistants may not only include administrative personnel but, for example in the case of major international sales, also include senior members of specialist departments who represent prospective buyers in the saleroom.

Saleroom The room or rooms in which the auction takes place. The saleroom increasingly has a standard layout with seating facing the rostrum, and the clerk and sale assistants positioned on either side of the auctioneer. Traditionally salerooms included the goods to be auctioned and enabled the auctioneer to point towards the particular lots as they came up for sale. In more general sales, furniture that was to be sold often provided participants with additional seating. The auction houses are increasingly using monitors to display each lot though it is not unusual to still find many lots displayed in the sale room during the auction.

Sale Sheets see Auctioneer's Book.

Selling Rate The selling rate is a calculation that summarises the number of lots sold and the revenue generated. How the selling rate is calculated and presented is ordinarily designed to maximise the impression of the success of the auction. For example, the figure is often expressed in terms of the overall value of the goods sold at the auction, especially if that is well in excess of the total predicted using the lower of the estimates for each lot. Increasingly the selling rate includes goods sold immediately after the sale through negotiation – goods that failed to reach their reserve during the auction.

Shill Bidding Shill bidding is a term widely used with regard to Internet auctions. It refers to the practice of a vendor, or his or her confederate, bidding on goods in which they have an interest in order to increase the selling price.

It is a violation federal law in the United States and of the rules of Internet auction providers such as eBay. Software systems have been developed and deployed to identify shill bidding during Internet auctions.

Sleeper An important work of art or antique that is submitted for sale but initially remains unrecognised. In many cases sleepers will have a low estimate and an inaccurate or ambivalent catalogue description. Before or during the auction 'interest' demonstrates that buyers have recognised its potential value and in consequence the price it achieves significantly exceeds expectations.

Spirited Competition Eager bidding during the sale of a particular lot – often consisting of a number of extensive runs and numerous prospective buyers declaring an interest.

Splitting the Increment During the sale of a particular lot the auctioneer may offer a bid that is half the projected next increment. Splitting the increment can also be requested by a prospective buyer. For the auctioneer a split increment may be offered in order to increase the price of goods to secure the reserve.

Strike of the Hammer The strike of the hammer marks the conclusion of the contract between the seller and buyer if the reserve has been met. It is typically followed by the auctioneer announcing the selling price and the buyer's number or name. In the case of goods failing to sell, the strike of the hammer is typically followed by an expression such as 'pass' that indicates the goods have not met their reserve.

Telephone Bids Most auction houses enable prospective buyers to participate in the sale by bidding by telephone. The arrangement is made in advance with the auction house. In the auction room the prospective buyer is represented by a sale assistant who provides information concerning bidding to the remote participant and where relevant invites him to bid and bids on his or her behalf.

Under Bidder A prospective buyer that has bid the current second highest price. During a run, the under bidder is typically the protagonist who made the previous bid.

Vendor Bids One of a variety of expressions (including for example Bids off the Wall, From the Chandelier, or Phantom Bids) used to describe bids placed by the auctioneer on behalf of the vendor – officially up until one increment below the reserve. Less scrupulous auctioneers are said to create bids to increase the price in excess of the reserve – to 'run the buyer up' or in some cases, create bids where there is no reserve at all.

Appendix II. Transcription Notation

The transcripts presented in the book have, where possible, been simplified and I have avoided including any of the original data maps that include reference to the visible conduct as well as the talk of the participants (see Heath et al. 2010). The orthography for transcribing talk, and now widely used within conversation analysis and cognate studies of language use and interaction, was developed by Gail Jefferson. Descriptions of the orthography can be found in various books and edited collections, including Drew and Heritage (1989), Streeck et al. (2011) and Heath et al. (2010).

Throughout the transcripts we have used 'A' to refer to the auctioneer. Bidders are represented by 'B'. The number following 'B' represents the order in which the bidder first enters the bidding. 'SA' represents sale assistants and 'OL' online bidders, also numbered in terms of the order in which they first enter the bidding.

Intervals between utterances

When there are intervals in a stream of talk, they are timed in tenths of a second and inserted within parentheses, either within an utterance:

A: At six million (0.2) six (.) hundred (0.2) thousand pounds

or between utterances

A: Two million six hundred thousand
(4.2)
B.3: Just knock it down and get on with it

A dot in parentheses (.) indicates a gap of less than two-tenths of a second

A: Four Five Two ladies and gentlemen, the solitaire ring seems to have er: (.) captured everybody's imagination.

Characteristics of speech delivery

Punctuation is used to capture various characteristics of speech delivery. For example, extensions of sounds or syllables are indicated by placing a colon (:) after the relevant syllable.

A: against your bidder, against you <u>Ro:bert</u>

More colons prolong the stretch, one colon for each tenth of a second.:

A: Lot Two Twenty Two:::::::::. I can start at <u>sixty</u> thousand.

Other punctuation marks are used as follows:

? A question mark for rising intonation.

. A full-stop (or period) for a fall in tone (not necessarily at the end of a sentence).

, A comma for continuing intonation.

! An exclamation mark indicates an animated tone.

- A single dash is used when the utterance is cut off.

Rising or falling shifts in intonation are indicated by up and down pointing arrows '↑' or '↓':

A: <u>Twenty five</u>: with↑Tina↓

Underlining shows where and utterance, or part of an utterance, is emphasised:

A: At twenty four <u>thou</u>sand <twenty <u>six</u> thousand.

Capital letters are used when part of an utterance is spoken much louder than the rest:

A: <u>Two</u> hu<u>nd</u>red thousand pounds.

(3.4)

A: At TWO HUNDRED thousand pounds

A degree sign is used when a passage of talk is quieter:

A: °No (.) it's Ben's bid. Victoria you're out

A: At eighty five thousand (.) Ben 's bidder

    (0.8)

SA.1: °Here°

    (0.4)

A: °I'm sorry°. Ninety thousand

Audible inhalations °hhh and aspirations hhh and are inserted in speech where they occur:

A: °hhh One million seven hundred thousand

When part of an utterance is delivered at a pace quicker than the surrounding talk, it is indicated by being preceded by a greater than '<' sign, a decrease in pace is indicated by a less than '>' sign.

A: At one mil(lion) < One million eight hundred >,

Transcription doubt

When it is unclear what is being said single parentheses mark the letter(s), word or phrase that is in doubt:

→A: At one mil(lion) < One million eight hundred >.

Simultaneous and overlapping utterances

When utterances overlap a bracket is used when the overlap begins:

A: At six⌈ty (0.5) thousand pounds

B.3:   ⌊°Sixty° two (thousand)

Contiguous utterances

When two speakers start talking at the same time, a bracket is used to denote synchronisation:

A: At one hundred and ten thousand

    (0.2)

A: ⌈At one hundred < One twenty in the room

B.3: ⌊One Twenty::

When there is no interval between adjacent utterances, they are 'latched'. This is indicated using equal signs:

A: Thirteen hundred, <u>ye</u>s::?

(0.5)

A: It's only money sir you could have a lot of fun with this=

SA.2   = °Thirteen°

A: <u>Thirteen</u> hundred pounds

Marking interesting parts of the transcript

An arrow (→) in the left-hand margin can be used to mark parts of the transcript that are being discussed.

A: At sixty two thousand in the room Not yours Paul nor yours Alice.

→ A: At sixty (0.3) <u>two</u> thousand

B.4:   [snaps fingers][B.3]

A: Sixty five thousand

(2.3)

A: Eight?

Describing an action or relevant feature of the activity

Where necessary descriptions are included within or alongside the transcript to indicate a relevant action. These are inserted in square brackets for example:

A: At three hundred [raises gavel] an eighty thousand.

References

Abolafia, M. Y. (1988) Markets as Cultures: An Ethnographic Approach. *Sociological Review* (69–85) reprinted in M. Callon (ed.) (1998). *The Laws of the Market.* Oxford, UK: Blackwell Publishers.

(1996) *Making Markets: Opportunism and Restraint on Wall Street.* Cambridge, MA: Harvard University Press.

Alexander, J. and P. Alexander (1987) Striking a Bargain in Javanese Markets. *Man* 22, 42–68.

(1991) What's a Fair Price? Price-Setting and Trading Partnerships in Javanese Markets. *Man* 26, 493–512.

Anderson, R. J., J. A. Hughes, and W. W. Sharrock (1989) *Working for Profit: The Social Organisation of Calculation in an Entrepreneurial Firm.* Aldershot: Avebury.

Antiques Trade Gazette: The Art Market Weekly. Buxton : Buxton Press

Appadurai, A. (1986) *The Social Life of Things.* Cambridge: Cambridge University Press.

Art Market Trends. Artprice.com.

Ashenfelter, O. and K. Graddy (2002) Art Auctions: A Survey of Empirical Studies. NBER Working Paper No. 8997: National Bureau of Economic Research, Cambridge, MA.

(2003) Auctions and the Price of Fine Art. *Journal of Economic Literature* Vol XLI: 763–86.

Aspers, P. (2001) *Markets in Fashion: A Phenomenological Approach.* Stockholm: City University Press.

Atkinson, J. M. and P. Drew (1979) *Order in Court: The Organisation of Verbal Interaction in Judicial Settings.* London: Macmillan.

Atkinson, J. M. and J. C. Heritage (eds.) (1984) *Structures of Social Action: Studies in Conversational Analysis.* Cambridge: Cambridge University Press.

Auer, P., E. Couper-Kuhlen, and F. Muller (1999) *Language in Time: The Rhythm and Tempo of Verbal Interaction.* Oxford: Oxford University Press.

Barley, S. R. and G. Kunda (2001) Bringing Work Back In. *Organization Science* 12(1): 76–97.

Beach, W. and C. LeBaron (2002) Body Disclosures: Attending to Personal Problems and Reported Sexual Abuse during a Medical Encounter. *Journal of Communication* 52(3): 617–39.

Beckert, J. (2002) *Beyond the Market: The Social Foundations of Economic Efficiency.* Trans. Barbara Harshaw. Princeton, NJ: Princeton University Press.

(2007) The Social Order of Markets. MPifG Discussion Paper 07/15 Koln: Max-Planck-Institut fur Gesellschaftsforschung.

Beckert, J. and P. Aspers (eds.) (2011) *The Worth of Goods: Valuation and Pricing in the Economy.* Oxford: Oxford University Press.

Bestor, T. C. (2004) *Tsukiji: The Fish Market at the Center of the World.* Berkeley: University of California Press.

Bittner, E. (1965) The Concept of Organisation. *Social Research* 32: 230–55.

Boden, D. and D. H. Zimmerman (eds.) (1991) *Talk and Social Structure.* Cambridge: Polity Press.

Boeck, G. A. (1990) *Texas Livestock Auctions: A Folklife Ethnography.* New York: AMS Press.

Button, G. and C. C. Heath (2002) Special Issue: Workplace Studies. *British Journal of Sociology* 53/2.

Caliskan, K. (2007). Price as a Market Device: Cotton Trading in Izmir Mercantile Exchange. *The Sociological Review* 55: 241–60.

Callon, M. (ed.) (1998) *The Laws of the Market.* Oxford: Blackwell.

Callon, M. (2005) Why Virtualism Paves the Way to Political Impotence: A Reply to Daniel Miller's Critique of *The Laws of the Markets*. In O. Velthius (ed.) *Economic Sociology European Electronic NewsLetter* 6(2) February: 26–42.

Callon, M., Y. Millo, and F. Muniesa (2007) *Market Devices.* Oxford: Blackwell.

Callon, M. and F. Muniesa (2005) Peripheral Vision: Economic Markets as Calculative Collective Devices. *Organization Studies* 26(8): 1229–50.

Cassady, R., Jr. (1967) *Auctions and Auctioneering.* California, USA: University of California Press.

Chichester, D., H. Edmeades, B. Strongin, D. Gregory, F. N. McEuen, and J. Krass (undated) *Guidelines for Auctioneers.* London: Christie's.

Christie's (6.7.2006) *Important Old Master Picture: Evening Sale* London: Christie's.

(16.10.2006) *The Italian Sale: 20th Century Art.* London: Christie's.

(14.5.2008) *Post-War and Contemporary Art.*New York: Christie's.

Clark, C, P. Drew, and T. Pinch (2003) Managing Prospect Affiliation and Rapport in Real-life Sales Encounters. *Discourse Studies* 5(1): 5–31.

Clark, C. and T. Pinch (1995) *The Hard Sell: The Language and Lessons of Street Wise Marketing.* New York: Harper Collins.

(1994) The Interactional Study of Exchange Relationships: an Analysis of Patter Merchants at Work on Street Markets. In N. de Marchi and M. S. Morgan (eds.) *Higgling: Transactors and Their Markets in the History of Economics.* Durham/London.

Clark, C., P. Drew, and T. Pinch (1994) Managing Customer 'Objections' During Real-Life Sales Encounters. *Discourse and Society* 5(4): 437–62.

Clayman, S. and J. C. Heritage (2002) *The News Interview: The History and Dynamics of a Social Form.* London: Sage.

Cohen, A. (2002) *The Perfect Store: Inside eBay.* London: Platkus.

Cooper, J. (1977) *Under the Hammer: The Auctions and Auctioneers of London.* London: Constable.

Coslor, E. (2009) Playing by the Rules: Competing Logics of Exchange in the Market for Contemporary Art. *Paper presented ASA Annual Meeting, San Francisco.*

Coulter, J. (2001) Human Practices and the Observability of the 'Macro-social'. In T. R. Schatzki, K. Knorr Cetina, and E. von Savigny (eds.) *The Practice Turn in Contemporary Theory.* Routledge: London.

Dargan, A. and S. Zeitlin (1983) American Talkers: Expressive Styles and Occupational Choice. *The Journal of American Folklore* 96(379): 3–33.

de la Pradelle, M. (2006) *Market Day in Provence.* Trans. Amy Jacobs. Chicago: Chicago University Press.

Durkheim, E. (1997/1893) *The Division of Labor in Society.* Trans. Lewis A. Coser. New York: Free Press.

Drew, P. and J. C. Heritage (1992) *Talk at Work: Interaction in Institutional Settings.* Cambridge: Cambridge University Press.

The Economist. London: The Economist Newspaper.

Elliot, G. (1871–2/1992) *Middlemarch: A Study of Provincial Life.* Harmondsworth, London: Penguin.

Engeström, Y. and D. Middleton (eds.) (1996) *Cognition and Communication at Work.* Cambridge: Cambridge University Press.

Finn, K. E., Sellen, A. J. and S. B. Wilbur (eds.) *Video-Mediated Communication: Computers, Cognition, and Work.* New Jersey: Lawrence Erlbaum.

Fligstein, N. (2001) *The Architecture of Markets: An Economic Sociology of the Twenty-First-Century Capitalist Societies.* Princeton: Princeton University Press.

Garcia, M. (1986) La construction sociale d'un march parfait: le marche au cadran de Fontaines-en-Solgne.*Actes de Recherche en Science Sociales* 65: 2–13.

Garfinkel, H. (1963) A Conception of and Experiments with "Trust" as a Condition of Stable Concerted Actions in O. J. Harvey (ed.) *Motivation and Social Interaction.* New York: The Ronald Press.

(1967) *Studies in Ethnomethodology.* Englewood Cliffs: Prentice-Hall.

Gaver, W. W., A. Sellen, C. C. Heath, and P. Luff (1993) One is not Enough: Multiple Views in a Media Space. In *Proceedings of INTERCHI '93,* Amsterdam, Netherlands, 335–41.

Geismar, H. (2004) What's in a Price? An Ethnography of Tribal Art at Auction. In A. Amin and N. Thrift (eds.) *The Blackwell Cultural Economy Reader.* Oxford: Blackwell.

Goffman, E. (1952) On Cooling the Mark Out: Some Aspects of Adaptation to Failure. *Psychiatry* 15(4): 451–63.

(1959) *The Presentation of Self in Everyday Life.* Garden City, NY: Doubleday.

(1964) The Neglected Situation. *American Anthropologist* 6(2): 133–56.

(1981) *Forms of Talk.* Philadelphia: University of Pennsylvania Press.

(1983) The Interaction Order. *American Sociological Review* 48: 1–17.

Goodwin, C. (1981) *Conversational Organization: Interaction between Speakers and Hearers.* New York: Academic Press.

(1993) Recording Interaction in Natural Settings. *Pragmatics* 3(2): 181–209.

(1994) Professional Vision. *American Anthropologist* 96: 606–33.

(1995) Seeing in Depth. *Social Studies of Science* 25(2): 237–74.

Goodwin, C. and M. H. Goodwin (1996) Seeing as a Situated Activity: Formulating Planes. In Y. Engeström and D. Middleton (eds.) *Cognition and Communication at Work*. Cambridge: Cambridge University Press, 61–95.

Goodwin, M. H. (2006) *The Hidden Life of Girls: Games of Stance, Status, and Exclusion*. Malden, MA: Blackwell.

Granovetter, M. (1985) Economic Action and Social Structure: The Problem of Embeddedness. *American Journal of Sociology* 91(3): 481–510.

Greatbatch, D., P. Luff, C. C. Heath, and P. Campion (1993) Interpersonal Communication and Human-Computer Interaction: An Examination of the Use of Computers in Medical Consultations. *Interacting With Computers* 5(2): 193–216.

Hardy, T. (1872) *Under the Greenwood Tree*. Harmondsworth, England: Penguin.

Harper, R. H. (1998) *Inside the IMF: An Ethnography of Documents, Technology and Organisational Action*. London: Academic Press.

Harrison, S. (ed.) *Media Space 20+ Years of Mediated Life*. New York: Springer.

Harvey, B. W. and F. Meisel (2006) *Auctions Law and Practice*. Oxford: Oxford University Press.

Heath, C. C. (1982) The Display of Recipiency: An Instance of a Sequential Organization in Speech and Body Movement. *Semiotica* 42–2/4: 147–61.

(1986) *Body Movement and Speech in Medical Interaction*. Cambridge: Cambridge University Press.

(1992) Gesture's Discreet Tasks: Body Movement and the Contextualisation of Language. In P. Auer and A. di Luzio (eds.) *The Contextualisation of Language*. Amsterdam: John Benjamins, 101–29.

Heath, C. C., J. Hindmarsh, and P. Luff (2010) *Video in Qualitative Research: Analysing Social Interaction in Everyday Life*. London: Sage.

Heath, C. C., M. Jirotka, P. Luff, and J. Hindmarsh (1995) Unpacking Collaboration: Interactional Organisation in a City Trading Room. *Journal of Computer Supported Cooperative Work* 3(1): 147–65.

Heath, C. C. and P. Luff (1996) Convergent Activities: Collaborative Work and Multimedia Technology in London Underground Line Control Rooms. In D. Middleton and Y. Engeström (eds). *Cognition and Communication at Work: Distributed Cognition in the Workplace*. Cambridge: Cambridge University Press, 96–130.

(2000) *Technology in Action*. Cambridge: Cambridge University Press.

Heath, C. C., P. Luff and M. Sanchez-Svensson (2002) 'Overseeing Organisations: Configuring Action and its Environment'. *British Journal of Sociology* 53(2): 181–201.

Heath, C. C., P. Luff, K. vom Lehn, J. Yamashita, and H. Kuzuoka (2009). Enhancing Remote Participation in Live Auctions: An 'Intelligent' Gavel. *Proceedings of CHI 2009*, Boston, 1427–36.

Herbert, J. (1990) *Inside Christie's*. London: Hodder and Stoughton.

Heritage, J. C. (1984) *Garfinkel and Ethnomethodology*. Cambridge: Polity Press.

(1997) Conversation Analysis and Institutional Talk: Analysing Data. In Silverman, D. (ed.) *Qualitative Research: Theory, Method and Practice*. London: Sage, 161–82.

Heritage, J. C. and D. Greatbatch (1991). On the Institutional Character of Institutional Talk: The Case of News Interviews. In D. Boden, and D. H. Zimmerman (eds.) *Talk and Social Structure*. Cambridge: Polity Press, 93–137.

Heritage, J. C. and D. W. Maynard (eds.) (2006) *Communication in Medical Care: Interaction Between Primary Care Physicians and Patients*. Cambridge: Cambridge University Press.

Herrmann, F. (1980) *Sotheby's: Portrait of an Auction House*. London: Chatto & Windus.

Hibbitts, B. J. (1992) Coming to Our Senses: Communication and Legal Expression in Performance Cultures. *Emory Law Journal* 41: 4.

Hindmarsh, J. and A. Pilnick (2002) The Tacit Order of Teamwork: Collaboration and Embodied Conduct in Anaesthesia. *Sociological Quarterly* 43(2): 139–64.

(2007) Knowing Bodies at Work: Embodiment and Ephemeral Teamwork in Anaesthesia. *Organization Studies* 28(9): 1395–1416.

Ho, K. (2009) *Liquidated: An Ethnography of Wall Street*. London: Duke University Press.

Hughes, E. C. (1958) *Men and their Work*. Glencoe: The Free Press.

Hutchins, E. L. (1998) *Cognition in the Wild*. Harvard: MIT Press.

Jarvenpa, R. (2003) Collective Witnessing: Performance, Drama, and Circulation of Valuables in the Rural Auction and Antiques Trade. *Journal of Contemporary Ethnography* 32(5): 555–91.

Jefferson, G. (1991) List Construction as a Task and Resource. In G. Psathas (ed.) *Interactional Competence*. New York, NY: Irvington, 63–92.

Kauffman, R. and C. Wood (2003) Running up the Bid: Detecting, Predicting, and Preventing Reserve Price Shilling in Online Auctions. *5th Int. Conf. on Electronic Commerce*. Pittsburgh: ACM, 259–65.

(2004) The Effects of Shilling on Final Bid Prices in Online Auctions. *Electronic Commerce Research and Applications* 4(1): 21–34.

Keynes, J. M. (1936) *The General Theory of Employment, Interest and Money*. New York: Harcourt, Brace and Co.

Klemperer, P. (1999) Auction Theory: A Guide to the Literature. *Journal of Economic Surveys* 13(3): 227–86.

(2004) *Auctions: Theory and Practice*. Oxford: Princeton University Press.

Knoblauch, H., B. Schnettler, J. Raab and H.- G. Söffner (eds.) (2006) *Video-Analysis: Methodology and Methods Qualitative Audiovisual Data Analysis in Sociology*. Frankfurt am Main: Lang-Verlag.

Knorr Cetina, K. and U. Bruegger (2002) Global Microstructures: The Virtual Societies of Financial Markets. *American Journal of Sociology* 107(4): 905–50.

(2004) Traders' Engagement with Markets: A Postsocial Relationship. In A. Amin and N. Thrift (eds.) *The Blackwell Cultural Economy Reader*. Oxford: Blackwell.

Knorr Cetina, K. (2009) The Synthetic Situation: Interactionism for a Global World. *Symbolic Interaction* 32(1): 61–87.

Koschmann, T., C. LeBaron, C. Goodwin, and P. Feltovich (2006) The Mystery of the Missing Referent: Objects, Procedures, and the Problem of the Instruction Follower. In S. Greenberg and G. Mark (eds.) *Computer Supported Cooperative Work*. New York: ACM, 373–82.

Koschmann, T., C. LeBaron, C. Goodwin, A. Zemel and G. Dunnington (2007) Formulating the Triangle of Doom. *Gesture* 7(1): 97–118.

Krishna, V. (2002) *Auction Theory*. London: Academic Press.

Kuiper, K. (1992) The English Oral Tradition in Auctions Speech. *American Speech* 67: 279–89.

(1995) *Smooth Talkers: The Linguistic Performance of Auctioneers and Sportscasters*. London: Routledge.

Kuiper, K. and D. C. Haggo (1984) Livestock Auctions, Oral Poetry and Ordinary Language. *Language in Society* 13: 205–34.

Kuiper, K. and F. Tillis (1986) The Chant of the Tobacco Auctioneer. *American Speech* 60: 141–9.

Lacey, R. (1998) *Sotheby's: Bidding for Class*. London: Little, Brown & Company.

Laurier, E. and C. Philo (2006) Natural Problems of Naturalistic Video Data. In H. Knoblauch, J. Raab, H.-G. Soefnner, and B. Schnettler (eds.) *Video Analysis: Methodology and Methods*. Frankfurt: Peter Lang, 181–90.

Lawson, T. (2002) Economics and Expectations. In J. Runde and S. Mizuhara (eds.) *Philosophy of Keynes' Economics Probability, Uncertainty and Convention*. London: Routledge.

Learmount, B. (1985) *The History of the Auction*. Ivers, England: Barnard & Learmount.

Llewellyn, N. and R. Burrow (2008) Streetwise Sales and the Social Order of City Streets. *British Journal of Sociology* 59(3): 561–83.

Llewellyn, N. and J. Hindmarsh (eds.) (2010) *Organisation, Interaction and Practice: Studies in Ethnomethodology and Conversation Analysis*. Cambridge: Cambridge University Press.

London Evening Standard. London: Newspapers Publishing.

Luff, P., H. Kuzuoka, C. C. Heath, K. Yamazaki, and J. Yamashita (2009) Creating Assemblies in Media Space: Recent Developments in Enhancing Access to Workspaces. In S. Harrison (ed.) *Media Space: 20+ Years of Mediated Life*. Springer, 27–56.

Luff, P., J. Hindmarsh and C. C. Heath (eds.) (2000) *Workplace Studies: Recovering Work Practice and Informing System Design*. Cambridge: Cambridge University Press.

Mackenzie, D. (2009) *Material Markets: How Economic Agents are Constructed*. Oxford: Oxford University Press.

Mackenzie, D. and Y. Millo (2003) Constructing a Market, Performing Theory: The Historical Sociology of a Financial Derivatives Exchange. *American Journal of Sociology* 109: 107–45.

Maynard, D. W. (2003) *Bad News, Good News: Conversational Order in Everyday Talk and Clinical Settings*. Chicago: University of Chicago Press.

(1988) Language, Interaction, and Social Problems. *Social Problems* 35: 311–34.

Mead, M. (1974/1995) Visual Anthropology and the Discipline of Words. In P. Hockings (ed.) *Principles of Visual Anthropology* (2nd Edition). Berlin and New York: Mouton de Gruyter, 3–10.

Mears, A. (2011) Pricing Looks: Circuits of Value in Fashioning Modelling Markets. In J. Beckert and P. Aspers (eds.) *The Worth of Goods: Valuation and Pricing in the Economy*. Oxford: Oxford University Press, 155–177.

Menzes, F. M. and P. K. Monteiro (2005) *An Introduction to Auction Theory*. Oxford: Oxford University Press.

Milgrom, P. R. (2004) *Putting Auction Theory to Work.* Cambridge: Cambridge University Press.

Mondada, L. (2003) Working with Video: How Surgeons Produce Video Records of Their Actions. *Visual Studies* 18: 58–73.

(2001) Interactions et pratiques professionnelles: un regard issu des studies of work. *Studies in Communication Sciences* 2/2: 47–82.

(2006) Video Recording as the Reflexive Preservation and Configuration of Phenomenal Features for Analysis. In H. Knoblauch, B. Schnettler, J. Raab, and H.-G. Soeffner (eds.) *Video Analysis: Methodology and Methods. Qualitative Audiovisual Analysis in Sociology.* Frankfurt/M: Peter Lang, 51–68.

(2007) Operating Together through Videoconference: Members' Procedures for Accomplishing a Common Space of Action. In S. Hester and D. Francis (eds.) *Orders of Ordinary Action.* Aldershot: Ashgate, 51–67.

(2008) Using Video for a Sequential and Multimodal Analysis of Social Interaction: Videotaping Institutional Telephone Calls. *Forum: Qualitative Social Research* 9: 1–35.

(2011) The Organisation of Concurrent Courses of Action in Surgical Demonstrations. In J. Streeck, C. Goodwin, and C. LeBaron (eds.) *Embodied Interaction: Language and Body in the Material World.* Cambridge: Cambridge University Press, 227–42.

Montias, J. M. (2002) *Art at Auction in 17th Century Amsterdam.* Amsterdam: Amsterdam University Press.

Moore, R., J. Whalen, and E. Cabell HankinsonGathman (2010). The Work of the Work Order: Document Practice in Face-to-face Service Encounters. In N. Llewellyn and J. Hindmarsh (eds.) *Organisation, Interaction and Practice.* Cambridge: Cambridge University Press, 172–97.

Muniesca, F. (2005) Containing the Market: The Transition from Open Outcry to Electronic Trading at the Paris Bourse. *Sociologie du Travail* 47: 485–501.

Muniesa, F. and Callon, M. (2007) Economic Experiments and the Construction of Markets. In D. Mackenzie, F. Muniesa and L. Siu (eds.) *Do Economists Make Markets? On the Performativity of Economics.* Princeton, NJ: Princeton University Press, 163–89.

Murphy, K. (2004) Imagination as Joint Activity: The Case of Architectural Interaction. *Mind, Culture, and Activity* 11(4): 267–78.

(2005) Collaborative Imagining: The Interactive Use of Gestures, Talk, and Graphic Representation in Architectural Practice. *Semiotica* 156(1/4): 113–45.

Ockenfels, A., D. Reiley, and A. Sadrieh (2006) Online Auctions, NBER Working Paper Series. *National Bureau of Economic Research:* Cambridge, MA.

Perakyla, A. (1995) *AIDS Counselling: Institutional Interaction and Clinical Practice.* Cambridge: Cambridge University Press.

Pepys, S. (1660) *The Diary of Samuel Pepys.* London.

Pinch, T. and C. Clark (1986) The Hard Sell: "Patter Merchanting" and the (Re)Production and Local Management of Economic Reasoning in the Sales Routines of Market Pitchers. *Sociology* 20: 169–91.

Polanyi, K. (1944/1957) *The Great Transformation: The Political and Economic Origins of Our Time.* Princeton: Princeton University Press.

Preda, A. (2009) Brief Encounters. Calculation and the Interaction Order of Anonymous Electronic Markets. *Accounting, Organization and Society* 34/5: 675–93.

(2009) *Information, Knowledge, and Economic Life: An Introduction to the Sociology of Markets.* Oxford: Oxford University Press.

Prus, R. (1985) Price-Setting as Social Activity: Defining Price, Value, and Profit in the Marketplace. *Journal of Contemporary Ethnography* 14: 59–93.

Resnick, P., R. Zeckhauser, E. Friedman, and K. Kuwabara (2000) Reputation Systems. *Communications of the ACM* 43(12): 45–8.

Rogers, A., D. Reily, N. R. Jennings, and J. Schiff (2007) The Effects of Proxy Bidding and Minimum Bid Increments within eBay Auction. *ACM Trans. Web*, 1(2).

Rothkopf, M. and R. M. Harstad (1994) Modelling Competitive Bidding: A Critical Essay. *Management Science* 40(3): 364–84.

Reitlinger, G. (1982) *The Economics of Taste. The Rise and Fall of Picture Prices 1760–1960 Volumes 1, II and III.* New York: Hacker Art Books.

Sacks, H., E. A. Schegloff and G. Jefferson (1973/1974) A Simplest Systematics for the Organisation of Turn-taking for Conversation. *Language* 50(4): 696–735. Republished in Schenkein, J. (1974) *Studies in the Organisation of Conversational Interaction.* New York: Academic Press, 7–55.

Sacks, H. (1992). *Lectures on Conversation.* Oxford: Blackwell.

Sanchez-Svensson, M., C. C. Heath, and P. Luff (2007) Instrumental Action: The Timely Exchange of Implements during Surgical Operations. In L. Bannon et al. *The Proceedings of the 10th European Conference on Computer Supported Cooperative Work.* London: Springer-Verlag, 41–61.

Sanchez-Svensson, M., P. Luff and C. C. Heath (2009) Embedding Instruction in Practice: Contingency and Collaboration during Surgical Training. *Sociology of Health and Illness* 31(6): 889–906.

Saxenian, A. (1994) *Regional Advantage: Culture and Competition in Silicon Valley and Route 128.* Cambridge, MA: Harvard University Press.

Schegloff, E. A. (2007) *Sequence Organisation in Interaction: A Primer in Conversation Analysis Volume 1.* Cambridge, MA: Cambridge University Press.

Schegloff, E. A. and H. Sacks (1974) Opening up Closings. In R. Turner (ed.) *Ethnomethodology: Selected Readings.* Harmondsworth: Penguin.

Schmidt, K. and L. Bannon (1992) Taking CSCW Seriously: Supporting Articulation Work *Computer Supported Cooperative Work* 1(1–2): 7–40.

Schutz, A. (1962) *Collected Papers I: The Problem of Social Reality.* Edited by M. A. Natanson and H. L. van Breda. Martinus Nijhoff: Dordrecht, The Netherlands.

Secrest, M. (2003) *Duveen: A Life in Art.* Chicago: Chicago University Press.

Seligman, A. B. (1997) *The Problem of Trust.* Princeton, NJ: Princeton University Press.

Silverman, D. (1997). *Discourses of Counselling: HIV Counselling as Social Interaction.* London: Sage.

Simmel, G. (1904/1971) Fashion. In D. Levine (ed.) *Georg Simmel on Individuality and Social Form.* Chicago: Chicago University Press, 294–323.

Smith, C. (1989). *Auctions: The Social Construction of Value*. California, USA: California University Press.

(1991) Comment on Siegelman's Review of Auctions. *American Journal of Sociology* 96(6): 1539–41.

Streeck, J. and S. Mehus (2005) Microethnography: The Study of Practices. In K. Fitch and R. Sanders (eds.) *Handbook of Language and Social Interaction*. Mahwah, NJ: Lawrence Erlbaum, 381–404.

Streeck, J., C. Goodwin and C. LeBaron (eds.) (2011) *Embodied Interaction in the Material World*. Cambridge: Cambridge University Press.

Suchman, L A. (1996) Constituting Shared Workspaces. In Y. Engeström and D. Middleton (eds.) *Cognition and Communication at Work*. Cambridge: Cambridge University Press, 35–60.

(2007). *Human-Machine Reconfigurations: Plans and Situated Actions* (2nd Edition). Cambridge: Cambridge University Press.

Swedberg, R. and M. Granovetter (eds.) (1992) *The Sociology of Economic Life*. Boulder, CO: Westview Press.

Szmanski, H. and J. Whalen (2011) *Making Work Visible: Ethnographically Grounded Case Studies of Work Practice*. Cambridge: Cambridge University Press.

Thevenot, L. (2001) Organized Complexity: Conventions of Coordination and the Composition of Economic Arrangement. *European Journal of Social Theory* 4(4): 379–458.

Towner, W. (1971) *The Elegant Auctioneers*. London: Victor Gollancz (completed by Stephen Varble).

Vargha, Z. (2011) From Long-term Savings to Instant Mortgages: Financial Demonstrations and the Role of Interaction in Markets. *Organization* 18: 215–36.

Velthuis, O. (2005) *Talking Prices: Symbolic Meanings of Prices on the Market for Contemporary Art*. Princeton: Princeton University Press.

(2011) Damien's Dangerous Game:Valuing Contemporary Art at Auction. In J. Beckert and P. Aspers (eds.) *The Worth of Goods: Valuation and Pricing in the Economy*. Oxford: Oxford University Press, 178–200.

Watson, P. (1997) *Sotheby's Inside Story*. London: Bloomsbury.

Whalen, J. (1995) A Technology of Order Production: Computer-Aided Dispatch in Public Safety Communications. In P. Have and G. Psathas (eds.) *Situated Order: Studies in the Social Organization of Talk and Embodied Action*. Washington, DC: University Press of America, 187–230.

Whalen, J. and E. Vinkhuyzen (2000) Expert Systems in (Inter)Action: Diagnosing Document Machine Problems Over the Telephone. In P. Luff, J. Hindmarsh, and C. C. Heath (eds.) *Workplace Studies: Recovering Work Practice and Informing System Design*. Cambridge: Cambridge University Press, 92–140.

Whalen, J., M. Whalen and K. Henderson (2002) Improvisational Choreography in a Teleservice Work. *British Journal of Sociology* 53(2): 239–59.

White, H. (1981) Where Do Markets Come From? *American Journal of Sociology* 87: 517–57.

Wieder, D. L. (1975) *Language and Social Reality: The Case of Telling the Convict Code*. Amsterdam: Mouton.

Woolgar, S. (2004) Marketing Ideas. *Economy and Society* 33(4): 448–62.

Zeitlin, A. D. (1993) *American Talkers: The Art of the Sideshow Carnival Pitchman and other Itinerant Showmen and Vendors.* PhD dissertation, University of Pennsylvania.

Zemel, A., T. Koschmann, and C. LeBaron (2011) Pursuing a Response: Prodding Recognition and Expertise within a Surgical Team. In J. Streeck, C. Goodwin, and C. LeBaron (eds.) *Embodied Interaction: Language and Body in the Material World.* Cambridge: Cambridge University Press, 227–42.

Index